MW00939500

A

HISTORY

OF

THE EARTH,

AND

ANIMATED NATURE.

By OLIVER GOLDSMITH.

ILLUSTRATED WITH COPPER PLATES.

WITH CORRECTIONS AND ADDITIONS

By W. TURTON, M.D.

FELLOW OF THE LINNÆAN SOCIETY.

A NEW EDITION; IN SIX VOLUMES.

VOL. II.

LONDON:

PRINTED FOR WINGRAVE AND COLLINGWOOD; F., C., AND J. RIVINGTON;
LONGMAN, HURST, REES, ORME, AND BROWN; CADELL AND DAVIES;
J. NUNN; J. RICHARDSON; J. M. RICHARDSON; S. BAGSTER; J. AND
A. ARCH; J. MAWMAN; J. BOOKER; BALDWIN, CRADOCK AND JOY;
J. BLACK; GALE AND FENNER; WALKER AND EDWARDS; J. ROBINSON;
AND B. REYNOLDS.

1816.

Printed by T. C. Hansard,
Peterborough-court, Fleet-street,
London.

CONTENTS

OF THE SECOND VOLUME.

CONTENTS.

A

HISTORY

OF

ANIMALS.

CHAP. I.

Of Sleep and Hunger.

As man, in all the privileges he enjoys, and the powers he is invested with, has a superiority over all other animals, so, in his necessities, he seems inferior to the meanest of them all. Nature has brought him into life with a greater variety of wants and infirmities, than the rest of her creatures, unarmed in the midst of enemies. The lion has natural arms; the bear natural clothing: but man is destitute of all such advantages; and, from the superiority of his mind alone, he is to supply the deficiency. The number of his wants, however, were merely given, in order to multiply the number of his enjoyments; since the possibility of being deprived of any good, teaches him the value of its possession. Were man born with those advantages which he learns to possess by industry, he would very probably enjoy them with a blunter relish: it is by being naked, that he knows the value of a covering; it is by being exposed to the weather, that he learns the comforts of an habitation. Every want thus becomes a means of pleasure, in the redressing; and the animal that has most desires, may be said to be capable of the greatest variety of happiness.

Beside the thousand imaginary wants peculiar to man, there are two, which he has in common with all other animals; and which he feels in a more necessary manner than they. These are the wants of sleep and hunger. Every animal that we are acquainted with, seems to endure the want of these with much less injury to health than man; and some are most surprisingly patient in sustaining both. The little domestic animals that we keep about us, may often set a lesson of calm resignation, in supporting want and watchfulness, to the boasted philosopher. They receive their pittance at uncertain intervals, and wait its coming with cheerful expectation. We have instances of the dog, and the cat, living, in this manner, without food for several days; and yet still preserving their attachment to the tyrant that oppresses them; still ready to exert their little services for his amusement or defence. But the patience of these is nothing to what the animals of the forest endure. As these mostly live upon accidental carnage, so they are often known to remain without food for several weeks together. Nature, kindly solicitous for their support, has also contracted their stomachs, to suit them for their precarious way of living; and kindly, while it abridges the banquet, lessens the necessity of providing for it. But the meaner tribes of animals are made still more capable of sustaining life without food, many of them remaining in a state of torpid indifference till their prey approaches, when they jump upon and seize it. In this manner, the snake, or the spider, continue, for several months together, to subsist upon a single meal; and some of the butterfly kinds live upon little or nothing. But it is very different with man: his wants daily make their importunate demands; and it is known that he cannot continue to live many days without eating, drinking, and sleeping.

Hunger is a much more powerful enemy to man than watchfulness, and kills him much sooner. It may be considered as a disorder that food removes; and that would quickly be fatal, without its proper antidote. In fact, it is so terrible to man, that to avoid it he even encounters certain death; and, rather than endure its tortures, exchanges them for immediate destruction. However, by what I have been told, it is much more dreadful in its approaches, than in its continuance; and the pains of a famishing wretch decrease as his strength diminishes. In the beginning, the desire of food is dreadful indeed, as we know by experience; for there are few who have not in some degree felt its approaches. But, after the first or second day, its tortures become less terrible, and a total insensibility at length comes kindly in to the poor wretch's assistance. I have talked with the captain of a ship, who was one of six that endured it in its extremities; and who was the only person that had not lost his senses, when they received accidental relief. He assured me, his pains at first were so great, as to be often tempted to eat a part of one of the men who died; and which the rest of his crew actually for some time lived upon : he said, that, during the continuance of this paroxysm, he found his pains insupportable ; and was desirous, at one time, of anticipating that death which he thought inevitable : but his pains, he said, gradually decreased, after the sixth day (for they had water in the ship, which kept them alive so long), and then he was in a state rather of languor than desire ; nor did he much wish for food, except when he saw others eating ; and that for a while revived his appetite, though with diminished importunity. The latter part of the time, when his health was almost destroyed, a thousand strange images rose upon his mind ; and every one of his senses began to bring him wrong information. The most fragrant perfumes appeared to him to have a fetid smell ; and every thing he looked at took a greenish hue, and sometimes a yellow. When he was presented with food by the ship's company that took him and his men up, four of whom died shortly after, he could not help looking upon it with lothing, instead of desire ; and it was not till after four days, that his stomach was brought to its natural tone ; when the violence of his appetite returned, with a sort of canine eagerness.

Thus dreadful are the effects of hunger ; and yet, when we come to assign the cause that produces them, we find the subject involved in doubt and intricacy. This longing eagerness is, no doubt, given for a very obvious purpose ; that of replenishing the body, wasted by fatigue and perspiration. Were not men stimulated by such a pressing monitor, they might be apt to pursue other amusements, with a perseverance beyond their power ; and forget the useful hours of refreshment, in those more tempting ones of pleasure. But hunger makes a demand that will not be refused; and, indeed, the generality of mankind seldom await the call.

Hunger has been supposed by some to arise from the rubbing of the coats of the stomach against each other, without having any intervening substance to prevent their painful attrition. Others have imagined, that its juices, wanting their necessary supply, turn acrid, or, as some say, pungent; and thus fret its internal coats, so as to produce a train of the most uneasy sensations. Boerhaave, who established his reputation in physic by uniting the conjectures of all those that preceded him, ascribes hunger to the united effect of both these causes; and asserts, that the pungency of the gastric juices, and the attrition of its coats against each other, cause those pains, which nothing but food can remove. These juices continuing still to be separated in the stomach, and every moment becoming more acrid, mix with the blood, and infect the circulation: the circulation being thus contaminated, becomes weaker, and more contracted; and the whole nervous frame sympathising, an hectic fever, and sometimes madness, is produced; in which state the faint wretch expires. In this manner, the man who dies of hunger may be said to be poisoned by the juices of his own body; and is destroyed less by the want of nourishment, than by the vitiated qualities of that which he had already taken. *

[* The pains of hunger are occasioned by the extreme irritability of the numerous ramifications of nerves about the stomach, in consequence of the abstraction of their usual stimulation by food.

The inactivity of an organ causes pain by the accumulation of

However this may be, we have but few instances of men dying, except at sea, of absolute hunger; the decline of those unhappy creatures who are destitute of food, at land, being more slow and unperceived. These, from being often in need, and as often receiving an accidental supply, pass their lives between surfeiting and repining; and their constitution is impaired by insensible degrees. Man is unfit for a state of precarious expectation. That share of provident precaution which incites him to lay up stores for a distant day, becomes his torment, when totally unprovided against an immediate call. The lower race of animals, when satisfied, for the instant moment, are perfectly happy: but it is otherwise with man; his mind anticipates distress, and feels the pang of want even before it arrests him. Thus the mind, being continually harassed by the situation, it at length influences the constitution, and unfits it for all its functions. Some cruel disorder, but no way like hunger, seizes the unhappy sufferer; so that almost all those men who have thus long lived by chance, and whose every day may be considered as an happy escape from famine, are known at last to die, in reality, of a

sensorial power, which, for want of stimulation, it cannot consume; as, in a cold frosty morning, the hands ache in consequence of the deficiency of the usual stimulus of heat.

In like manner, in thirst, the membrane of the upper end of the gullet becomes torpid, and consequently painful, when there is a deficiency of aqueous fluid in the general system; because it then wants its proper stimulus. It is for this reason that seals, on the coast of Greenland, are known to swallow stones, for want of other food, that they may exhaust the exuberant and painful accumulation of sensorial powers.]

disorder caused by hunger; but which, in the common language, is often called a broken heart. Some of these I have known myself, when very little able to relieve them; and I have been told, by a very active and worthy magistrate, that the number of such as die in London for want, is much greater than one would imagine—I think he talked of two thousand in a year.

But how numerous soever those who die of hunger may be, many times greater, on the other hand, are the number of those who die by repletion. It is not the province of the present page to speculate, with the physician, upon the danger of surfeits; or, with the moralist, upon the nauseousness of gluttony: it will only be proper to observe, that as nothing is so prejudicial to health as hunger by constraint, so nothing is more beneficial to the constitution than voluntary abstinence. It was not without reason that religion enjoined this duty; since it answered the double purpose of restoring the health oppressed by luxury, and diminished the consumption of provisions; so that a part might come to the poor. It should be the business of the legislature, therefore, to enforce this divine precept; and thus, by restraining one part of mankind in the use of their superfluities, to consult for the benefit of those who want the necessaries of life. The injunctions for abstinence are strict over the whole Continent; and were rigorously observed, even among ourselves, for a long time after the Reformation. Queen Elizabeth, by giving her commands, upon this head, the air of a political injunction, lessened, in a great measure, and, in my opinion, very unwisely, the religious force of the obligation. She

enjoined that her subjects should fast from flesh on
Fridays and Saturdays; but at the same time
declared, that this was not commanded from motives
of religion, as if there were any differences in meats,
but merely to favour the consumption of fish, and
thus to multiply the number of mariners; and also
to spare the stock of sheep, which might be more
beneficial in another way. In this manner the injunction defeated its own force; and this most
salutary law became no longer binding, when it
was supposed to come purely from man. How far
it may be enjoined in the Scriptures, I will not take
upon me to say; but this may be asserted, that if
the utmost benefit to the individual, and the most
extensive advantage to society, serve to mark any
institution as of Heaven, this of abstinence may be
reckoned among the foremost.

Were we to give a history of the various benefits
that have arisen from this command, and how conducive it has been to long life, the instances would
fatigue with their multiplicity. It is surprising to
what a great age the primitive Christians of the
East, who retired from persecution in the deserts of
Arabia, continued to live in all the bloom of health,
and yet all the rigours of abstemious discipline.
Their common allowance, as we are told, for four
and twenty hours, was twelve ounces of bread, and
nothing but water. On this simple beverage, St.
Anthony is said to have lived a hundred and five
years; James, the hermit, a hundred and four;
Arsenius, tutor to the emperor Arcadius, a hundred
and twenty; St. Epiphanius, a hundred and
fifteen; Simeon, a hundred and twelve; and Rom-
bald, a hundred and twenty. In this manner did

these holy temperate men live to an extreme old age, kept cheerful by strong hopes, and healthful by moderate labour.

Abstinence, which is thus voluntary, may be much more easily supported than constrained hunger. Man is said to live without food for seven days; which is the usual limit assigned him : and, perhaps, in a state of constraint, this is the longest time he can survive the want of it. But, in cases of voluntary abstinence, of sickness, or sleeping, he has been known to live much longer.

In the records of the Tower, there is an account of a Scotchman, imprisoned for felony, who, for the space of six weeks, took not the least sustenance, being exactly watched during the whole time; and for this he received the king's pardon.

When the American Indians undertake long journies, and when, consequently, a stock of provisions sufficient to support them the whole way would be more than they could carry, in order to obviate this inconvenience, instead of carrying the necessary quantity, they contrive a method of palliating their hunger, by swallowing pills, made of calcined shells and tobacco. These pills take away all appetite, by producing a temporary disorder in the stomach ; and, no doubt, the frequent repetition of this wretched expedient, must at last be fatal. By these means, however, they continue several days without eating, cheerfully bearing such extremes of fatigue and watching, as would quickly destroy men bred up in a greater state of delicacy. For those arts by which we learn to obviate our necessities, do not fail to unfit us for their accidental encounter.

Upon the whole, therefore, man is less able to support hunger than any other animal; and he is not better qualified to support a state of watchfulness. Indeed, sleep seems much more necessary to him than to any other creature; as, when awake, he may be said to exhaust a greater proportion of the nervous fluid; and, consequently, to stand in need of an adequate supply. Other animals, when most awake, are but little removed from a state of slumber; their feeble faculties, imprisoned in matter, and rather exerted by impulse than deliberation, require sleep rather as a cessation from motion, than from thinking. But it is otherwise with man; his ideas, fatigued with their various excursions, demand a cessation, not less than the body, from toil; and he is the only creature that seems to require sleep from double motives; not less for the refreshment of the mental than of the bodily frame.

There are some lower animals, indeed, that seem to spend the greatest part of their lives in sleep; but, properly speaking, the sleep of such may be considered as a kind of death; and their waking, a resurrection. Flies, and insects, are said to be asleep, at a time that all the vital motions have ceased; without respiration, without any circulation of their juices; if cut in pieces, they do not awake, nor does any fluid ooze out at the wound. These may be considered rather as congealed than as sleeping animals; and their rest, during winter, rather as a cessation from life, than a necessary refreshment: but in the higher races of animals, whose blood is not thus congealed, and thawed by heat, these all bear the want of sleep much better than man;

and some of them continue a long time without
seeming to take any refreshment from it whatsoever.

But man is more feeble; he requires its due
return; and if it fails to pay the accustomed visit, his
whole frame is in a short time thrown into disorder;
his appetite ceases; his spirits are dejected; his
pulse becomes quicker and harder; and his mind,
abridged of its slumbering visions, begins to adopt
waking dreams. A thousand strange phantoms
arise, which come and go without his will: these,
which are transient in the beginning, at last take
firm possession of the mind, which yields to their
dominion, and, after a long struggle, runs into
confirmed madness. In that horrid state, the mind
may be considered as a city without walls, open to
every insult, and paying homage to every invader:
every idea that then starts, with any force, becomes
a reality; and the reason, over fatigued with its
former importunities, makes no head against the
tyrannical invasion, but submits to it from mere
imbecility.

But it is happy for mankind, that this state of
inquietude is seldom driven to an extreme; and
that there are medicines which seldom fail to give
relief. However, man finds it more difficult than
any other animal to procure sleep: and some are
obliged to court its approaches for several hours
together, before they incline to rest. It is in vain
that all light is excluded; that all sounds are
removed; that warmth and softness conspire to
invite it; the restless and busy mind still retains its
former activity; and reason, that wishes to lay
down the reins, in spite of herself, is obliged to
maintain them. In this disagreeable state, the

mind passes from thought to thought, willing to lose the distinctness of perception, by increasing the multitude of the images. At last, when the approaches of sleep are near, every object of the imagination begins to mix with that next it; their outlines become, in a manner, rounder; a part of their distinctions fade away; and sleep, that ensues, fashions out a dream from the remainder.

If then it should be asked from what cause this state of repose proceeds, or in what manner sleep thus binds us for several hours together, I must fairly confess my ignorance, although it is easy to tell what philosophers say upon the subject. Sleep, says one of them,* consists in a scarcity of spirits, by which the orifices or pores of the nerves in the brain, through which the spirits used to flow into the nerves, being no longer kept open by the frequency of the spirits, shut of themselves; thus the nerves, wanting a new supply of spirits, become lax, and unfit to convey any impression to the brain. All this, however, is explaining a very great obscurity by somewhat more obscure; leaving, therefore, those spirits to open and shut the entrances to the brain, let us be contented with simply enumerating the effects of sleep upon the human constitution.†

---

* Rohault.

[† Sleep seems to be the provision of nature for supplying the waste of sensorial power, which is gradually exhausted by the various external stimulants of food, thought, exercise, &c. during the day. The common effects of all the exciting powers to produce sleep, is proved by every day's experience. After great fatigue of mind or body, or after a full meal and much wine, we feel the powers of volition gradually suspended, and an inclination

In sleep, the whole nervous frame is relaxed, while the heart and the lungs seem more forcibly exerted. This fuller circulation produces also a swelling of the muscles, as they always find who sleep with ligatures on any part of their body. This increased circulation, also, may be considered as a kind of exercise, which is continued through the frame; and, by this, the perspiration becomes more copious, although the appetite for food is entirely taken away. Too much sleep dulls the apprehension, weakens the memory, and unfits the body for labour. On the contrary, sleep too much abridged, emaciates the frame, produces melancholy, and consumes the constitution. It requires some care, therefore, to regulate the quantity of sleep, and just to take as much as will completely restore Nature, without oppressing it. The poor, as Otway says, sleep little; forced, by their situation, to lengthen out their labour to their necessities, they have but a short interval for this pleasing refreshment; and I have ever been of opinion, that bodily labour demands a less quantity of sleep than mental. Labourers and artizans are generally satisfied with about seven hours; but I have known some scholars who usually slept nine, and perceived their faculties no way impaired by over-sleeping.

The famous Philip Barrettiere, who was considered as a prodigy of learning at the age of fourteen, was known to sleep regularly twelve hours in the

to sleep. After a sound night's repose, the irritations occasioned by the exertions of the day are allayed, the mind becomes tranquil and placid, the emaciated muscles are enlarged and invigorated, and man rises refreshed and fitted for the labours of the day before him.]

twenty-four; the extreme activity of his mind, when awake, in some measure called for an adequate alternation of repose: and, I am apt to think, that when students stint themselves in this particular, they lessen the waking powers of the imagination, and weaken its most strenuous exertions. Animals, that seldom think, as was said, can very easily dispense with sleep; and of men, such as think least, will very probably be satisfied with the smallest share. A life of study, it is well known, unfits the body for receiving this gentle refreshment; the approaches of sleep are driven off by thinking: when, therefore, it comes at last, we should not be too ready to interrupt its continuance.

Sleep is, indeed, to some, a very agreeable period of their existence: and it has been a question in the schools, which was most happy, the man who was a beggar by night, and a king by day; or he who was a beggar by day, and a king by night? It is given in favour of the nightly monarch, by him who first started the question: for the dream, says he, gives the full enjoyment of the dignity, without its attendant inconveniences; while, on the other hand, the king, who supposes himself degraded, feels all the misery of his fallen fortune, without trying to find the comforts of his humble situation. Thus, by day, both states have their peculiar distresses: but, by night the exalted beggar is perfectly blessed, and the king completely miserable. All this, however, is rather fanciful than just; the pleasure dreams can give us, seldom reaches to our waking pitch of happiness; the mind often in the midst of its highest visionary satisfactions, demands of itself, whether it does not owe them to a dream; and frequently awakes with the reply.

But it is seldom, except in cases of the highest delight, or the most extreme uneasiness, that the mind has power thus to disengage itself from the dominion of fancy. In the ordinary course of its operations, it submits to those numberless fantastic images that succeed each other; and which, like many of our waking thoughts, are generally forgotten. Of these, however, if any, by their oddity, or their continuance, affect us strongly, they are then remembered; and there have been some who felt their impressions so strongly, as to mistake them for realities, and to rank them among the past actions of their lives.

There are others upon whom dreams seem to have a very different effect; and who, without seeming to remember their impressions the next morning, have yet shewn, by their actions during sleep, that they were very powerfully impelled by their dominion. We have numberless instances of such persons, who, while asleep, have performed many of the ordinary duties to which they had been accustomed, when waking; and with a ridiculous industry, have completed by night, what they failed doing by day. We are told, in the German Ephemerides, of a young student, who being enjoined a severe exercise by his tutor, went to bed, despairing of accomplishing it. The next morning awaking, to his great surprise, he found the task fairly written out, and finished in his own hand-writing. He was at first, as the account has it, induced to ascribe this strange production to the operations of an infernal agent; but his tutor, willing to examine the affair to the bottom, set him another exercise, still more severe than the former; and took precautions to observe his conduct the whole night. The young gentleman, upon being so severely tasked, felt the same inquietude that he had done on the former occasion; went to bed gloomy and pensive, pondering on the next day's duty, and, after some time, fell asleep. But shortly after, his tutor, who continued to observe him from a place that was concealed, was surprised to see him get up, and very deliberately go to the table; there he took out pen, ink, and paper, drew himself a chair, and sate very methodically to thinking; it seems, that his being asleep only served to strengthen the powers of his imagination; for he very quickly and easily went through the task assigned him, put his chair aside, and then returned to bed to take the rest of his nap. What credit we are to give to this account I will not pretend to determine; but this may be said, that the book from whence it is taken, has some good marks of veracity; for it is very learned and very dull, and is written in a country noted, if not for truth, at least for want of invention.

The ridiculous history of Arlotto is well known, who has had a volume written, containing a narrative of the actions of his life, not one of which was performed while he was awake. He was an Italian Franciscan friar, extremely rigid in his manners, and remarkably devout and learned in his daily conversation. By night, however, and during his sleep, he played a very different character from what he did by day, and was often detected in very atrocious crimes. He was at one time detected

†

in actually attempting a rape, and did not awake till the next morning, when he was surprised to find himself in the hands of justice. His brothers of the convent often watched him while he went very deliberately into the chapel, and there attempted to commit sacrilege. They sometimes permitted him to carry the chalice and the vestments away into his own chamber, and the next morning amused themselves at the poor man's consternation for what he had done. But of all his sleeping transgressions, that was the most ridiculous, in which he was called to pray for the soul of a person departed. Arlotto, after having very devoutly performed his duty, retired to a chamber which was shewn him, to rest; but there he had no sooner fallen asleep, than he began to reflect that the dead body had got a ring upon one of the fingers, which might be useful to him : accordingly, with a pious resolution of stealing it, he went down, undressed as he was, into a room full of women, and, with great composure, endeavoured to seize the ring. The consequence was, that he was taken before the inquisition for witchcraft: and the poor creature had like to have been condemned, till his peculiar character accidentally came to be known : however, he was ordered to remain for the rest of his life in his own convent, and upon no account whatsoever to stir abroad.

What are we to say to such actions as these ; or how account for this operation of the mind in dreaming ? It should seem, that the imagination, by day, as well as by night, is always employed ; and that often against our wills, it intrudes where it is least commanded or desired. While awake, and in health, this busy principle cannot much delude us : it may build castles in the air, and raise a thousand phantoms before us ; but we have every one of the senses alive, to bear testimony to its false-hood. Our eyes shew us that the prospect is not present ; our hearing, and our touch, depose against its reality ; and our taste and smelling are equally vigilant in detecting the impostor. Reason, there-fore, at once gives judgment upon the cause ; and the vagrant intruder, imagination, is imprisoned, or banished from the mind. But in sleep it is otherwise ; having, as much as possible, put our senses from their duty, having closed the eyes from seeing, and the ears, taste, and smelling, from their peculiar functions, and having diminished even the touch itself, by all the arts of softness, the imagination is then left to riot at large, and to lead the under-standing without an opposer. Every incursive idea then becomes a reality ; and the mind, not having one power that can prove the illusion, takes them for truths. As in madness, the senses, from strug-gling with the imagination, are at length forced to submit, so, in sleep, they seem for a while soothed into the like submission : the smallest violence exerted upon any one of them, however, rouzes all the rest in their mutual defence ; and the imagina-tion, that had for a while told its thousand false-hoods, is totally driven away, or only permitted to pass under the custody of such as are every moment ready to detect its imposition.*

[* Dreams seem to be the delirium of sleep : as in waking all those ideas where the imagination exceeds probability, constitute a greater or less degree of delirium ; so in sleep, where no external irritations are attended to, and where the power of

CHAP. II.

Of Seeing.*

" HAVING mentioned the senses as correcting the errors of the imagination, and as forcing it, in some measure, to bring us just information, it will naturally follow that we should examine the nature of those senses themselves : we shall thus be enabled to see how far they also impose on us, and how far they contribute to correct each other. Let it be observed, however, that in this we are neither giving a treatise of optics or phonics, but a history of our own perceptions ; and to those we chiefly confine ourselves."

The eyes very soon begin to be formed in the human embryo, and in the chicken also. Of all the parts which the animal has double, the eyes are produced the soonest, and appear the most prominent. It is true, indeed, that in viviparous animals, and particularly in man, they are not so large in proportion, at first, as in the oviparous kinds ; nevertheless, they are more speedily developed, when they begin to appear, than any other parts of the body. It is the same with the organ of hearing ; the little bones that compose the internal parts of

volition is totally suspended, the endless trains of our sleeping ideas are excited by the mere sensation of pleasure and pain with their association.]

* This chapter is taken from Mr. Buffon. I believe the reader will readily excuse any apology; and, perhaps, may wish that I had taken this liberty much more frequently. What I add is marked, as in a former instance, with inverted commas, " thus."

the ear, are entirely formed before the other bones, though much larger, have acquired any part of their growth, or solidity. Hence it appears, that those parts of the body which are furnished with the greatest quantity of nerves, are the first in forming. Thus the brain, and the spinal marrow, are the first seen begun in the embryo ; and in general, it may be said, that wherever the nerves go, or send their branches in great numbers, there the parts are soonest begun, and the most completely finished.

If we examine the eyes of a child, some hours, or even some days after its birth, it will be easily discerned that it, as yet, makes no use of them. The humours of the organ not having acquired a sufficient consistence, the rays of light strike but confusedly upon the retina, or expansion of nerves at the back of the eye. It is not till about a month after they are born, that children fix them upon objects ; for, before that time, they turn them indiscriminately every where, without appearing to be affected by any. At six or seven weeks old, they plainly discover a choice in the objects of their attention ; they fix their eyes upon the most brilliant colours, and seem peculiarly desirous of turning them towards the light. Hitherto, however, they only seem to fortify the organ for seeing distinctly ; but they have still many illusions to correct.

The first great error in vision is, that the eye inverts every object ; and it in reality appears to the child, until the touch has served to undeceive it, turned upside down. A second error in vision is, that every object appears double. The same object forms itself distinctly upon each eye ; and is consequently seen twice. This error, also, can only be corrected by the touch; and although, in reality, every object we see appears inverted and doubled, yet the judgment, and habit, have so often corrected the sense, that we no longer submit to its imposition, but see every object in its just position, the very instant it appears. Were we, therefore, deprived of feeling, our eyes would not only misrepresent the situation, but also the number of all things round us.

To convince us that we see objects inverted, we have only to observe the manner in which images are represented, coming through a small hole, in a darkened room. If such a small hole be made in a dark room, so that no light can come in, but through it, all the objects without will be painted on the wall behind, but in an inverted position, their heads downwards. For as all the rays which pass from the different parts of the object without, cannot enter the hole in the same extent which they had in leaving the object, since, if so, they would require the aperture to be as large as the object; and, as each part, and every point of the object sends forth the image of itself on every side, and the rays, which form these images, pass from all points of the object as from so many centres; so such only can pass through the small aperture as come in opposite directions. Thus the little aperture becomes a centre for the entire object; through which the rays from the upper parts, as well as from the lower parts of it, pass in converging directions; and, consequently, they must cross each other in the central point, and thus paint the objects behind, upon the wall, in an inverted position.

It is, in like manner, easy to conceive, that we see

all objects double, whatever our present sensations may seem to tell us to the contrary. For, to convince us of this, we have only to compare the situation of any one object on shutting one eye, and then compare the same situation by shutting the other. If, for instance, we hold up a finger, and shut the right eye, we shall find it hide a certain part of the room ; if again we shut the other eye, we shall find that part of the room visible, and the finger seeming to cover a part of the room that had been visible before. If we open both eyes, however, the part covered will appear to lie between the two extremes. But, the truth is, we see the object our finger had covered, one image of it to the right, and the other to the left ; but, from habit, suppose that we see but one image placed between both ; our sense of feeling having corrected the errors of sight. And thus, also, if instead of two eyes, we had two hundred, we should, at first, fancy the objects increased in proportion, until one sense had corrected the errors of another.

" The having two eyes might thus be said to be rather an inconvenience than a benefit, since one eye would answer the purposes of sight as well, and be less liable to illusion. But it is otherwise ; two eyes greatly contribute, if not to distinct, at least to extensive vision.* When an object is placed at a moderate distance, by the means of both eyes we see a larger share of it than we possibly could with one ; the right eye seeing a greater portion of its right side, and the left eye of its correspondent side.

* Leonardo da Vinci.

Thus both eyes, in some measure, see round the object; and it is this that gives it, in nature, that bold relievo, or swelling, with which they appear; and which no painting, how exquisite soever, can attain to. The painter must be contented with shading on a flat surface; but the eyes, in observing nature, do not behold the shading only, but a part of the figure also, that lies behind those very shadings, which gives it that swelling, which painters so ardently desire, but can never fully imitate.

"There is another defect, which either of the eyes, taken singly, would have, but which is corrected by having the organ double. In either eye there is a point which has no vision whatsoever; so that if one of them only is employed in seeing, there is a part of the object to which it is always totally blind. This is that part of the optic nerve where its vein and artery run; which being insensible, that point of the object that is painted there must continue unseen. To be convinced of this we have only to try a very easy experiment. If we take three black patches, and stick them upon a white wall, about a foot distance from each other, each about as high as the eye that is to observe them; then retiring six or seven feet back, and shutting one eye, by trying for some time we shall find, that while we distinctly behold the black spots that are to the right and left, that which is in the middle remains totally unseen. Or, in other words, when we bring that part of the eye, where the optic artery runs, to fall upon the object it will then become invisible. This defect, however, in either eye, is always corrected by both, since the part of the object, that is unseen by one, will be very distinctly perceived by the other."

Besides the former defects, we can have no idea of distances from the sight, without the help of touch. Naturally, every object we see appears to be within our eyes; and a child, who has as yet made but little use of the sense of feeling, must suppose that every thing it sees makes a part of itself. Such objects are only seen more or less bulky as they approach or recede from its eyes; so that a fly that is near will appear larger than an ox at a distance. It is experience alone that can rectify this mistake; and a long acquaintance with the real size of every object, quickly assures us of the distance at which it is seen. The last man in a file of soldiers appears in reality much less, perhaps ten times more diminutive, than the man next to us; however, we do not perceive this difference, but continue to think him of equal stature; for the numbers we have seen thus lessened by distance, and have found, by repeated experience, to be of the natural size, when we come closer, instantly correct the sense, and every object is perceived with nearly its natural proportion. But it is otherwise, if we observe objects in such situations as we have not had sufficient experience to correct the errors of the eye; if, for instance, we look at men from the top of a high steeple, they in that case appear very much diminished, as we have not had a habit of correcting the sense in that position.

Although a small degree of reflection will serve to convince us of the truth of these positions, it may not be amiss to strengthen them by an authority which cannot be disputed. Mr. Cheselden having couched a boy of thirteen for a cataract, who had hitherto been blind, and thus at once having restored him to sight, curiously marked the progress of his mind, upon that occasion. This youth, though he had been till then incapable of seeing, yet was not totally blind, but could tell day from night, as persons in his situation always may. He could also, with a strong light, distinguish black from white, and either from the vivid colour of scarlet; however, he saw nothing of the form of bodies; and, without a bright light, not even colours themselves. He was, at first, couched only in one of his eyes; and, when he saw for the first time, he was so far from judging of distances, that he supposed his eyes touched every object that he saw, in the same manner as his hands might be said to feel them. The objects that were most agreeable to him were such as were of plain surfaces and regular figures; though he could as yet make no judgment whatever of their different forms, nor give a reason why one pleased him more than another. Although he could form some idea of colours during his state of blindness, yet that was not sufficient to direct him at present; and he could scarcely be persuaded that the colours he now saw were the same with those he had formerly conceived such erroneous ideas of. He delighted most in green; but black objects, as if giving him an idea of his former blindness, he regarded with horror. He had, as was said, no idea of forms; and was unable to distinguish one object from another, though never so different. When those things were shewn him, which he had been formerly familiarized to by his feeling, he beheld them with earnestness, in order to remember them a second time; but, as he had too many to recollect at once, he forgot the greatest number; and for one he could tell, after seeing, there was a thousand he was totally unacquainted with. He was very much surprised to find that those things and persons he loved best were not the most beautiful to be seen; and even testified displeasure in not finding his parents so handsome as he conceived them to be. It was near two months before he could find that a picture resembled a solid body. Till then he only considered it as a flat surface variously shadowed; but, when he began to perceive that these kind of shadings actually represented human beings, he then began to examine, by his touch, whether they had not the usual qualities of such bodies, and was greatly surprised to find, what he expected a very unequal surface to be smooth and even. He was then shewn a miniature picture of his father, which was contained in his mother's watch-case, and he readily perceived the resemblance; but asked, with great astonishment, how so large a face could be contained in so small a compass? it seemed as strange to him as if a bushel was contained in a pint vessel. At first, he could bear but a very small quantity of light, and he saw every object much greater than the life; but in proportion as he saw objects that were really large, he seemed to think the former were diminished; and although he knew the chamber where he was contained in the house, yet until he saw the latter he could not be brought to conceive how a house could be larger than a chamber. Before the ope-

ration he had no great expectations from the pleasure he should receive from a new sense ; he was
only excited by the hopes of being able to read
and write; he said, for instance, that he could
have no greater pleasure in walking, in the garden,
with his sight, than he had without it, for he walked
there at his ease, and was acquainted with all the
walks. He remarked also, with great justice,
that his former blindness gave him one advantage
over the rest of mankind, which was that of being
able to walk in the night, with confidence and
security. But; when he began to make use of
his new sense, he seemed transported beyond
measure. He said that every new object was
a new source of delight, and that his pleasure
was so great as to be past expression. About a
year after, he was brought to Epsom, where there
is a very fine prospect, with which he seemed
greatly charmed; and he called the landscape
before him a new method of seeing. He was
couched in the other eye, a year after the former,
and the operation succeeded equally well: when
he saw with both eyes, he said that objects appeared
to him twice as large as when he saw but with one;
however, he did not see them doubled, or at least
he shewed no marks as if he saw them so. Mr.
Cheselden mentions instances of many more that
were restored to sight in this manner; they all
seemed to concur in their perceptions with this
youth; and they all seemed particularly embarrassed
in learning how to direct their eyes to the objects
they wished to observe.

In this manner it is that our feeling corrects the
sense of seeing, and that objects which appear of

very different sizes, at different distances, are all
reduced, by experience, to their natural standard.
" But not the feeling only, but also the colour,
and brightness of the object, contributes, in some
measure, to assist us in forming an idea of the
distance at which it appears.* Those which we
see most strongly marked with light and shade, we
readily know to be nearer than those on which
the colours are more faintly spread, and that, in
some measure, take a part of their hue from the air
between us and them. Bright objects also are seen
at a greater distance than such as are obscure;
and, most probably, for this reason, that being less
similar in colour to the air which interposes, their
impressions are less effaced by it, and they continue
more distinctly visible. Thus a black and distant
object is not seen so far off as a bright and glit-
tering one : and a fire by night is seen much farther
off than by day."

The power of seeing objects at a distance is very
rarely equal in both eyes. When this inequality is
in any great degree, the person so circumstanced
then makes use only of one eye, shutting that which
sees the least, and employing the other with all its
power. And hence proceeds that awkward look
which is known by the name of strabism.

There are many reasons to induce us to think
that such as are near-sighted see objects larger
than other persons; and yet the contrary is most
certainly true, for they see them less. Mr. Buffon
informs us that he himself is short-sighted, and

* Mr. Buffon gives a different theory, for which I must refer
the reader to the original. That I have given, I take to be easy
and satisfactory enough.

that his left eye is stronger than his right. He has very frequently experienced, upon looking at any object, such as the letters of a book, that they appear less to the weakest eye; and that when he places the book, so as that the letters appear double, the images of the left eye, which is strongest, are greater than those of the right, which is the most feeble. He has examined several others who were in similar circumstances, and has always found that the best eye saw every object the largest. This he ascribes to habit; for near-sighted people being accustomed to come close to the object, and view but a small part of it at a time, the habit ensues, when the whole of an object is seen, and it appears less to them than to others.

Infants having their eyes less than those of adults, must see objects also smaller in proportion. For the image formed on the back of the eye will be large, as the eye is capacious; and infants, having it not so great, cannot have so large a picture of the object. This may be a reason also why they are unable to see so distinctly, or at such distances as persons arrived at maturity.

Old men, on the contrary, see bodies close to them very indistinctly, but bodies at a great distance from them with more precision; and this may happen from an alteration in the coats, or, perhaps, humours of the eye; and not, as is supposed, from their diminution. The cornea, for instance, may become too rigid to adapt itself, and take a proper convexity for seeing minute objects; and its very flatness will be sufficient to fit it for distant vision.

When we cast our eyes upon an object extremely brilliant, or when we fix and detain them too long upon the same object, the organ is hurt and fatigued, its vision becomes indistinct, and the image of the body, which has thus too violently, or too perseveringly employed us, is painted upon every thing we look at, and mixes with every object that occurs. " And this is an obvious consequence of the eye taking in too much light, either immediately, or by reflection. Every body exposed to the light, for a time, drinks in a quantity of its rays, which, being brought into darkness, it cannot instantly discharge. Thus the hand, if it be exposed to broad day-light, for some time, and then immediately snatched into a dark room, will appear still luminous; and it will be some time before it is totally darkened. It is thus with the eye; which, either by an instant gaze at the sun, or a steady continuance, upon some less brilliant object, has taken in too much light; its humours are, for a while, unfit for vision, until that be discharged, and room made for rays of a milder nature." How dangerous the looking upon bright and luminous objects is to the sight, may be easily seen, from such as live in countries, covered, for most part of the year, with snow, who become generally blind before their time. Travellers who cross these countries, are obliged to wear a crape before their eyes, to save their eyes, which would otherwise be rendered totally unserviceable; and it is equally dangerous in the sandy plains of Africa. The reflection of the light is there so strong that it is impossible to sustain the effect, without incurring the danger of

†

losing one's sight entirely. Such persons, therefore, as read, or write for any continuance, should choose a moderate light, in order to save their eyes; and, although it may seem insufficient at first, the eye will accustom itself to the shade, by degrees, and be less hurt by the want of light than the excess.

"It is, indeed, surprising how far the eye can accommodate itself to darkness, and make the best of a gloomy situation. When first taken from the light, and brought into a dark room, all things disappear; or, if any thing is seen, it is only the remaining radiations that still continue in the eye. But, after a very little time, when these are spent, the eye takes the advantage of the smallest ray that happens to enter; and this alone would, in time, serve for many of the purposes of life. There was a gentleman of great courage and understanding who was a major under King Charles the First. This unfortunate man sharing in his master's misfortunes, and being forced abroad, ventured at Madrid to do his king a signal service; but, unluckily, failed in the attempt. In consequence of this, he was instantly ordered to a dark and dismal dungeon, into which the light never entered, and into which there was no opening but by a hole at the top, down which the keeper put his provisions, and presently closed it again on the other side. In this manner the unfortunate loyalist continued for some weeks, distressed and disconsolate; but, at last, began to think he saw some little glimmering of light. This internal dawn seemed to increase from time to time, so that he could not only discover the parts of his bed,

and such other large objects, but, at length, he
even began to perceive the mice that frequented
his cell; and saw them as they ran about the floor,
eating the crumbs of bread that happened to fall.
After some months' confinement, he was at last set
free; but, such was the effect of the darkness upon
him, that he could not for some days venture to
leave his dungeon, but was obliged to accustom
himself by degrees to the light of the day.*

[* According to Dr. Darwin's reasoning on the motions of the
retina, it appears, that neither mechanical impressions nor chemical combinations of light, but the animal activity of the muscles
and fibres of the retina, constitutes vision. These, like all other
animal muscles and fibres, are susceptible of external excitement,
and retain or lose their powers by the different combinations of
the stimulus of light.

"On looking long on an area of scarlet silk of about an inch
in diameter, laid on white paper, the scarlet colour becomes
fainter, till at length it entirely vanishes, though the eye is kept
uniformly steady upon it. Now if the change or motion of the
retina was a mechanical impression, or a chemical tinge of
coloured light, the perception would every minute become
stronger and stronger; whereas, in this experiment, it becomes
every instant weaker and weaker. The same circumstance
obtains in the continued application of sound, or of sapid bodies,
or of odorous ones, or of tangible ones, to their adapted organs
of sense.

"Thus, when a circular coin, as a shilling, is pressed on the
palm of the hand, the sense of touch is mechanically compressed;
but it is the stimulus of this pressure that excites the organs of
touch into animal action, which constitutes the perception of
hardness, and figure: for in some minutes the perception ceases,
though the mechanical pressure of the object remains."

All the organs of sense are animal motions. They are originally excited into action by the irritation of external objects, like
the larger muscles of the body, are associated together like our
muscular actions, act in similar time like them, are fatigued like
them by continual exertion in the same manner as the muscular

CHAP. III.

Of Hearing.*

AS the sense of hearing, as well as of sight, gives us notice of remote objects, so, like that, it is subject to similar errors, being capable of imposing on us upon all occasions, where we cannot rectify it by the sense of feeling. We can have from it no distinct intelligence of the distance from whence a sounding body is heard; a great noise far off, and a small one very near, produce the same sensation; and, unless we receive information from some other sense, we can never distinctly tell whether the sound be a great or a small one. It is not till we have learned, by experience, that the particular sound, which is heard, is of a peculiar kind; then we can judge of the distance from whence we hear it. When we know the tone of the bell, we can then judge how far it is from us.

Every body that strikes against another produces a sound, which is simple, and but one in bodies which are not elastic, but which is often repeated in such as are. If we strike a bell, or a stretched string, for instance, which are both elastic, a single blow produces a sound, which is repeated by the undulations of the sonorous body, and which is multiplied as often as it happens to un-

fibres, are subject to inflammations, numbness, palsy, convulsion, and the defects of old age.]

* This chapter is taken from M. Buffon, except where marked by inverted commas.

dulate, or vibrate. These undulations each strike their own peculiar blow; but they succeed so fast, one behind the other, that the ear supposes them one continued sound; whereas, in reality, they make many. A person who should, for the first time hear the toll of the bell, would very probably be able to distinguish these breaks of sound; and, in fact, we can readily ourselves perceive an intension and remission in the sound.

In this manner, sounding bodies are of two kinds; those unelastic ones, which being struck, return but a single sound; and those more elastic returning a succession of sounds; which uniting together form a tone. This tone may be considered as a great number of sounds, all produced one after the other, by the same body, as we find in a bell, or the string of a harpsichord, which continues to sound for some time after it is struck. A continuing tone may be also produced from a non-elastic body, by repeating the blow quick and often, as when we beat a drum, or when we draw a bow along the string of a fiddle.

Considering the subject in this light, if we should multiply the number of blows, or repeat them at quicker intervals upon the sounding body, as upon the drum, for instance, it is evident that this will have no effect in altering the tone; it will only make it either more even or more distinct. But it is otherwise, if we increase the force of the blow; if we strike the body with double weight, this will produce a tone twice as loud as the former. If, for instance, I strike a table with a switch, this will be very different from the sound produced by striking it with a cudgel. Hence, therefore,

we may infer, that all bodies give a louder
and graver tone, not in proportion to the number
of times they are struck, but in proportion to
the force that strikes them. And, if this be so,
those philosophers who make the tone of a sonorous
body of a bell, or the string of a harpsichord,
for instance, to depend upon the number only
of its vibrations, and not the force, have mistaken
what is only an effect for a cause. A bell, or
an elastic string, can only be considered as a
drum beaten; and the frequency of the blows can
make no alteration whatever in the tone. The
largest bells, and the longest and thickest strings,
have the most forceful vibrations; and, therefore, their tones are the most loud and the most
grave.

To know the manner in which sounds thus produced become pleasing, it must be observed, no
one continuing tone, how loud or swelling soever,
can give us satisfaction; we must have a succession
of them, and those in the most pleasing proportion.
The nature of this proportion may be thus conceived. If we strike a body incapable of vibration
with a double force, or, what amounts to the
same thing, with a double mass of matter, it
will produce a sound that will be doubly grave.
Music has been said by the ancients, to have been
first invented from the blows of different hammers
on an anvil. Suppose then we strike an anvil with
a hammer of one pound weight, and again with
a hammer of two pounds, it is plain that the
two-pound hammer will produce a sound twice
as grave as the former. But if we strike with
a two-pound hammer, and then with a three-

pound, it is evident that the latter will produce a sound one third more grave than the former. If we strike the anvil with a three-pound hammer, and then with a four-pound, it will likewise follow that the latter will be a quarter part more grave than the former. Now, in the comparing between all those sounds, it is obvious that the difference between one and two is more easily perceived than between two and three, three and four, or any numbers succeeding in the same proportion. The succession of sounds will be, therefore, pleasing in proportion to the ease with which they may be distinguished. That sound which is double the former, or, in other words, the octave to the preceding tone, will of all others be the most pleasing. The next to that, which is as two to three, or, in other words, the third, will be most agreeable. And thus, universally, those sounds whose difference may be most easily compared are the most agreeable.

" Musicians, therefore, have contented themselves with seven different proportions of sound, which are called notes, and which sufficiently answer all the purposes of pleasure. Not but that they might adopt a greater diversity of proportions ; and some have actually done so ; but in these, the differences of the proportion are so imperceptible, that the ear is rather fatigued than pleased in making the distinction. In order, however, to give variety, they have admitted half tones ; but, in all the countries where music is yet in its infancy, they have rejected such ; and they can find music in none but the obvious ones. The Chinese, for instance, have neither flats nor sharps in their music; but the intervals between their other notes are in the same proportion with ours.

" Many more barbarous nations have their peculiar instruments of music; and, what is remarkable, the proportion between their notes is in all the same as in ours. This is not the place for entering into the nature of these sounds, their effects upon the air, or their consonances with each other. We are not now giving a history of sound, but of human perception.

" All countries are pleased with music; and, if they have not skill enough to produce harmony, at least they seem willing to substitute noise. Without all question, noise alone is sufficient to operate powerfully on the spirits; and, if the mind be already predisposed to joy, I have seldom found noise fail of increasing it into rapture. The mind feels a kind of distracted pleasure in such powerful sounds, braces up every nerve, and riots in the excess. But, as in the eye, an immediate gaze upon the sun will disturb the organs, so, in the ear, a loud unexpected noise disorders the whole frame, and sometimes disturbs the sense ever after. The mind must have time to prepare for the expected shock, and to give its organs the proper tension for its arrival.

" Musical sounds, however, seem of a different kind. Those are generally most pleasing, which are most unexpected. It is not from bracing up the nerves, but from the grateful succession of the sounds, that these become so charming. There are few, how indifferent soever, but have at times felt their pleasing impression; and, perhaps, even those who have stood out against the powerful persuasion of sounds, only wanted the proper tune, or the proper instrument, to allure them.

" The ancients give us a thousand strange instances of the effects of music, upon men and animals. The story of Arion's harp, that gathered the dolphins to the ship side, is well known ; and, what is remarkable, Schotteus assures us,* that he saw a similar instance of fishes being allured by music. They tell us of diseases that have . been cured, unchastity corrected, seditions quelled, passions removed, and sometimes excited even to madness. Doctor Wallis has endeavoured to account for these surprising effects, by ascribing them to the novelty of the art. For my own part, I can scarcely hesitate to impute them to the exaggeration of the writers. They are as hyperbolical in the effects of their oratory ; and yet we well know there is nothing in the orations which they have left us, capable of exciting madness, or of raising the mind to that ungovernable degree of fury which they describe. As they have exaggerated, therefore, in one instance, we may naturally suppose that they have done the same in the other : and, indeed, from the few remains we have of their music, collected by Meibomius, one might be apt to suppose, there was nothing very powerful in what is lost. Nor does any one of the ancient instruments such as we see them represented in statues, appear comparable to our fiddle.

" However this be, we have many odd accounts,

---

* Quod oculis meis spectavi. Scotti Magic. universalis, pars ii L 1, p. 26.

not only among them, but the moderns, of the
power of music; and it must not be denied,
but that, on some particular occasions, musical
sounds may have a very powerful effect. I have
seen all the horses and cows in a field, where there
were above a hundred, gather round a person that
was blowing a French horn, and seeming to testify
an awkward kind of satisfaction. Dogs are well
known to be very sensible of different tones in
music; and I have sometimes heard them sustain
a very ridiculous part in a concert, where their
assistance was neither expected nor desired.

" We are told of Henry IV. of Denmark,* that,
being one day desirous of trying in person whether
a musician who boasted that he could excite men
to madness, was not an impostor, he submitted to
the operation of his skill : but the consequence was
much more terrible than he expected; for, becoming
actually mad, he killed four of his attendants, in
the midst of his transports. A contrary effect of
music we have,† in the cure of a madman of
Alais, in France, by music. This man, who was
a dancing-master, after a fever of five days, grew
furious, and so ungovernable, that his hands were
obliged to be tied to his sides: what at first was
rage, in a short time was converted into silent
melancholy, which no arts could exhilarate, nor no
medicines remove. In this sullen and dejected
state, an old acquaintance accidentally came to
enquire after his health ; he found him sitting up in
bed, tied, and totally regardless of every external
object round him. Happening, however, to take

* Olai Magni, l. 15. hist. c. 28. † Hist. de l'Acad. 1708, p. 22.

up a fiddle that lay in the room, and touching a
favourite air, the poor madman instantly seemed to
brighten up at the sound; from a recumbent posture, he began to sit up; and as the musician continued playing, the patient seemed desirous of
dancing to the sound; but he was tied, and incapable
of leaving his bed, so that he could only humour
the tune with his head, and those parts of his
arms which were at liberty. Thus the other continued playing, and the dancing-master practised
his own art, as far as he was able, for about a
quarter of an hour, when suddenly falling into a
deep sleep, in which his disorder came to a crisis,
he awaked perfectly recovered.

" A thousand other instances might be added,
equally true : let it suffice to add one more, which
is not true; I mean that of the tarantula. Every
person who has been in Italy, now well knows,
that the bite of this animal, and its being cured
by music, is all a deception. When strangers
come into that part of the country, the country
people are ready enough to take money for dancing
to the tarantula. A friend of mine had a servant
who suffered himself to be bit; the wound, which
was little larger than the puncture of a pin, was
uneasy for a few hours, and then became well
without any farther assistance. Some of the
country people, however, still make a tolerable
livelihood of the credulity of strangers, as the
musician finds his account in it not less than the
dancer."

Sounds, like light, are not only extensively diffused, but are frequently reflected. The laws of
this reflection, it is true, are not as well under-

stood as those of light; all we know is, that sound
is principally reflected by hard bodies; and their
being hollow, also, sometimes increases the rever-
beration. "No art, however, can make an echo;
and some, who have bestowed great labour and
expense upon such a project, have only erected
shapeless buildings, whose silence was a mortifying
lecture upon their presumption."

The internal cavity of the ear seems to be fitted
up for the purpose of echoing sound with the
greatest precision. This part is fashioned out in
the temporal bone, like a cavern cut into a rock.
"In this the sound is repeated and articulated;
and, as some anatomists tell us, (for we have as
yet but very little knowledge on this subject) is
beaten against the tympanum, or drum of the ear,
which moves four little bones joined thereto; and
these move and agitate the internal air which lies
on the other side; and lastly, this air strikes and
affects the auditory nerves, which carry the sound
to the brain."

One of the most common disorders in old age is
deafness; which probably proceeds from the rigidity of the nerves in the labyrinth of the ear. This
disorder also, sometimes, proceeds from a stoppage
of the wax, which art may easily remedy. In
order to know whether the defect be an internal or
an external one, let the deaf person put a repeating
watch into his mouth; and if he hears it strike, he
may be assured that his disorder proceeds from an
external cause, and is, in some measure, curable:
" for there is a passage from the ears into the
mouth, by what anatomists call the eustachian
tube; and, by this passage people often hear

sounds, when they are utterly without hearing
through the larger channel: and this also is the
reason that we often see persons who listen with
great attention, hearken with their mouths open, in
order to catch all the sound at every aperture."

It often happens, that persons hear differently
with one ear from the other; and it is generally
found that these have what is called, by musicians,
a bad ear. M. Buffon, who has made many trials
upon persons of this kind, always found that their
defect in judging properly of sounds, proceeded
from the inequality of their ears; and receiving
by both, at the same time, unequal sensations,
they form an unjust idea. In this manner, as those
people hear false, they also without knowing it,
sing false. Those persons also frequently deceive
themselves with regard to the side from whence the
sound comes, generally supposing the noise to
come on the part of the best ear.

Such as are hard of hearing find the same advantage in the trumpet made for this purpose, that
short-sighted persons do from glasses. These
trumpets might easily be improved so as to increase
sounds, in the same manner that the telescope does
objects: however, they could be used to advantage
only in a place of solitude and stillness, as the
neighbouring sounds would mix with the more
distant, and the whole would produce in the ear
nothing but tumult and confusion.

Hearing is a much more necessary sense to man
than to animals. With these it is only a warning
against danger, or an encouragement to mutual
assistance. In man it is the source of most of his
pleasure; and without which, the rest of his

senses would be of little benefit. A man born
deaf, must necessarily be dumb ; and his whole
sphere of knowledge must be bounded only by
sensual objects. We have an instance of a young
man who, being born deaf, was restored, at
the age of twenty-four, to perfect hearing: the
account is given in the Memoirs of the Academy of
Sciences, 1703, page 18.

A young man of the town of Chartres, between
the age of twenty-three and twenty-four, the son
of a tradesman, and deaf and dumb from his birth,
began to speak all of a sudden, to the great astonishment of the whole town. He gave them to
understand that, about three or four months before,
he had heard the sound of the bells for the first
time, and was greatly surprised at this new and
unknown sensation. After some time, a kind of
water issued from his left ear, and he then heard
perfectly well with both. During these three
months, he was sedulously employed in listening,
without saying a word, and accustoming himself
to speak softly, so as not to be heard, the words
pronounced by others. He laboured hard also in
perfecting himself in the pronunciation, and in
the ideas attached to every sound. At length,
having supposed himself qualified to break silence,
he declared, that he could now speak, although
as yet but imperfectly. Soon after, some able
divines questioned him concerning his ideas of
his past state ; and principally with respect to God,
his soul, the morality or turpitude of actions.
The young man, however, had not driven his
solitary speculations into that channel. He had gone
to mass indeed with his parents, had learned to

sign himself with the cross, to kneel down and
assume all the grimaces of a man that was praying:
but he did all this without any manner of knowledge
of the intention or the cause; he saw others
do the like, and that was enough for him; he
knew nothing even of death, and it never entered
into his head; he led a life of pure animal instinct;
entirely taken up with sensible objects, and such
as were present; he did not seem even to make as
many reflections upon these, as might reasonably
be expected from his improving situation: and yet,
the young man was not in want of understanding;
but the understanding of a man deprived of all
commerce with others, is so very confined, that the
mind is in some measure totally under the control
of its immediate sensations.

 Notwithstanding, it is very possible to communicate ideas to deaf men, which they previously
wanted, and even give them very precise notions
of some abstract subjects, by means of signs and
of letters. A person born deaf, may, by time,
and sufficient pains, be taught to write and read,
to speak, and, by the motions of the lips, to understand what is said to him; however, it is probable
that, as most of the motions of speech are made
within the mouth by the tongue, the knowledge
from the motion of the lips, is but very confined:
" nevertheless, I have conversed with a gentleman
thus taught, and in all the commonly occurring
questions, and the usual salutations, he was ready
enough, merely by attending to the motion of
the lips alone. When I ventured to speak for a
short continuance, he was totally at a loss, although
he understood the subject, when written, extremely

well." Persons taught in this manner, were at first considered as prodigies; but there have been so many instances of success of late, and so many are skilful in the art of instructing in this way, that, though still a matter of some curiosity, it ceases to be an object of wonder.

CHAP. IV.

Of Smelling, Feeling, and Tasting.

AN animal may be said to fill up that sphere which he can reach by his senses; and is actually large in proportion to the sphere to which its organ extends. By sight, man's enjoyments are diffused into a wide circle; that of hearing, though less widely diffused, nevertheless extends his powers; the sense of smelling is more contracted still; and the taste and touch are the most confined of all. Thus man enjoys very distant objects, but with one sense only; more nearly he brings two senses at once to bear upon them; his sense of smelling assists the other two, at its own distance; and of such objects, as a man, he may be said to be in perfect possession.

Each sense, however, the more it acts at a distance, the more capable it is of making combinations; and is, consequently, the more improveable.

Refined imaginations, and men of strong minds, take more pleasure, therefore, in improving the delights of the distant senses than in enjoying such as are scarce capable of improvement.

By combining the objects of the extensive senses,

all the arts of poetry, painting, and harmony, have been discovered; but the closer senses, if I may so call them, such as smelling, tasting, and touching, are, in some measure, as simple as they are limited, and admit of little variety. The man of imagination makes a great and an artificial happiness, by the pleasure of altering and combining; the sensualist just stops where he began, and cultivates only those pleasures which he cannot improve. The sensualist is contented with those enjoyments that are already made to his hand; but the man of pleasure is best pleased with growing happiness.

Of all the senses, perhaps, there is not one in which man is more inferior to other animals than in that of smelling. With man, it is a sense that acts in a narrow sphere, and disgusts almost as frequently as it gives him pleasure. With many other animals it is diffused to a very great extent; and never seems to offend them. Dogs not only trace the steps of other animals, but also discover them by scent, at a very great distance; and, while they are thus exquisitely sensible of all smells, they seem no way disgusted by any.

But, although this sense is, in general, so very inferior in man, it is much stronger in those nations that abstain from animal food, than among Europeans. The Bramins of India have a power of smelling, as I am informed, equal to what it is in most other creatures. They can smell the water which they drink, that to us seems quite inodorous; and have a word, in their language, which denotes a country of fine water. We are told, also, that the Negroes of the Antilles, by the smell

alone, can distinguish between the footsteps of a
Frenchman and a Negro. It is possible, therefore,
that we may dull this organ by our luxurious way
of living; and sacrifice to the pleasures of taste
those which might be received from perfume.

However, it is a sense that we can, in some
measure, dispense with; and I have known many
that wanted it entirely, with but very little inconvenience from its loss. In a state of nature, it is
said to be useful in guiding us to proper nourishment, and deterring us from that which is unwholesome; but, in our present situation, such
information is but little wanted; and, indeed, but
little attended to. In fact, the sense of smelling
gives us very often false intelligence. Many things
that have a disagreeable odour are, nevertheless,
wholesome and pleasant to the taste; and such as
make eating an art, seldom think a meal fit to
please the appetite till it begins to offend the nose.
On the other hand, there are many things that
smell most gratefully, and yet are noxious, or fatal
to the constitution. Some physicians think that
perfumes, in general, are unwholesome; that they
relax the nerves, produce head-aches, and even
retard digestion. The manchineel apple, which
is known to be deadly poison, is possessed of the
most grateful odour. Some of those mineral
vapours that are often found fatal in the stomach,
smell like the sweetest flowers, and continue thus
to flatter till they destroy. This sense, therefore,
as it should seem, was never meant to direct us in
the choice of food, but appears rather as an
attendant than a necessary pleasure.

Indeed, if we examine the natives of different

countries, or even different natives of the same, we shall find no pleasure in which they differ so widely as that of smelling. Some persons are pleased with the smell of a rose; while I have known others that could not abide to have it approach them. The savage nations are highly delighted with the smell of assafœtida, which is to us the most nauseous stink in nature. It would in a manner seem that our delight in perfumes was made by habit; and that a very little industry could bring us totally to invert the perception of odours.

Thus much is certain, that many bodies which at one distance are an agreeable perfume, when nearer are a most ungrateful odour. Musk, and ambergrise, in small quantities, are considered by most persons as highly fragrant; and yet, when in larger masses, their scent is insufferable. From a mixture of two bodies, each whereof is, of itself, void of all smell, a very powerful smell may be drawn. Thus, by grinding quick lime with sal-ammoniac, may be produced a very fœtid mixture. On the contrary, from a mixture of two bodies, that are separately disagreeable, a very pleasant aromatic odour may be gained. A mixture of aqua fortis with spirit of wine produces this effect. But not only the alterations of bodies by each other, but the smallest change in us, makes a very great alteration in this sense, and frequently deprives us of it totally. A slight cold often hinders us from smelling; and as often changes the nature of odours. Some persons, from disorder, retain an incurable aversion to those smells which most pleased them before; and many have been known to have an antipathy to some animals, whose presence they instantly perceived by the smell. From all this, therefore, the sense of smelling appears to be an uncertain monitor, easily disordered, and not much missed when totally wanting.

The sense most nearly allied to smelling is that of tasting. This some have been willing to consider merely as a nicer kind of touch, and have undertaken to account, in a very mechanical manner, for the difference of savours. Such bodies, said they, as are pointed, happening to be applied to the papillæ of the tongue, excite a very powerful sensation, and give us the idea of saltness. Such, on the contrary, as are of a rounder figure, slide smoothly along the papillæ, and are perceived to be sweet. In this manner they have, with minute labour, gone through the variety of imagined forms in bodies, and have given them as imaginary effects. All we can precisely determine upon the nature of tastes is, that the bodies to be tasted must be either somewhat moistened, or, in some measure, dissolved by the saliva before they can produce a proper sensation : when both the tongue itself, and the body to be tasted, are extremely dry, no taste whatever ensues. The sensation is then changed ; and the tongue, instead of tasting, can only be said, like any other part of the body, to feel the object.

It is for this reason, that children have a stronger relish of tastes than those who are much advanced in life. This organ with them, from the greater moisture of their bodies, is kept in greater perfection ; and is, consequently, better adapted to perform its functions. Every person remembers how great a pleasure he found in sweets, while a child : but his taste growing more obtuse with age, he is obliged to use artificial means to excite it. It is then that he is found to call in the assistance of poignant sauces, and strong relishes, of salts and aromatics ; all which the delicacy of his tender organ, in childhood, was unable to endure. His taste grows callous to the natural relishes ; and is artificially formed to others more unnatural ; so that the highest epicure may be said to have the most depraved taste ; as it is owing to the bluntness of his organ that he is obliged to have recourse to such a variety of expedients, to gratify his appetite.

As smells are often rendered agreeable by habit, so also tastes may be. Tobacco, and coffee, so pleasing to many, are yet, at first, very disagreeable to all. It is not without perseverance that we begin to have a relish for them ; we force nature so long, that what was constraint in the beginning, at last becomes inclination.

The grossest, and yet the most useful of all the senses, is that of feeling. We are often seen to survive under the loss of the rest : but of this we can never be totally deprived, but with life. Although this sense is diffused over all parts of the body, yet it most frequently happens that those parts which are most exercised in touching, acquire the greatest degree of accuracy. Thus the fingers, by long habit, become greater masters in the art than any others, even where the sensation is more delicate and fine.* It is from this habit,

* Buffon, vol. vi. p. 80.

therefore, and their peculiar formation, and not, as is supposed, from their being furnished with a greater quantity of nerves, that the fingers are thus perfectly qualified to judge of forms. Blind men, who are obliged to use them much oftener, have this sense much finer; so that the delicacy of the touch arises rather from the habit of constantly employing the fingers, than from any fancied nervousness in their conformation.

All animals that are furnished with hands,* seem to have more understanding than others. Monkeys have so many actions, like those of men, that they appear to have similar ideas of the form of bodies. All other creatures, deprived of hands, can have no distinct ideas of the shape of the objects by which they are surrounded, as they want this organ, which serves to examine and measure their forms, their risings and depressions. A quadruped probably conceives as erroneous an idea of any thing near him, as a child would of a rock or a mountain, that it beheld at a distance. It may be for this reason that we often see them frighted at things with which they ought to be better acquainted. Fishes, whose bodies are covered with scales, and who have no organs for feeling, must be the most stupid of all animals. Serpents, that are likewise destitute, are yet, by winding round several bodies, better capable of judging of their form. All these, however, can have but very imperfect ideas from feeling; and we have already seen, when deprived of this sense, how little the rest of the senses are to be relied on.

* Buffon, vol. vi. p. 82.

The feeling, therefore, is the guardian, the judge, and the examiner of all the rest of the senses. It establishes their information, and detects their errors. All the other senses are altered by time, and contradict their former evidence; but the touch still continues the same; and though extremely confined in its operations, yet it is never found to deceive. The universe, to a man who had only used the rest of his senses, would be but a scene of illusion; every object misrepresented, and all its properties unknown. M. Buffon has imagined a man just newly brought into existence, describing the illusion of his first sensations, and pointing out the steps by which he arrived at reality. He considers him as just created, and, awaking amidst the productions of nature; and, to animate the narrative still more strongly, has made his philosophical man a speaker. The reader will no doubt recollect Adam's speech in Milton, as being similar. All that I can say to obviate the imputation of plagiarism is, that the one treats the subject more as a poet, the other more as a philosopher. The philosopher's man describes his first sensations in the following manner.*

I well remember that joyful anxious moment when I first became acquainted with my own existence. I was quite ignorant of what I was, how I was produced, or from whence I came. I opened my eyes: what an addition to my surprize! The light of the day, the azure vault of heaven, the verdure of the earth, the crystal of the waters, all employed me at once, and animated and filled me

* Buffon, vol. vi. p. 88.

with inexpressible delight. I at first imagined that all those objects were within me, and made a part of myself.

Impressed with this idea, I turned my eyes to the sun ; its splendor dazzled and overpowered me ; I shut them once more ; and, to my great concern, I supposed that during this short interval of darkness, I was again returning to nothing.

Afflicted, seized with astonishment, I pondered a moment on this great change, when I heard a variety of unexpected sounds. The whistling of the wind, and the melody of the groves, formed a concert, the soft cadence of which sunk upon my soul. I listened for some time, and was persuaded that all this music was within me.

Quite occupied with this new kind of existence, I had already forgotten the light which was my first inlet into life ; when I once more opened my eyes, and found myself again in possession of my former happiness. The gratification of the two senses at once, was a pleasure too great for utterance.

I turned my eyes upon a thousand various objects : I soon found that I could lose them, and restore them at will: and amused myself more at leisure with a repetition of this new-made power.

I now began to gaze without emotion, and to hearken with tranquillity, when a light breeze, the freshness of which charmed me, wafted its perfumes to my sense of smelling, and gave me such satisfaction as even increased my self-love.

Agitated, rouzed by the various pleasures of my new existence, I instantly arose, and perceived myself moved along, as if by some unknown and secret power.

I had scarcely proceeded forward, when the novelty of my situation once more rendered me immoveable. My surprise returned; I supposed that every object around me had been in motion: I gave to them that agitation which I produced by changing place; and the whole creation seemed once more in disorder.

I lifted my hand to my head; I touched my forehead; I felt my whole frame: I then supposed that my hand was the principal organ of my existence; all its informations were distinct and perfect; and so superior to the senses I had yet experienced, that I employed myself for some time in repeating its enjoyments: every part of my person I touched, seemed to touch my hand in turn, and gave back sensation for sensation.

I soon found that this faculty was expanded over the whole surface of my body; and I now first began to perceive the limits of my existence, which I had in the beginning supposed spread over all the objects I saw.

Upon casting my eyes upon my body, and surveying my own form, I thought it greater than all the objects that surrounded me. I gazed upon my person with pleasure; I examined the formation of my hand and all its motions; it seemed to me large or little in proportion as I approached it to my eyes; I brought it very near, and it then hid almost every other object from my sight. I began soon, however, to find that my sight gave me uncertain information, and resolved to depend upon my feeling for redress.

This precaution was of the utmost service; I renewed my motions, and walked forward with my face turned towards the heavens. I happened to strike lightly against a palm-tree, and this renewed my surprise : I laid my hand on this strange body ; it seemed replete with new wonders, for it did not return me sensation for sensation, as my former feelings had done. I perceived that there was something external, and which did not make a part of my own existence.

I now, therefore, resolved to touch whatever I saw, and vainly attempted to touch the sun ; I stretched forth my arm, and felt only yielding air : at every effort, I fell from one surprise into another, for every object appeared equally near me ; and it was not till after an infinity of trials, that I found some objects farther removed than the rest.

Amazed with the illusions, and the uncertainty of my state, I sat down beneath a tree ; the most beautiful fruits hung upon it, within my reach ; I stretched forth my hand, and they instantly separated from the branch. I was proud of being able to grasp a substance without me ; I held them up, and their weight appeared to me like an animated power that endeavoured to draw them to the earth. I found a pleasure in conquering their resistance.

I held them near my eye ; I considered their form and beauty ; their fragrance still more allured me to bring them nearer ; I approached them to my lips, and drank in their odours ; the perfume inviting my sense of tasting, and I soon tried a new sense—How new ! how exquisite ! Hitherto I tasted only of pleasure; but now it was luxury. The power of tasting gave me the idea of possession.

Flattered with this new acquisition, I continued its exercise, till an agreeable languor stealing upon my mind, I felt all my limbs become heavy, and all my desire suspended. My sensations were now no longer vivid and distinct; but seemed to lose every object, and presented only feeble images confusedly marked. At that instant I sunk upon the flowery bank, and slumber seized me. All now seemed once more lost to me. It was then as if I was returning to my former nothing. How long my sleep continued, I cannot tell; as I yet had no perception of time. My awaking appeared like a second birth; and I then perceived that I had ceased for a time to exist. This produced a new sensation of fear; and from this interruption in life, I began to conclude that I was not formed to exist for ever.

In this state of doubt and perplexity, I began to harbour new suspicions; and to fear that sleep had robbed me of some of my late powers; when, turning on one side, to resolve my doubts, what was my amazement, to behold another being, like myself, stretched by my side! New ideas now began to arise; new passions, as yet unperceived, with fears, and pleasures, all took possession of my mind, and prompted my curiosity: love served to complete that happiness which was begun in the individual; and every sense was gratified in all its varieties.

CHAP. V.

*Of Old Age and Death.**

EVERY thing in nature has its improvement and decay. The human form is no sooner arrived at its state of perfection than it begins to decline. The alteration is, at first, insensible ; and, often, several years are elapsed before we find ourselves grown old. The news of this disagreeable change, too generally, comes from without, and we learn from others that we grow old, before we are willing to believe the report.

When the body has come to its full height, and is extended into its just dimensions ; it then also begins to receive an additional bulk, which rather loads than assists it. This is formed from fat ; which generally, at the age of thirty-five, or forty, covers all the muscles, and interrupts their activity. Every action is then performed with greater labour, and the increase of size only serves as a forerunner of decay.

The bones, also, become every day more solid. In the embryo they are as soft almost as the muscles of the flesh ; but, by degrees, they harden, and acquire their natural vigour ; but still, however, the circulation is carried on through them ; and, how hard soever the bones may seem, yet the blood holds its current through them as through

* This chapter is taken from M. Buffon, except where it is marked by inverted commas.

all other parts of the body. Of this we may be
convinced, by an experiment, which was first accidentally discovered, by our ingenious countryman
Mr. Belcher. Perceiving, at a friend's house, that
the bones of hogs, which were fed upon madder,
were red, he tried it upon various animals, by
mixing this root with their usual food; and he
found that it tinctured the bones in all: an evident
demonstration that the juices of the body had a
circulation through the bones. He fed some
animals alternately upon madder and their common
food, for some time, and he found their bones
tinctured with alternate layers, in conformity to
their manner of living. From all this, he naturally
concluded, that the blood circulated through the
bones as it does through every other part of the
body; and that, how solid soever they seemed, yet,
like the softest parts, they were furnished, through
all their substance, with their proper canals. Nevertheless, these canals are of very different capacities,
during the different stages of life. In infancy they
are capacious; and the blood flows almost as freely
through the bones as through any other part of the
body; in manhood their size is greatly diminished;
the vessels are almost imperceptible; and the circulation through them is proportionably slow. But,
in the decline of life, the blood, which flows
through the bones, no longer contributing to their
growth, must necessarily serve to increase their
hardness. The channels, that every where run
through the human frame, may be compared to
those pipes that we every where see crusted on the
inside, by the water, for a long continuance, running
through them. Both every day grow less and less,

¶

by the small rigid particles which are deposited within them. Thus, as the vessels are by degrees diminished, the juices, also, which were necessary for the circulation through them, are diminished in proportion; till, at length, in old age, those props of the human frame are not only more solid, but more brittle.

The cartilages, or gristles, which may be considered as bones beginning to be formed, grow also more rigid. The juices circulating through them, for there is a circulation through all parts of the body, every day contribute to render them harder; so that these substances, which in youth are elastic and pliant, in age become hard and bony. As these cartilages are generally placed near the joints, the motion of the joints also must, of consequence, become more difficult. Thus, in old age, every action of the body is performed with labour; and the cartilages, formerly so supple, will now sooner break than bend.

" As the cartilages acquire hardness, and unfit the joints for motion, so also that mucous liquor, which is always separated between the joints, and which serves, like oil to a hinge, to give them an easy and ready play, is now grown more scanty. It becomes thicker, and more clammy, more unfit for answering the purposes of motion; and from thence, in old age, every joint is not only stiff, but awkward. At every motion, this clammy liquor is heard to crack; and it is not without the greatest effort of the muscles that its resistance is overcome. I have seen an old person, who never moved a single joint that did not thus give notice of the violence done to it."

The membranes that cover the bones, the joints,

and the rest of the body, become, as we grow old,
more dense and more dry. These which surround
the bones, soon cease to be ductile. The fibres, of
which the muscles or flesh is composed, become
every day more rigid ; and, while to the touch the
body seems, as we advance in years, to grow softer,
it is, in reality, increasing in hardness. It is the
skin and not the flesh, that we feel upon such occasions. The fat, and the flabbiness of that, seems
to give an appearance of softness, which the flesh
itself is very far from having. There are few can
doubt this after trying the difference between the
flesh of young and old animals. The first is soft
and tender, the last is hard and dry.

· The skin is the only part of the body that age
does not contribute to harden. That stretches to
every degree of tension ; and we have horrid
instances of its pliancy, in many disorders incident
to humanity. In youth, therefore, while the body
is vigorous and increasing, it still gives way to its
growth. But, although it thus adapts itself to our
increase, it does not in the same manner conform to
our decay. The skin, which in youth was filled,
and glossy, when the body begins to decline, has
not elasticity enough to shrink entirely with its
diminution. It hangs, therefore, in wrinkles,
which no art can remove. The wrinkles of the
body, in general, proceed from this cause. But those
of the face seem to proceed from another ; namely,
from the many varieties of positions into which it
is put by the speech, the food, or the passions.
Every grimace, and every passion, wrinkles up the
visage into different forms. These are visible
enough in young persons ; but what at first was

accidental, or transitory, becomes unalterably fixed
in the visage as it grows older. " Hence we may
conclude, that a freedom from passions not only
adds to the happiness of the mind, but preserves
the beauty of the face; and the person that has
not felt their influence, is less strongly marked by
the decays of nature."

. Hence, therefore, as we advance in age, the
bones, the cartilages, the membranes, the flesh, the
skin, and every fibre of the body, become more
solid, more brittle, and more dry. Every part
shrinks, every motion becomes more slow; the
circulation of the fluids is performed with less
freedom; perspiration diminishes; the secretions
alter; the digestion becomes slow and laborious;
and the juices, no longer serving to convey their
accustomed nourishment, those parts may be said
to live no longer when the circulation ceases. Thus
the body dies by little and little : all its functions
are diminished by degrees; life is driven from one
part of the frame to another; universal rigidity
prevails; and death at last seizes upon the little
that is left.

As the bones, the cartilages, the muscles, and all
other parts of the body are softer in women than
in men, these parts must, of consequence, require a
longer time to come to that hardness which hastens
death. Women, therefore, ought to be a longer
time in growing old than men; and this is actually
the case. If we consult the tables which have
been drawn up respecting human life, we shall
find, that after a certain age they are more long-
lived than men, all other circumstances the same.
A woman of sixty has a better chance than a man

of the same age to live till eighty. Upon the whole we may infer, that such persons as have been slow in coming up to maturity, will also be slow in growing old; and this holds as well with regard to other animals as to man.

The whole duration of the life of either vegetables, or animals, may be, in some measure, determined from their manner of coming to maturity. The tree, or the animal, which takes but a short time to increase to its utmost pitch, perishes much sooner than such as are less premature. In both, the increase upwards is first accomplished; and not till they have acquired their greatest degree of height do they begin to spread in bulk. Man grows in stature till about the age of seventeen; but his body is not completely developed till about thirty. Dogs, on the other hand, are at their utmost size in a year, and become as bulky as they usually are in another. However, man, who is so long in growing, continues to live for fourscore or a hundred years; but the dog seldom above twelve or thirteen. In general also it may be said that large animals live longer than little ones, as they usually take a larger time to grow. But in all animals one thing is equally certain, that they carry the cause of their own decay about them; and that their deaths are necessary and inevitable. The prospects which some visionaries have formed of perpetuating life by remedies, have been often enough proved false by their own example. Such unaccountable schemes would, therefore, have died with them, had not the love of life always augmented our credulity.

When the body is naturally well-formed, it is

possible to lengthen out the period of life for some years by management. Temperance in diet is often found conducive to this end. The famous Cornaro, who lived to above a hundred years, although his constitution was naturally feeble, is a strong instance of the benefit of an abstemious life. Moderation in the passions also may contribute to extend the term of our existence. "Fontenelle, the celebrated writer, was naturally of a very weak and delicate habit of body. He was affected by the smallest irregularities; and had frequently suffered severe fits of illness from the slightest causes. But the remarkable equality of his temper, and his seeming want of passion, lengthened out his life to above a hundred. It was remarkable of him, that nothing could vex or make him uneasy; every occurrence seemed equally pleasing: and no event, however unfortunate, seemed to come unexpected." However, the term of life can be prolonged but for a very little time by any art we can use. We are told of men who have lived beyond the ordinary duration of human existence; such as Par, who lived to a hundred and forty-four; and Jenkins to a hundred and sixty-five: yet these men used no peculiar arts to prolong life; on the contrary, it appears that these, as well as some others, remarkable for their longevity, were peasants, accustomed to the greatest fatigues, who had no settled rules of diet, but who often indulged in accidental excesses. Indeed, if we consider that the European, the Negro, the Chinese, and the American, the civilized man and the savage, the rich and the poor, the inhabitant of the city, and of the country, though all so different

in other respects, are yet entirely similar in the
period allotted them for living; if we consider
that neither the difference of race, of climate, of
nourishment, of convenience, or of soil, makes any
difference in the term of life; if we consider that
those men who live upon raw flesh, or dried fishes,
upon sago, or rice, upon cassava, or upon roots,
nevertheless live as long as those who are fed upon
bread and meat, we shall readily be brought to
acknowledge, that the duration of life depends
neither upon habit, customs, or the quantity of
food; we shall confess, that nothing can change
the laws of that mechanism which regulates the
number of our years, and which can chiefly be
affected only by long fasting, or great excess.

If there be any difference in the different periods
of man's existence, it ought principally to be
ascribed to the quality of the air.   It has been
observed, that, in elevated situations there have been
found more old people than in those that were low.
The mountains of Scotland, Wales, Auvergne, and
Switzerland, have furnished more instances of
extreme old age than the plains of Holland,
Flanders; Germany, or Poland: But, in general,
the duration of life is nearly the same in most
countries.   Man, if not cut off by accidental
diseases, is often found to live to ninety or a
hundred years.   Our ancestors did not live beyond
that date ; and, since the times of David, this term
has undergone little alteration.

If we be asked how in the beginning men lived
so much longer than at present, and by what
means their lives were extended to nine hundred
and thirty, or even nine hundred and sixty years,

it may be answered, that the productions of the earth, upon which they fed, might be of a different nature at that time, from what they are at present. " It may be answered, that the term was abridged by Divine command, in order to keep the earth from being over-stocked with human inhabitants ; since, if every person were now to live and generate for nine hundred years, mankind would be increased to such a degree, that there would be no room for subsistence ; so that the plan of Providence would be altered ; which is seen not to produce life, without providing a proper supply."

But, to whatever extent life may be prolonged, or however some may have delayed the effects of age, death is the certain goal to which all are hastening. All the causes of decay which have been mentioned, contribute to bring on this dreaded dissolution. However nature approaches to this awful period, by slow and imperceptible degrees ; life is consumed day after day ; and some one of our faculties, or vital principles, is every hour dying before the rest ; so that death is only the last shade in the picture ; and it is probable, that man suffers a greater change in going from youth to age, than from age into the grave. When we first begin to live, our lives may scarcely be said to be our own ; as the child grows, life increases in the same proportion ; and is at its height in the prime of manhood. But as soon as the body begins to decrease, life decreases also ; for as the human frame diminishes, and its juices circulate in smaller quantity, life diminishes and circulates with less vigour ; so that as we begin to live by degrees, we begin to die in the same manner.

Why then should we fear death, if our lives have been such as not to make eternity dreadful? Why should we fear that moment which is prepared by a thousand other moments of the same kind? the first pangs of sickness being probably greater than the last struggles of departure. Death, in most persons, is as calmly endured as the disorder that brings it on. If we inquire from those whose business it is to attend the sick and the dying, we shall find that except in a very few acute cases, where the patient dies in agonies, the greatest number die quietly, and seemingly without pain: and even the agonies of the former, rather terrify the spectators than torment the patient; for how many have we not seen who have been accidentally relieved from this extremity, and yet had no memory of what they then endured? In fact, they had ceased to live, during that time when they ceased to have sensation; and their pains were only those of which they had an idea.

The greatest number of mankind die, therefore, without sensation; and of those few that still preserve their faculties entire to the last moment, there is scarcely one of them that does not also preserve the hopes of still out-living his disorder. Nature, for the happiness of mankind, has rendered this sentiment stronger than his reason. A person dying of an incurable disorder, which he must know to be so, by frequent examples of his case; which he perceives to be so, by the inquietude of all around him, by the tears of his friends, and the departure or the face of the physician, is, nevertheless, still in hopes of getting over it. His interest is so great that he only attends to his own representa-

tions; the judgment of others is considered as a hasty
conclusion; and while death every moment makes
new inroads upon his constitution, and destroys life
in some part, hope still seems to escape the universal
ruin, and is the last that submits to the blow.

Cast your eyes upon a sick man, who has a
hundred times told you that he felt himself dying,
that he was convinced he could not recover, and
that he was ready to expire; examine what passes
on his visage, when, through zeal or indiscretion,
any one comes to tell him that his end is at hand.
You will see him change like one who is told an
unexpected piece of news. He now appears not to
have thoroughly believed what he had been telling
you himself; he doubted much; and his fears were
greater than his hopes: but he still had some feeble
expectations of living, and would not have seen the
approaches of death, unless he had been alarmed
by the mistaken assiduity of his attendants.

Death, therefore, is not that terrible thing which
we suppose it to be. It is a spectre which frights
us at a distance, but which disappears when we
come to approach it more closely. Our ideas of
its terrors are conceived in prejudice, and dressed
up by fancy; we regard it not only as the greatest
misfortune, but as also an evil accompanied with
the most excruciating tortures: we have even increased our apprehensions, by reasoning on the
extent of our sufferings. It must be dreadful, say
some, since it is sufficient to separate the soul from
the body; it must be long, since our sufferings are
proportioned to the succession of our ideas; and
these being painful, must succeed each other with
extreme rapidity. In this manner has false philo-

sophy laboured to augment the miseries of our
nature ; and to aggravate that period, which Nature
has kindly covered with insensibility.   Neither the
mind, nor the body, can suffer these calamities ;
the mind is, at that time, mostly without ideas ;
and the body too much enfeebled to be capable of
perceiving its pain.   A very acute pain produces
either death, or fainting, which is a state similar to
death ; the body can suffer but to a certain degree ;
if the torture becomes excessive, it destroys itself ;
and the mind ceases to perceive, when the body
can no longer endure.

In this manner, excessive pain admits of no reflection ; and wherever there are any signs of it,
we may be sure that the sufferings of the patient
are no greater than what we ourselves may have
remembered to endure.

But in the article of death, we have many instances
in which the dying person has shown that very
reflection which pre-supposes an absence of the
greatest pain ; and, consequently, that pang which
ends life, cannot even be so great as those which
have preceded.   Thus, when Charles XII. was
shot at the siege of Frederickshall, he was seen to
clap his hand on the hilt of his sword ; and although
the blow was great enough to terminate one of the
boldest and bravest lives in the world, yet it was
not painful enough to destroy reflection.   He
perceived himself attacked ; he reflected that he
ought to defend himself, and his body obeyed the
impulse of his mind, even in the last extremity.
Thus it is the prejudice of persons in health,
and not the body in pain, that makes us suffer
from the approach of death: we have, all our

lives, contracted a habit of making out excessive
pleasures and pains; and nothing but repeated
experience shows us, how seldom the one can be
suffered, or the other enjoyed to the utmost.

If there be any thing necessary to confirm what
we have said, concerning the gradual cessation of
life, or the insensible approaches of our end,
nothing can more effectually prove it, than the
uncertainty of the signs of death. If we consult
what Winslow or Bruhier have said upon this
subject, we shall be convinced, that between life
and death, the shade is so very undistinguishable,
that even all the powers of art can scarcely determine
where the one ends, and the other begins. The
colour of the visage, the warmth of the body, the
suppleness of the joints, are but uncertain signs
of life still subsisting; while, on the contrary,
the paleness of the complexion, the coldness of the
body, the stiffness of the extremities, the cessation
of all motion, and the total insensibility of the
parts, are but uncertain marks of death begun.
In the same manner also, with regard to the pulse,
and the breathing, these motions are often so kept
under, that it is impossible to perceive them. By
approaching a looking-glass to the mouth of the
person supposed to be dead, people often expect
to find whether he breathes or not. But this is a
very uncertain experiment: the glass is frequently
sullied by the vapour of the dead man's body; and
often the person is still alive, although the glass is
no way tarnished. In the same manner, neither
burning, nor scarifying, neither noises in the ears,
nor pungent spirits applied to the nostrils, give
certain signs of the discontinuance of life; and

there are many instances of persons who have
endured them all, and afterwards recovered, without
any external assistance, to the astonishment of
the spectators. How careful, therefore, should we
be, before we commit those who are dearest to us
to the grave, to be well assured of their departure?
Experience, justice, humanity, all persuade us not
to hasten the funerals of our friends, but to keep
their bodies unburied, until we have certain signs
of their real decease.

CHAP. VI.

Of the Varieties in the Human Race.

HITHERTO we have compared man with
other animals; we now come to compare men
with each other. We have hitherto considered
him as an individual, endowed with excellencies
above the rest of the creation; we now come to
consider the advantages which men have over
men, and the various kinds with which our earth is
inhabited.

If we compare the minute differences of mankind,
there is scarcely one nation upon the earth that
entirely resembles another; and there may be said
to be as many different kinds of men as there are
countries inhabited. One polished nation does
not differ more from another, than the merest
savages do from those savages that lie even contiguous to them; and it frequently happens that a
river, or a mountain, divides two barbarous tribes
that are unlike each other in manners, customs,

features, and complexion. But these differences, however perceivable, do not form such distinctions as come within a general picture of the varieties of mankind. Custom, accident, or fashion, may produce considerable alterations in neighbouring nations; their being derived from ancestors of a different climate, or complexion, may contribute to make accidental distinctions, which every day grow less; and it may be said, that two neighbouring nations, how unlike soever at first, will assimilate by degrees; and, by long continuance, the difference between them will at last become almost imperceptible. It is not, therefore, between contiguous nations we are to look for any strong marked varieties in the human species; it is by comparing the inhabitants of opposite climates, and distant countries; those who live within the polar circle with those beneath the equator; those that live on one side of the globe with those that occupy the other.

Of all animals, the differences between mankind are the smallest. Of the lower races of creatures, the changes are so great as often entirely to disguise the natural animal, and to distort, or to disfigure its shape. But the chief differences in man are rather taken from the tincture of his skin than the variety of his figure; and in all climates he preserves his erect deportment, and the marked superiority of his form. If we look round the world there seem to be not above six * distinct

* I have taken four of these varieties from Linnæus; those of the Laplanders and Tartars from M. Buffon.

varieties in the human species, each of which is
strongly marked, and speaks the kind seldom to
have mixed with any other. But there is nothing
in the shape, nothing in the faculties, that shows
their coming from different originals; and the
varieties of climate, of nourishment, and custom, are
sufficient to produce every change.

The first distinct race of men is found round
the polar regions. The Laplanders, the Esquimaux Indians, the Samoeid Tartars, the inhabitants of Nova Zembla, the Borandians, the Greenlanders, and the natives of Kamtschatka, may be
considered as one peculiar race of people, all
greatly resembling each other in their stature,
their complexion, their customs, and their ignorance. These nations being under a rigorous
climate, where the productions of nature are but
few, and the provisions coarse and unwholesome,
their bodies have shrunk to the nature of their food;
and their complexions have suffered, from cold,
almost a similar change to what heat is known to
produce; their colour being a deep brown, in some
places inclining to actual blackness. These, therefore, in general, are found to be a race of short
stature, and odd shape, with countenances as savage
as their manners are barbarous. The visage, in
these countries, is large and broad, the nose flat
and short, the eyes of a yellowish brown, inclining
to blackness, the eye-lids drawn towards the
temples, the cheek-bones extremely high, the mouth
very large, the lips thick and turned outwards, the
voice thin and squeaking, the head large, the hair
black and straight, the colour of the skin of a dark

The Laplander.

greyish.* They are short in stature, the generality
not being above four feet high, and the tallest not
above five. Among all these nations the women
are as deformed as the men, and resemble them so
nearly that one cannot, at first, distinguish the
sexes among them.

These nations not only resemble each other in
their deformity, their dwarfishness, the colour of
their hair and eyes, but they have, in a great measure, the same inclinations, and the same manners,
being all equally rude, superstitious, and stupid.
The Danish Laplanders have a large black cat, to
which they communicate their secrets, and consult
in all their affairs. Among the Swedish Laplanders there is in every family a drum for con-
sulting the devil; and although these nations are
robust, and nimble, yet they are so cowardly,
that they never can be brought into the field. Gus-
tavus Adolphus attempted to form a regiment of
Laplanders, but he found it impossible to accom-
plish his design; for it should seem that they can
live only in their own country, and in their own
manner. They make use of skates, which are
made of fir, of near three feet long, and half a
foot broad; these are pointed, and raised before,
and tied to the foot by straps of leather. With
these they skate upon the icy snow with such
velocity, that they very easily overtake the swiftest
animals. They make use also of a pole, pointed
with iron at one end, and rounded at the other.
This pole serves to push them along, to direct
their course, to support them from falling, to stop

* Krantz.

the impetuosity of their motion, and to kill that
game which they have overtaken. Upon these
skates they descend the steepest mountains, and
scale the most craggy precipices; and, in these
exercises, the women are not less skilful than the
men. They have all the use of the bow and arrow,
which seems to be a contrivance common to all
barbarous nations; and which, however, at first,
required no small skill to invent. They launch a
javelin also, with great force; and some say that
they can hit a mark, no larger than a crown, at thirty
yards distance, and with such force as would pierce
a man through. They are all hunters; and particularly pursue the ermine, the fox, the ounce, and
the martin, for the sake of their skins. These they
barter with their southern neighbours, for brandy
and tobacco; both which they are fond of to excess.
Their food is principally dried fish, the flesh of
rein-deer and bears. Their bread is composed
of the bones of fishes, pounded and mixed with
the inside tender bark of the pine-tree. Their
drink is train-oil, or brandy, and, when deprived
of these, water in which juniper berries have been
infused. With regard to their morals, they have
all the virtues of simplicity, and all the vices of
ignorance. They offer their wives and daughters
to strangers; and seem to think it a particular
honour if their offer be accepted. They have no
idea of religion, or a Supreme being; the greatest
number of them are idolaters; and their supersti-
tion is as profound as their worship is contemptible.
Wretched and ignorant as they are, yet they do
not want pride; they set themselves far above
the rest of mankind; and Krantz assures us, that

when the Greenlanders are got together, nothing is so customary among them as to turn the Europeans into ridicule. They are obliged, indeed, to yield them the pre-eminence in understanding and mechanic arts; but they do not know how to set any value upon these. They therefore count themselves the only civilized and well-bred people in the world; and it is common with them, when they see a quiet, or a modest stranger, to say that he is almost as well-bred as a Greenlander.

From this description, therefore, this whole race of people may be considered as distinct from any other. Their long continuance in a climate the most inhospitable, their being obliged to subsist on food the most coarse and ill-prepared, the savageness of their manners, and their laborious lives, all have contributed to shorten their stature, and to deform their bodies.* In proportion as we approach towards the north pole, the size of the natives appears to diminish, growing less and less as we advance higher, till we come to those latitudes that are destitute of all inhabitants whatsoever.

The wretched natives of these climates seem fitted by nature to endure the rigours of their situation. As their food is but scanty and precarious, their patience in hunger is amazing.† A man who has eaten nothing for four days, can manage his little canoe, in the most furious waves, and calmly subsist in the midst of a tempest, that would quickly dash an European boat to pieces. Their strength is not less amazing than their

* Ellis's Voyage, p. 256.   † Krantz, p. 134, vol. i.

patience; a woman among them will carry a piece
of timber, or a stone, near double the weight of what
an European can lift. Their bodies are of a dark
grey all over; and their faces brown, or olive.
The tincture of their skins partly seems to arise
from their dirty manner of living, being generally
daubed with train-oil; and partly from the rigours
of climate, as the sudden alterations of cold and
raw air in winter, and of burning heats in summer,
shade their complexions by degrees, till, in a succession of generations, they at last become almost
black. As the countries in which these reside are
the most barren, so the natives seem the most barbarous of any part of the earth. Their more
southern neighbours of America treat them with
the same scorn that a polished nation would treat
a savage one; and we may readily judge of the
rudeness of those manners, which even a native
of Canada can think more barbarous than his
own.

But the gradations of nature are imperceptible;
and, while the north is peopled with such miserable
inhabitants, there are here and there to be found,
upon the edges of these regions, people of larger
stature and completer figure. A whole race of
the dwarfish breed is often found to come down
from the north, and settle more to the southward;
and, on the contrary, it sometimes happens that
southern nations are seen higher up, in the midst
of these diminutive tribes, where they have continued for time immemorial. Thus the Ostiac
Tartars seem to be a race that have travelled
down from the north, and to be originally sprung
from the minute savages we have been describing.

There are also Norwegians, and Finlanders, of proper stature, who are seen to inhabit in latitudes higher even than Lapland. These, however, are but accidental migrations, and serve as shades to unite the distinct varieties of mankind.

The second great variety, in the human species, seems to be that of the Tartar race; from whence, probably, the little men we have been describing originally proceeded. The Tartar country, taken in general, comprehends the greatest part of Asia; and is, consequently, a general name given to a number of nations, of various forms and complexions. But, however, they seem to differ from each other, they all agree in being very unlike the people of any other country. All these nations have the upper part of the visage very broad, and wrinkled even while yet in their youth. Their noses are short and flat; their eyes little and sunk in their heads; and, in some of them, they are seen five or six inches asunder. Their cheek-bones are high, the lower part of their visage narrow, the chin long and advanced forward, their teeth of an enormous size and growing separate from each other, their eye-brows thick, large, and covering their eyes, their eyelids thick, the face broad and flat, the complexion olive-coloured, and the hair black. They are of a middle size, extremely strong, and very robust. They have but little beard, which grows stragglingly on the chin. They have large thighs, and short legs. The ugliest of all are the Calmoucks, in whose appearance there seems to be something frightful. They all lead an erratic life, remaining under tents of hair, or skins. They live upon horse-flesh and that of camels, either raw or a little sodden between the horse and the saddle. They eat also fish dried in the sun. Their most usual drink is mares' milk fermented with millet ground into meal. They all have the head shaven, except a lock of hair, on the top, which they let grow sufficiently long to form into tresses, on each side of the face. The women, who are as ugly as the men, wear their hair, which they bind up with bits of copper and other ornaments of a like nature. The majority of these nations have no religion, no settled notions of morality, no decency of behaviour. They are chiefly robbers; and the natives of Dagestan, who live near their more polished neighbours, make a traffic of Tartar slaves who have been stolen, and sell them to the Turks and the Persians. Their chief riches consist in horses, of which perhaps there are more in Tartary, than in any other part of the world. The natives are taught by custom to live in the same place with their horses; they are continually employed in managing them, and at last bring them to such great obedience, that the horse seems actually to understand the rider's intention.

To this race of men, also, we must refer the Chinese and the Japanese, however different they seem in their manners and ceremonies. It is the form of the body we are now principally considering; and there is, between these countries, a surprising resemblance. It is in general allowed that the Chinese have broad faces, small eyes, flat noses, and scarcely any beard; that they are broad and square-shouldered, and rather less in stature than Europeans. These are marks common to them and the Tartars, and they may, there-

†

3

Warner sc.

The Chinefe.

fore, be considered as being derived from the
same original. "I have observed," says Chardin,
"that in all the people from the east and the
north of the Caspian sea, to the peninsula of
Malacca, that the lines of the face, and the formation of the visage, is the same. This has induced
me to believe, that all these nations are derived
from the same original, however different either
their complexions or their manners may appear;
for as to the complexion, that proceeds entirely
from the climate and the food; and as to the
manners, these are generally the result of their
different degrees of wealth or power." That they
come from one stock is evident, also, from this:
that the Tartars who settle in China quickly
resemble the Chinese; and, on the contrary,
the Chinese who settle in Tartary, soon assume
the figure and the manners of the Tartars.

The Japanese so much resemble the Chinese,
that one cannot hesitate to rank them in the same
class. They only differ in being rather browner,
as they inhabit a more southern climate. They
are, in general, described, as of a brown complexion, a short stature, a broad flat face, a very
little beard, and black hair. Their customs and
ceremonies are nearly the same; their ideas of
beauty similar; and their artificial deformities of
blackening the teeth, and bandaging the feet, entirely
alike in both countries. They both, therefore,
proceed from the same stock; and although they
differ very much from their brutal progenitors,
yet they owe their civilization wholly to the mildness of the climate in which they reside, and to
the peculiar fertility of the soil. To this tribe,

also, we may refer the Cochin-Chinese, the Siamese, the Tonquinese, and the inhabitants of Aracan, Laos, and Pegu, who, though all differing from the Chinese, and each other, nevertheless, have too strong a resemblance, not to betray their common original.

Another, which makes the third variety in the human species, is that of the southern Asiatics; the form of whose features and persons may be easily distinguished from those of the Tartar races. The nations that inhabit the peninsula of India seem to be the principal stock from whence the inhabitants of the islands that lie scattered in the Indian ocean have been peopled. They are, in general, of a slender shape, with long, strait black hair, and often with Roman noses. Thus they resemble the Europeans in stature and features; but greatly differ in colour and habit of body. The Indians are of an olive colour, and, in the more southern parts, quite black; although the word Mogul, in their language, signifies a white man. The women are extremely delicate, and bathe very often: they are of an olive colour, as well as the men; their legs and thighs are long, and their bodies short, which is the opposite to what is seen among the women of Europe. They are, as I am assured, by no means so fruitful as the European women; but they feel the pains of child-birth with much less sensibility, and are generally up and well the day following. In fact, these pains seem greatest in all countries where the women are most delicate, or the constitution enfeebled by luxury or indolence. The women of savage nations seem, in a great measure, exempt from painful labours ; and even the hard-working wives of the peasants among ourselves have this advantage, from a life of industry, that their child-bearing is less painful. Over all India, the chil-dren arrive sooner at maturity, than with us of Europe. They often marry, and consummate, the husband at ten years old, and the wife at eight; and they frequently have children at that age. However, the women who are mothers so soon, cease bearing before they are arrived at thirty, and, at that time, they appear wrinkled, and seem marked with all the deformities of age. The Indians have long been remarkable for their cowardice and effeminacy; every conqueror that has attempted the invasion of their country, having succeeded. The warmth of the climate entirely influences their manners; they are slothful, submissive and luxu-rious : satisfied with sensual happiness alone, they find no pleasure in thinking ; and contented with slavery, they are ready to obey any master. Many tribes among them eat nothing that has life ; they are fearful of killing the meanest insect ; and have even erected hospitals for the maintenance of all kinds of vermin. The Asiatic dress is a loose flowing garment, rather fitted for the purposes of peace and indolence, than of industry or war. The vigour of the Asiatics is in general conformable to their dress and nourishment; fed upon rice, and clothed in effeminate silk vestments, their soldiers are unable to oppose the onset of an European army; and from the times of Alexander to the present day, we have scarcely any instances of their success in arms. Upon the whole, there-fore, they may be considered as a feeble race of

sensualists, too dull to find rapture in any pleasures,
and too indolent to turn their gravity into wisdom.
To this class we may refer the Persians and Arabians, and, in general, the inhabitants of the islands
that lie scattered in the Indian ocean.

The fourth striking variety in the human species,
is to be found among the Negroes of Africa. This
gloomy race of mankind is found to blacken all
the southern parts of Africa, from eighteen degrees
north of the line, to its extreme termination, at
the Cape of Good Hope. I know it is said, that
the Caffres, who inhabit the southern extremity
of that large continent, are not to be ranked among
the Negro race; however, the difference between
them, in point of colour and features, is so small,
that they may very easily be grouped in this general
picture; and in the one or two that I have seen,
I could not perceive the smallest difference. Each
of the Negro nations, it must be owned, differ
from each other; they have their peculiar countries
for beauty, like us; and different nations, as in
Europe, pride themselves upon the regularity of their
features. Those of Guinea, for instance, are extremely ugly, and have an insupportable scent;
those of Mosambique are reckoned beautiful, and
have no ill smell whatsoever. The Negroes in
general are of a black colour, with a smooth, soft
skin. This smoothness proceeds from the downy
softness of the hair which grows upon it; the
strength of which gives a roughness to the feel, in
those of a white complexion. Their skins, therefore, have a velvet smoothness, and seem less
braced upon the muscles than ours. The hair of
their heads differs entirely from what we are

4

The African.

accustomed to, being soft, woolly, and short. The beard also partakes of the same qualities; but in this it differs, that it soon turns grey, which the hair is seldom found to do; so that several are seen with white beards, and black hair, at the same time. Their eyes are generally of a deep hazle; their noses flat and short; their lips thick and tumid; and their teeth of an ivory whiteness. This their only beauty, however, is set off by the colour of their skin; the contrast between the black and white being the more observable. It is false to say that their features are deformed by art; since, in the Negro children born in European countries, the same deformities are seen to prevail; the same flatness in the nose; and the same prominence in the lips. They are, in general, said to be well shaped; but of such as I have seen, I never found one that might be justly called so; their legs being mostly ill formed, and commonly bending outward on the shin-bone. But it is not only in those parts of their bodies that are obvious, that they are disproportioned; those parts which among us are usually concealed by dress, with them are large and languid.* The women's breasts, after bearing one child, hang down below the navel; and it is customary, with them, to suckle the child at their backs, by throwing the breast over the shoulder. As their persons are thus naturally deformed, at least to our imaginations, their minds are equally

* Linnæus, in prima linea sua, fœminas Africanas depingit sicut aliquid deforme in parte genitali gestantes, quod signum pudoris nuncupat. Attamen nihil differunt a nostratibus in hac parte nisi quod labia pudendæ sint aliquantulum tumidiora. In hominibus etiam penis est longior et multo laxior.

incapable of strong exertions. The climate seems
to relax their mental powers still more than those
of the body; they are, therefore, in general, found
to be stupid, indolent, and mischievous. The
Arabians themselves, many colonies of whom have
migrated southward into the most inland parts of
Africa, seem to have degenerated from their ancestors; forgetting their ancient learning, and losing
their beauty, they have become a race scarcely any
way distinguishable from the original natives.
Nor does it seem to have fared otherwise with
the Portuguese, who, about two centuries ago,
settled along this coast. They also are become
almost as black as the Negroes; and are said, by
some, to be even more barbarous.

The inhabitants of America make a fifth race, as
different from all the rest in colour, as they are distinct in habitation. The natives of America (except
in the northern extremity, where they resemble
the Laplanders) are of a red or copper colour;
and although, in the old world, different climates
produce a variety of complexions and customs, the
natives of the new continent seem to resemble each
other in almost every respect. They are all nearly
of one colour; all have black thick straight hair, and
thin black beards; which, however, they take care
to pluck out by the roots. They have, in general,
flat noses, with high cheek-bones, and small eyes;
and these deformities of nature they endeavour to
increase by art: they flatten the nose, and often
the whole head of their children, while the bones
are yet susceptible of every impression. They
paint the body and face of various colours, and
consider the hair upon any part of it, except the

5

Werner sc.

The American.

head, as a deformity which they are careful to
eradicate. Their limbs are generally slighter made
than those of the Europeans; and I am assured
they are far from being so strong. All these
savages seem to be cowardly; they seldom are
known to face their enemies in the field, but fall
upon them at an advantage; and the greatness of
their fears serves to increase the rigours of their
cruelty. The wants which they often sustain, make
them surprisingly patient in adversity; distress, by
being grown familiar, becomes less terrible; so that
their patience is less the result of fortitude than of
custom. They have all a serious air, although they
seldom think; and, however cruel to their enemies,
are kind and just to each other. In short, the
customs of savage nations in every country are
almost the same; a wild, independent, and precarious life, produces a peculiar train of virtues and
vices: and patience and hospitality, indolence and
rapacity, content and sincerity, are found not less
among the natives of America, than all the barbarous nations of the globe.

The sixth and last variety of the human species
is that of the Europeans, and the nations bordering
on them. In this class we may reckon the Geor-
gians, Circassians, and Mingrelians, the inhabitants
of Asia Minor, and the northern parts of Africa,
together with a part of those countries which lie
north-west of the Caspian Sea. The inhabitants
of these countries differ a good deal from each
other; but they generally agree in the colour of
their bodies, the beauty of their complexions, the
largeness of their limbs, and the vigour of their
understandings. Those arts which might have

had their invention among the other races of mankind, have come to perfection there. In barbarous countries, the inhabitants go either naked, or are awkwardly clothed in furs or feathers; in countries semi-barbarous, the robes are loose and flowing; but here the clothing is less made for show than expedition, and unites, as much as possible, the extremes of ornament and dispatch.

To one or other of these classes, we may refer the people of every country; and as each nation has been less visited by strangers, or has had less commerce with the rest of mankind, we find their persons, and their manners, more strongly impressed with one or other of the characters mentioned above. On the contrary, in those places where trade has long flourished, or where enemies have made many incursions, the races are usually found blended, and properly fall beneath no one character. Thus, in the islands of the Indian Ocean, where a trade has been carried on for time immemorial, the inhabitants appear to be a mixture of all the nations upon the earth; white, olive, brown, and black men, are all seen living together in the same city, and propagate a mixed breed, that can be referred to none of the classes into which naturalists have thought proper to divide mankind.

Of all the colours by which mankind is diversified, it is easy to perceive, that ours is not only the most beautiful to the eye, but the most advantageous. The fair complexion seems, if I may so express it, as a transparent covering to the soul; all the variations of the passions, every expression of joy or sorrow, flows to the cheek, and, without language, marks the mind. In the slightest change of health, also, the colour of the European face is the most exact index, and often teaches us to prevent those disorders that we do not as yet perceive : not but that the African black, and the Asiatic olive complexions, admit of their alterations also ; but these are neither so distinct, nor so visible, as with us ; and, in some countries, the colour of the visage is never found to change ; but the face continues in the same settled shade, in shame and in sickness, in anger and despair.

The colour, therefore, most natural to man, ought to be that which is most becoming ; and it is found, that, in all regions, the children are born fair, or at least red ; and that they grow more black, or tawny, as they advance in age. It should seem, consequently, that man is naturally white ; since the same causes that darken the complexion in infants, may have originally operated, in slower degrees in blackening whole nations. We could, therefore, readily account for the blackness of different nations, did we not see the Americans, who live under the line, as well as the natives of Negroland, of a red colour, and but a very small shade darker than the natives of the northern latitudes in the same continent. For this reason, some have sought for other causes of blackness than the climate ; and have endeavoured to prove that the blacks are a race of people, bred from one man, who was marked with accidental blackness. This, however, is but mere ungrounded conjecture ; and, although the Americans are

not so dark as the Negroes, yet we must still
continue in the ancient opinion, that the deep-
ness of the colour proceeds from the excessive
heat of the climate: for, if we compare the
heats of Africa with those of America, we shall
find they bear no proportion to each other. In
America, all that part of the continent which lies
under the line is cool and pleasant, either shaded
by mountains, or refreshed by breezes from the
sea; but, in Africa, the wide tract of country that
lies under the line is very extensive, and the soil
sandy; the reflection of the sun, therefore, from
so large a surface of earth, is almost intolerable;
and it is not to be wondered at, that the inhabitants should bear, in their looks, the marks of the
inhospitable climate. In America, the country
is but thinly inhabited; and the more torrid tracts
are generally left desert by the inhabitants; for
which reasons they are not so deeply tinged by the
beams of the sun. But in Africa the whole
face of the country is fully peopled; and the
natives are obliged to endure their situation,
without a power of migration. It is there, consequently, that they are in a manner tied down
to feel all the severity of the heat; and their complexions take the darkest hue they are capable of
receiving. We need not, therefore, have recourse
to any imaginary propagation, from persons accidentally black, since the climate is a cause obvious,
and sufficient to produce the effect.

In fact, if we examine the complexion of different countries, we shall find them darken in proportion to the heat of their climate; and the
shades gradually to deepen as they approach the

line. Some nations, indeed, may be found not
so much tinged by the sun as others, although
they lie nearer the line. But this ever proceeds
from some accidental causes; either from the
country lying higher, and consequently being
colder; or from the natives bathing oftener, and
leading a more civilized life. In general, it may
be asserted, that, as we approach the line, we find
the inhabitants of each country grow browner,
until the colour deepens into perfect blackness.
Thus taking our standard from the whitest race
of people, and beginning with our own country,
which, I believe, bids fairest for the pre-eminence,
we shall find the French, who are more southern,
a slight shade deeper than we; going farther
down, the Spaniards are browner than the French;
the inhabitants of Fez darker than they; and the
natives of Negroland the darkest of all. In what
manner the sun produces this effect, and how the
same luminary which whitens wax and linen,
should darken the human complexion, is not easy
to conceive. Sir Thomas Brown first supposed
that a mucous substance, which had something of
a vitriolic quality, settled under the reticular membrane, and grew darker with heat. Others have
supposed that the blackness lay in the epidermis,
or scarf skin, which was burnt up like leather.
But nothing has been satisfactorily discovered upon
the subject: it is sufficient that we are assured of
the fact; and that we have no doubt of the sun's
tinging the complexion in proportion to its
vicinity.

But we are not to suppose that the sun is the
only cause of darkening the skin; the wind,

extreme cold, hard labour, or coarse and sparing
nourishment, are all found to contribute to this
effect. We find the peasants of every country,
who are most exposed to the weather, a shade
darker than the higher ranks of people. The
savage inhabitants of all places are exposed still
more, and, therefore, contract a still deeper hue;
and this will account for the tawny colour of the
North American Indians. Although they live in
a climate the same, or even more northerly than
ours, yet they are found to be of complexions
very different from those of Europe. But it must
be considered that they live continually exposed
to the sun; that they use many methods to darken
their skins by art, painting them with red ochre,
and anointing them with the fat of bears. Had
they taken, for a succession of several generations,
the same precautions to brighten their colour that
an European does, it is very probable that they
would in time come to have similar complexions;
and, perhaps, dispute the prize of beauty.

The extremity of cold is not less productive of
a tawny complexion than that of heat. The
natives of the arctic circle, as was observed, are
all brown; and those that lie most to the north
are almost entirely black. In this manner both
extremes are unfavourable to the human form and
colour, and the same effects are produced under the
poles that are found at the line.

With regard to the stature of different countries,
that seems chiefly to result from the nature of the
food, and the quantity of the supply.—Not but
that the severity of heat or cold may, in some
measure, diminish the growth, and produce a

dwarfishness of make. But, in general, the food is the great agent in producing this effect; where that is supplied in large quantities, and where its quality is wholesome and nutrimental, the inhabitants are generally seen above the ordinary stature. On the contrary, where it is afforded in a sparing quantity, or very coarse, and void of nourishment in its kind, the inhabitants degenerate, and sink below the ordinary size of mankind. In this respect they resemble other animals, whose bodies, by proper feeding, may be greatly augmented. An ox, on the fertile plains of India, grows to a size four times as large as the diminutive animal of the same kind bred in the Alps. The horses bred in the plains are larger than those of the mountain. So it is with man; the inhabitants of the valley are usually found taller than those of the hill; the natives of the Highlands of Scotland, for instance, are short, broad, and hardy; those of the Lowlands are tall and shapely. The inhabitants of Greenland, who live upon dried fish and seals, are less than those of Gambia or Senegal, where Nature supplies them with vegetable and animal abundance.

The form of the face seems rather to be the result of custom. Nations who have long considered some artificial deformity as beautiful, who have industriously lessened the feet, or flattened the nose, by degrees, begin to receive the impression they are taught to assume; and nature, in the course of ages, shapes itself to the constraint, and assumes hereditary deformity. We find nothing more common in births than for children to inherit sometimes even the accidental deformities of their parents. We have many instances of squinting in the father, which he received from fright, or habit, communicated to the offspring: and I myself have seen a child distinctly marked with a scar, similar to one the father had received in battle. In this manner accidental deformities may become natural ones; and by assiduity may be continued, and even increased, through successive generations. From this, therefore, may have arisen the small eyes and long ears of the Tartars, and Chinese nations. From hence originally may have come the flat noses of the blacks, and the flat heads of the American Indians.

In this slight survey, therefore, I think we may see that all the variations in the human figure, as far as they differ from our own, are produced either by the rigour of the climate, the bad quality or the scantiness of the provisions, or by the savage customs of the country. They are actual marks of the degeneracy in the human form; and we may consider the European figure and colour as standards to which to refer all other varieties, and with which to compare them. In proportion as the Tartar or American approaches nearer to European beauty, we consider the race as less degenerated; in proportion as he differs more widely, he has made greater deviations from his original form.

That we have all sprung from one common parent, we are taught, both by reason and religion, to believe; and we have good reason also to think that the Europeans resemble him more than any of the rest of his children. However, it must not be concealed that the olive-coloured Asiatic, and even the jet black Negro, claim this honour of hereditary resemblance ; and assert that white men are mere deviations from original perfection. Odd as this opinion may seem, they have Linnæus, the celebrated naturalist, on their side ; who supposes man a native of the tropical climates, and only a sojourner more to the north. But, not to enter into a controversy upon a matter of very remote speculation, I think one argument alone will suffice to prove the contrary, and show that the white man is the original source from whence the other varieties have sprung. We have frequently seen white children produced from black parents, but have never seen a black offspring the production of two whites. From hence we may conclude that whiteness is the colour to which mankind naturally tends ; for, as in the tulip, the parent stock is known, by all the artificial varieties breaking into it ; so in man, that colour must be original which never alters, and to which all the rest are accidentally seen to change. I have seen in London, at different times, two white Negroes, the issue of black parents, that served to convince me of the truth of this theory. I had before been taught to believe that the whiteness of the Negro skin was a disease, a kind of milky whiteness, that might be called rather a leprous crust than a natural complexion. I was taught to suppose that the numberless white Negroes, found in various parts of Africa, the white men that go by the name of Chacrelas in the East Indies, and the white Americans, near the Isthmus of Darien, in the West Indies, were all so many diseased persons, and even more deformed than the blackest of the natives. But, upon examining that Negro which was last shown in London, I found the colour to be exactly like that of an European; the visage white and ruddy, and the lips of the proper redness. However, there were sufficient marks to convince me of its descent. The hair was white and woolly, and very unlike any thing I had seen before. The iris of the eye was yellow, inclining to red; the nose was flat, exactly resembling that of a Negro; and the lips thick, and prominent. No doubt, therefore, remained of the child's having been born of Negro parents; and the person who showed it had attestations to convince the most incredulous. From this then we see that the variations of the Negro colour is into whiteness, whereas the white are never found to have a race of Negro children. Upon the whole, all those changes which the African, the Asiatic, or the American undergo, are but accidental deformities, which a kinder climate, better nourishment, or more civilized manners, would, in a course of centuries, very probably, remove.

CHAP. VII.

Of Monsters.

HITHERTO I have only spoken of those varieties in the human species, that are common to whole nations: but there are varieties of another kind, which are only found in the individual; and, being more rarely seen, are, therefore, called monstrous. If we examine into the varieties of dis-

torted nature, there is scarcely a limb of the body,
or a feature in the face, that has not suffered some
reprobation, either from art or nature; being enlarged or diminished, lengthened or wrested, from
its due proportion. Linnæus, after having given
a catalogue of monsters, particularly adds, the flat
heads of Canada, the long heads of the Chinese,
and the slender waists of the women of Europe,
who, by strait lacing, take such pains to destroy
their health, through a mistaken desire to improve
their beauty.* It belongs more to the physician
than the naturalist to attend to these minute deformities; and, indeed, it is a melancholy contem-
plation to speculate upon a catalogue of calamities, inflicted by unpitying nature, or brought
upon us by our own caprice. Some, however, are
fond of such accounts; and there have been books
filled with nothing else. To these, therefore, I
refer the reader; who may be better pleased with
accounts of men with two heads, or without any
head, of children joined in the middle, of bones
turned into flesh, or flesh converted into bones,
than I am.† It is sufficient here to observe, that

---

* Linnæi Syst. vol. i. p. 29. Monorchides ut minus fertiles.

† Vide Phil. Trans. passim. Miscellan. Curios. Johan. Baptist.
Wenck. Dissertatio Physica an ex virilis humani seminis cum bru-
tali per nefarium coitum commixtione, aut vicissim ex bruti maris
cum muliebri humano seminis commixtione possit verus homo
generari. Vide etiam Johnstoni Thaumatographia Naturalis.
Vide Adalberti Disquisitio Physica ostenti duorum puerorum
unus quorum dente aureo alter cum capite giganteo Biluæ specta-
bantur. A man without lungs and stomach; Journal des Sçavans,
1682, p. 301. Another without any brain; Andreas Caroli
Memorabilia, p. 167, an. 1676. Another without any head;
Giornale di Roma, anno 1675, p. 26. Another without any
*

every day's experience must have shown us miserable instances of this kind, produced by nature, or affectation; calamities that no pity can soften, nor assiduity relieve.

Passing over, therefore, every other account, I shall only mention the famous instance, quoted by Father Malbranche; upon which he founds his beautiful theory of monstrous productions. A woman of Paris, the wife of a tradesman, went to see a criminal broke alive upon the wheel, at the place of public execution. She was at that time two months advanced in her pregnancy, and no way subject to any disorders to affect the child in her womb. She was, however, of a tender habit of body; and, though led by curiosity to this horrid spectacle, very easily moved to pity and compassion. She felt, therefore, all those strong emotions which so terrible a sight must naturally inspire; shuddered at every blow the criminal received, and almost swooned at his cries. Upon returning from this scene of blood, she continued for some days pensive, and her imagination still wrought upon the spectacle she had lately seen. After some time, however, she seemed perfectly recovered from her fright, and had almost forgotten her former uneasiness. When the time of her delivery approached, she seemed no ways mindful of her former terrors, nor were her pains in labour more than usual in such circumstances. But, what was the amazement of her friends and assistants, when the child came into the world! It was found that

arms; New Memoirs of Literature, vol. iv. p. 446. In short, the variety of these accounts is almost infinite: and, perhaps their use is as much circumscribed as their variety is extensive.

every limb in its body was broken like those of the malefactor, and just in the same place. This poor infant, that had suffered the pains of life, even before its coming into the world, did not die, but lived in a hospital, in Paris, for twenty years after, a wretched instance of the supposed powers of imagination in the mother, of altering and distorting the infant in the womb. The manner in which Malbranche reasons upon this fact, is as follows: The Creator has established such a sympathy between the several parts of nature, that we are led not only to imitate each other, but also to partake in the same affections and desires. The animal spirits are thus carried to the respective parts of the body, to perform the same actions which we see others perform, to receive in some measure their wounds, and take part in their sufferings. Experience tells us, that if we look attentively on any person severely beaten, or sorely wounded, the spirits immediately flow into those parts of the body which correspond to those we see in pain. The more delicate the constitution, the more it is thus affected; the spirits making a stronger impression on the fibres of a weakly habit than of a robust one. Strong vigorous men see an execution without much concern, while women of nicer texture are struck with horror and concern. This sensibility in them must, of consequence, be communicated to all parts of their body; and, as the fibres of the child, in the womb, are incomparably finer than those of the mother, the course of the animal spirits must, consequently, produce greater alterations. Hence, every stroke given to the criminal, forcibly struck the imagination of the woman;

and by a kind of counter stroke, the delicate tender frame of the child.

Such is the reasoning of an ingenious man, upon a fact of the veracity of which many since have called in question.* They have allowed, indeed, that such a child might have been produced, but have denied the cause of its deformity. How could the imagination of the mother, say they, produce such dreadful effects upon her child? She has no communication with the infant; she scarcely touches it in any part; quite unaffected with her concerns, it sleeps in security, in a manner secluded by a fluid in which it swims, from her that bears it. With what a variety of deformities, say they, would all mankind be marked, if all the vain and capricious desires of the mother were thus readily written upon the body of the child? Yet notwithstanding this plausible way of reasoning, I cannot avoid giving some credit to the variety of instances I have either read, or seen, upon this subject. If it be a prejudice, it is as old as the days of Aristotle, and to this day as strongly believed, by the generality of mankind, as ever. It does not admit of a reason; and, indeed, I can give none even why the child should, in any respect, resemble the father, or the mother. The fact we generally find to be so. But why it should take the particular print of the father's features in the womb, is as hard to conceive, as why it should be affected by the mother's imagination. We all know what a strong effect the imagination has on those parts in particular, without being able to

* Buffon, vol. iv. p. 9.

assign a cause how this effect is produced; and why
the imagination may not produce the same effect
in marking the child that it does in forming it, I
see no reason. Those persons whose employment
it is to rear up pigeons of different colours, can
breed them, as their expression is, to a feather. In
fact, by properly pairing them, they can give what
colour they will to any feather, in any part of the
body. Were we to reason upon this fact, what
could we say? Might it not be asserted, that the
egg, being distinct from the body of the female,
cannot be influenced by it? Might it not be plausi-
bly said, that there is no similitude between any
part of the egg and any particular feather, which
we expect to propagate? and yet, for all this, the
fact is known to be true, and what no speculation
can invalidate. In the same manner, a thousand
various instances assure us that the child, in the
womb, is sometimes marked by the strong affections of the mother: how this is performed we
know not; we only see the effect, without any
connexion between it and the cause. The best
physicians have allowed it; and have been satisfied
to submit to the experience of a number of ages;
but many disbelieve it, because they expect a reason
for every effect. This, however, is very hard to
be given, while it is very easy to appear wise by
pretending incredulity.

Among the number of monsters, dwarfs and
giants are usually reckoned; though not, perhaps,
with the strictest propriety, since they are no way
different from the rest of mankind, except in stature.
It is a dispute, however, about words; and, therefore, scarcely worth contending about. But there

is a dispute, of a more curious nature, on this subject; namely, whether there are races of people
thus very diminutive, or vastly large; or whether
they be merely accidental varieties, that now and
then are seen in the country, in a few persons,
whose bodies some external cause has contributed
to lessen or enlarge.

With regard to men of diminutive stature, all
antiquity has been unanimous in asserting their
national existence. Homer was the first who has
given us an account of the pigmy nation, contending with the cranes; and what poetical licence
might be supposed to exaggerate, Athenæus has
attempted seriously to confirm by historical asser-
tion.[*] If we attend to these, we must believe that,
in the internal parts of Africa, there are whole
nations of pigmy beings, not more than a foot in
stature, who continually wage an unequal war with
the birds and beasts that inhabit the plains in
which they reside. Some of the ancients, however, and Strabo in particular, have supposed all
these accounts to be fabulous; and have been
more inclined to think this supposed nation of
pigmies nothing more than a species of apes, well
known to be numerous in that part of the world.
With this opinion the moderns have all concurred; and that diminutive race, which was
described as human, has been long degraded into a
class of animals that resemble us but very imperfectly.

The existence, therefore, of a pigmy race of
mankind being founded in error, or in fable, we

* Athenæus, ix. 390.

can expect to find men of diminutive stature only by accident, among men of the ordinary size. Of these accidental dwarfs, every country, and almost every village, can produce numerous instances. There was a time, when these unfavoured children of Nature were the peculiar favourites of the great; and no prince, or nobleman, thought himself completely attended, unless he had a dwarf among the number of his domestics. These poor little men were kept to be laughed at, or to raise the barbarous pleasure of their masters, by their contrasted inferiority. Even in England, as late as the times of king James the First, the court was at one time furnished with a dwarf, a giant, and a jester: these the king often took a pleasure in opposing to each other, and often fomented quarrels among them, in order to be a concealed spectator of their animosity. It was a particular entertainment of the courtiers at that time, to see little Jeffery, for so the dwarf was called, ride round the lists, expecting his antagonist; and discovering, in his actions, all the marks of contemptible resolution.

It was in the same spirit, that Peter of Russia, in the year 1710, celebrated a marriage of dwarfs. This monarch, though raised by his native genius far above a barbarian, was, nevertheless, still many degrees removed from actual refinement. His pleasures, therefore, were of the vulgar kind; and this was among the number. Upon a certain day, which he had ordered to be proclaimed several months before, he invited the whole body of his courtiers, and all the foreign ambassadors, to be present at the marriage of a pigmy man and woman. The preparations for this wedding were not only very grand, but executed in a style of barbarous ridicule. He ordered, that all the dwarf men and women, within two hundred miles, should repair to the capital; and also insisted, that they should be present at the ceremony. For this purpose he supplied them with proper vehicles; but so contrived it, that one horse was seen carrying in a dozen of them into the city at once, while the mob followed shouting and laughing from behind. Some of them were at first unwilling to obey an order, which they knew was calculated to turn them into ridicule, and did not come; but he soon obliged them to obey; and, as a punishment, enjoined, that they should wait upon the rest at dinner. The whole company of dwarfs amounted to seventy, besides the bride and bridegroom, who were richly adorned, and in the extremity of the fashion. For this little company in miniature, every thing was suitably provided; a low table, small plates, little glasses, and, in short, every thing was so fitted, as if all things had been dwindled to their own standard. It was his great pleasure to see their gravity and their pride; the contention of the women for places, and the men for superiority. This point he attempted to adjust, by ordering, that the most diminutive should take the lead; but this bred disputes, for none would then consent to sit foremost. All this, however, being at last settled, dancing followed the dinner, and the ball was opened with a minuet by the bridegroom, who measured exactly three feet two inches high. In the end, matters were so contrived, that this little company, who met together in

gloomy pride, and unwilling to be pleased, being
at last familiarized to laughter, joined in the diversion, and became, as the journalist has it,* extremely sprightly and entertaining.

But whatever may be the entertainment such
guests might afford, when united, I never found a
dwarf capable of affording any when alone. I
have sometimes conversed with some of those that
were exhibited at our fairs about town, and have
ever found their intellects as contracted as their
persons. They, in general, seemed to me to have
faculties very much resembling those of children,
and their desires of the same kind; being
diverted with the same sports, and best pleased
with such companions. Of all those I have seen,
which may amount to five or six, the little man,
whose name was Coan, that died lately at Chelsea,
was the most intelligent and sprightly. I have
heard him and the giant, who sung at the theatres,
sustain a very ridiculous duet, to which they were
taught to give great spirit. But this mirth, and
seeming sagacity, were but assumed. He had, by
long habit, been taught to look cheerful upon the
approach of company; and his conversation was
but the mere etiquette of a person that had been
used to receive visitors. When driven out of his
walk, nothing could be more stupid or ignorant,
nothing more dejected or forlorn. But, we have
a complete history of a dwarf, very accurately re-
lated by M. Daubenton, in his part of the His-

* Die dench wurdige. Iwerg. Hockweit, &c. Lipsiæ, 1713, vol,
viii. page 102. seq.

toire Naturelle; which I will here take leave to
translate.

The dwarf, whose name was Baby, was well
known, having spent the greatest part of his life
at Lunenville, in the palace of Stanislaus, the
titular king of Poland. He was born in the village
of Plaisne, in France, in the year 1741. His father
and mother were peasants, both of good constitutions, and inured to a life of husbandry and labour.
Baby, when born, weighed but a pound and a
quarter. We are not informed of the dimensions
of his body at that time; but we may conjecture
they were very small, as he was presented on a
plate to be baptized, and for a long time lay in a
slipper. His mouth, although proportioned to the
rest of his body, was not, at that time, large
enough to take in the nipple; and he was, therefore, obliged to be suckled by a she-goat that was
in the house; and that served as a nurse, attending
to his cries with a kind of maternal fondness. He
began to articulate some words when eighteen
months old; and at two years he was able to walk
alone. He was then fitted with shoes that were
about an inch and a half long. He was attacked
with several acute disorders; but the small-pox
was the only one which left any marks behind it.
Until he was six years old, he eat no other food
but pulse, potatoes, and bacon.. His father and
mother were, from their poverty, incapable of
affording him any better nourishment; and his
education was little better than his food, being
bred up among the rustics of the place. At six
years old he was about fifteen inches high; and

his whole body weighed but thirteen pounds.
Notwithstanding this, he was well proportioned,
and handsome; his health was good, but his understanding scarcely passed the bounds of instinct.
It was at that time that the king of Poland, having
heard of such a curiosity, had him conveyed to
Lunenville, gave him the name of Baby, and kept
him in his palace.

Baby, having thus quitted the hard condition of
a peasant, to enjoy all the comforts and the conveniences of life, seemed to receive no alteration
from his new way of living, either in mind or
person; he preserved the goodness of his constitution till about the age of sixteen; but his body
seemed to increase very slowly during the whole
time; and his stupidity was such, that all instructions
were lost in improving his understanding. He could
never be brought to have any sense of religion,
nor even to show the least signs of a reasoning
faculty. They attempted to teach him dancing
and music, but in vain; he never could make any
thing of music; and as for dancing, although he
beat time tolerably exact, yet he could never
remember the figure, but while his dancing-master
stood by to direct his motions. Notwithstanding,
a mind thus destitute of understanding was not
without its passions; anger and jealousy harassed
it at times; nor was he without desires of another
nature.

At the age of sixteen, Baby was twenty-nine
inches tall; at this he rested; but having thus
arrived at his acme, the alterations of puberty, or
rather, perhaps, of old age, came fast upon him.
From being very beautiful, the poor little creature

now became quite deformed; his strength quite forsook him; his back-bone began to bend; his head hung forward; his legs grew weak; one of his shoulders turned awry; and his nose grew disproportionably large. With his strength, his natural spirits also forsook him; and, by the time he was twenty, he was grown feeble, decrepid, and marked with the strongest impressions of old age. It had been before remarked by some, that he would die of old age before he arrived at thirty; and, in fact, by the time he was twenty-two, he could scarcely walk a hundred paces, being worn with the multiplicity of his years, and bent under the burden of protracted life. In this year he died; a cold attended with a slight fever, threw him into a kind of lethargy, which had a few momentary intervals; but he could scarcely be brought to speak. However, it is asserted, that in the five last years of his life, he showed a clearer understanding, than in his times of best health: but at length he died, after enduring great agonies, in the twenty-second year of his age.

Opposite to this accidental diminution of the human race, is that of its extraordinary magnitude. Concerning the reality of a nation of Giants, there have been many disputes among the learned. Some have affirmed the probability of such a race; and others, as warmly have denied the possibility of their existence. But it is not from any speculative reasonings, upon a subject of this kind, that information is to be obtained: it is not from the disputes of the scholar, but the labours of the enterprising, that we are to be instructed in this inquiry. Indeed, nothing can be more absurd than what some learned men have advanced upon this subject. It is very unlikely, says Grew, that there should either be dwarfs or giants; or if such, they cannot be fitted for the usual enjoyment of life and reason. Had man been born a dwarf, he could not have been a reasonable creature; for to that end he must have a jolt head, and then he would not have body and blood enough to supply his brain with spirits: or if he had a small head, proportionable to his body, there would not be brain enough for conducting life. But it is still worse with giants; and there could never have been a nation of such, for there would not be food enough found in any country to sustain them; or if there were beasts sufficient for this purpose, there would not be grass enough for their maintenance. But what is still more, add others, giants could never be able to support the weight of their own bodies; since a man of ten feet high must be eight times as heavy as one of the ordinary stature; whereas, he has but twice the size of muscles to support such a burden; and, consequently, would be overloaded with the weight of his own body. Such are the theories upon this subject; and they require no other answer, but that experience proves them both to be false: dwarfs are found capable of life and reason; and giants are seen to carry their own bodies. We have several accounts from mariners, that a nation of giants actually exists; and mere speculation should never induce us to doubt their veracity.

Ferdinand Magellan was the first who discovered this race of people along the coast towards the extremity of South America. Magellan was a Por-

tuguese, of noble extraction, who having long
behaved with great bravery, under Albuquerque, the
conqueror of India, he was treated with neglect by
the court, upon his return. Applying, therefore,
to the king of Spain, he was entrusted with the
command of five ships, to subdue the Molucca
islands: upon one of which he was slain. It was
in his voyage thither, that he happened to winter
in St. Julian's Bay, an American harbour, forty-
nine degrees south of the line. In this desolate
region, where nothing was seen but objects of
terror, where neither trees nor verdure drest the
face of the country, they remained for some months
without seeing any human creature. They had
judged the country to be utterly uninhabitable;
when one day they saw approaching, as if he had
been dropt from the clouds, a man of enormous
stature, dancing and singing, and putting dust upon
his head, as they supposed, in token of peace.
This overture for friendship was, by Magellan's
command, quickly answered by the rest of his
men; and the giant approaching, testified every
mark of astonishment and surprise. He was so
tall, that the Spaniards only reached his waist;
his face was broad, his colour brown, and painted
over with a variety of tints; each cheek had the
resemblance of a heart drawn upon it; his hair
was approaching to whiteness; he was clothed in
skins, and armed with a bow. Being treated with
kindness, and dismissed with some trifling presents,
he soon returned, with many more of the same
stature; two of whom the mariners decoyed on
shipboard: nothing could be more gentle than
they were in the beginning; they considered the

fetters that were preparing for them, as ornaments, and played with them, like children with their toys; but when they found for what purpose they were intended, they instantly exerted their amazing strength, and broke them in pieces with a very easy effort. This account, with a variety of other circumstances, has been confirmed by succeeding travellers: Herrera, Sebald Wert, Oliver Van Noort, and James le Maire, all correspond in affirming the fact, although they differ in many particulars of their respective descriptions. The last voyager we have had, that has seen this enormous race, is Byron. I have talked with the person who first gave the relation of that voyage, and who was the carpenter of the Commodore's ship. By him I was assured, in the most solemn manner, of the truth of his relation; and this account has since been confirmed by one or two publications; in all which the particulars are pretty nearly the same.* One of the circumstances which most puzzled me to reconcile to probability, was that of the horses, on which they are described as riding down to the shore. We know the American horse to be of European breed; and, in some measure, to be degenerated from the original. I was at a loss, therefore, to account how a horse of not more than fourteen hands high, was capable of carrying a man of nine feet; or, in other words, an animal almost as large as itself. But the wonder will cease, when we consider, that so small a beast as an ass will carry a man of ordinary size tolerably well; and the pro-

---

* Later voyagers have not confirmed this account, in some particulars.

portion between this and the former instance, is nearly exact. We can no longer, therefore, refuse our assent to the existence of this gigantic race of mankind. In what manner they are propagated, or under what regulations they live, is a subject that remains for future investigation. It should appear, however, that they are a wandering nation, changing their abode with the course of the sun, and shifting their situation, for the convenience of food, climate, or pasture.

This race of giants are described as possessed of great strength; and, no doubt, they must be very different from those accidental giants that are to be seen in different parts of Europe. Stature, with these, seems rather their infirmity than their pride; and adds to their burthen, without increasing their strength. Of those I have seen, the generality were ill-formed and unhealthful; weak in their persons, or incapable of exerting what strength they were possessed of. The same defects of understanding that attended those of suppressed stature, were found in those who were thus overgrown: they were heavy, phlegmatic, stupid, and inclined to sadness. Their numbers, however, are but few; and it is thus kindly ordered by Providence, that as the middle state is the best fitted for happiness, so the middle ranks of mankind are produced in the greatest variety.

However, mankind seems naturally to have a respect for men of extraordinary stature; and it has been a supposition of long standing, that our ancestors were much taller, as well as much more beautiful than we. This has been, indeed, a theme of poetical declamation from the beginning; and man was scarcely formed, when he began to deplore an imaginary decay. Nothing is more natural than this progress of the mind, in looking up to antiquity with reverential wonder. Having been accustomed to compare the wisdom of our fathers with our own in early imbecility, the impression of their superiority remains when they no longer exist, and when we cease to be inferior. Thus the men of every age consider the past as wiser than the present; and the reverence seems to accumulate as our imaginations ascend. For this reason, we allow remote antiquity many advantages, without disputing their title: the inhabitants of uncivilized countries represent them as taller and stronger; and the people of a more polished nation, as more healthy and more wise. Nevertheless, these attributes seem to be only the prejudices of ingenuous minds; a kind of gratitude which we hope in turn to receive from posterity. The ordinary stature of men, Mr. Derham observes, is in all probability the same now as at the beginning. The oldest measure we have of the human figure, is in the monument of Cheops, in the first pyramid of Egypt. This must have subsisted many hundred years before the times of Homer, who is the first that deplores the decay. This monument, however, scarcely exceeds the measure of our ordinary coffins: the cavity is no more than six feet long, two feet wide, and deep in about the same proportion. Several mummies, also, of a very early age, are found to be only of the ordinary stature; and show that for these three thousand years at least, men have not suffered the least diminution. We have many corroborating proofs of this, in the ancient pieces of armour which are dug up in different parts of Europe. The brass helmet dug up at Medauro, fits one of our men, and yet is allowed to have been left there at the overthrow of Asdrubal. Some of our finest antique statues, which we learn from Pliny, and others, to be exactly as big as the life, still continue to this day, remaining monuments of the superior excellence of their workmen, indeed, but not of the superiority of their stature. We may conclude, therefore, that men have been in all ages pretty much of the same size they are at present; and that the only difference must have been accidental, or perhaps national.

As to the superior beauty of our ancestors, it is not easy to make the comparison; beauty seems a very uncertain charm; and frequently is less in the object than in the eye of the beholder. Were a modern lady's face formed exactly like the Venus of Medicis, or the sleeping vestal, she would scarcely be considered beautiful, except by the lovers of antiquity, whom, of all her admirers, perhaps, she would be least desirous of pleasing. It is true, that we have some disorders among us that disfigure the features, and from which the ancients were exempt; but it is equally true, that we want some which were common among them, and which were equally deforming. As for their intellectual powers, these also were probably the same as ours; we excel them in the sciences,

§

which may be considered as a history of accumulated experience; and they excel us in the poetic
arts, as they had the first rifling of all the striking
images of Nature.

CHAP. VIII.

Of Mummies, Wax-works, &c.

" MAN * is not content with the usual term of
life, but he is willing to lengthen out his existence
by art; and although he cannot prevent death, he
tries to obviate his dissolution. It is natural
to attempt to preserve even the most trifling
relics of what has long given us pleasure; nor
does the mind separate from the body without
a wish, that even the wretched heap of dust it
leaves behind, may yet be remembered. The
embalming, practised in various nations, probably
had its rise in this fond desire: an urn filled with
ashes, among the Romans, served as a pledge of
continuing affection; and even the grassy graves
in our own church-yards are raised above the
surface, with the desire that the body below should
not be wholly forgotten. The soul, ardent after
eternity for itself, is willing to procure, even for
the body, a prolonged duration."

But of all nations, the Egyptians carried this
art to the highest perfection: as it was a principle
of their religion, to suppose the soul continued

* This chapter I have, in a great measure, translated from M.
Daubenton. Whatever is added from others, is marked with
inverted commas.

only coeval with the duration of the body, they
tried every art to extend the life of the one, by
preventing the dissolution of the other. In this
practice they were exercised from the earliest
ages; and the mummies they have embalmed in
this manner, continue in great numbers to the
present day. We are told, in Genesis, that Joseph
seeing his father expire, gave orders to his
physicians to embalm the body, which they executed in the compass of forty days, the usual
time of embalming. Herodotus, also, the most
ancient of the prophane historians, gives us a
copious detail of this art, as it was practised in his
time among the Egyptians. There are certain
men among them, says he, who practise embalming
as a trade; which they perform with all expedition possible. In the first place, they draw out
the brain through the nostrils, with irons adapted
to this purpose; and in proportion as they evacuate
it in this manner, they fill up the cavity with
aromatics; they next cut open the belly, near the
sides, with a sharpened stone, and take out the
entrails, which they cleanse, and wash in palm-
oil: having performed this operation, they roll
them in aromatic powder, fill them with myrrh,
cassia, and other perfumes, except incense; and
replace them, sewing up the body again. After
these precautions, they salt the body with nitre,
and keep it in the salting-place for seventy days,
it not being permitted to preserve it so any longer.
When the seventy days are accomplished, and the
body washed once more, they swathe it in bands
made of linen, which have been dipt in a gum
the Egyptians use instead of salt. When the

friends have taken back the body, they make a hollow trough, something like the shape of a man, in which they place the body; and this they inclose in a box preserving the whole as a most precious relic, placed against the wall. Such are the ceremonies used with regard to the rich; as for those who are contented with a humbler preparation, they treat them as follows: they fill a syringe with an odoriferous liquor extracted from the cedar tree, and, without making any incision, inject it up the body of the deceased, and then keep it in nitre, as long as in the former case. When the time is expired, they evacuate the body of the cedar liquor which had been injected; and such is the effect of this operation, that the liquor dissolves the intestines, and brings them away: the nitre also serves to eat away the flesh; and leaves only the skin and the bones remaining. This done, the body is returned to the friends, and the embalmer takes no farther trouble about it. The third method of embalming those of the meanest condition, is merely by purging and cleansing the intestines by frequent injections, and preserving the body for a similar term in nitre, at the end of which it is restored to the relations.

Diodorus Siculus, also, makes mention of the manner in which these embalmings are performed. According to him, there were several officers appointed for this purpose: the first of them, who was called the scribe, marked those parts of the body, on the left side, which were to be opened; the cutter made the incision; and one of those that were to salt it, drew out all the bowels, except the heart and the kidnies; another washed them in palm-wine, and odoriferous liquors; afterwards, they anointed, for above thirty days, with cedar, gum, myrrh, cinnamon, and other perfumes. These aromatics preserved the body entire for a long time, and gave it a very agreeable odour. It was not in the least disfigured by this preparation; after which it was returned to the relations, who kept it in a coffin, placed upright against a wall.

Most of the modern writers who have treated on this subject, have merely repeated what has been said by Herodotus; and if they add any thing of their own, it is but merely from conjecture. Dumont observes, that it is very probable, that aloes, bitumen, and cinnamon, make a principal part of the composition which is used on this occasion; he adds, that after embalming, the body is put into a coffin, made of the sycamore-tree; which is almost incorruptible. Mr. Grew remarks, that in an Egyptian mummy, in the possession of the Royal Society, the preparation was so penetrating, as to enter into the very substance of the bones, and rendered them so black, that they seemed to have been burnt. From this he is induced to believe, that the Egyptians had a custom of embalming their dead, by boiling them in a kind of liquid preparation, until all the aqueous parts of the body were exhaled away; and until the oily or gummy matter had penetrated throughout. He proposes, in consequence of this, a method of macerating, and afterwards of boiling the dead body in oil of walnut.

I am, for my own part, of opinion; that there

were several ways of preserving dead bodies from putrefaction; and that this would be no difficult matter, since different nations have all succeeded in the attempt. We have an example of this kind among the Guanches, the ancient inhabitants of the island of Teneriff. Those who survived the general destruction of this people, by the Spaniards, when they conquered this island, informed them, that the art of embalming was still preserved there; and that there was a tribe of priests among them, possessed of the secret, which they kept concealed as a sacred mystery. As the greatest part of the nation was destroyed, the Spaniards could not arrive at a complete knowledge of this art; they only found out a few of the particulars. Having taken out the bowels, they washed the body several times in a lee, made of the dried bark of the pine-tree, warmed, during the summer, by the sun, or by a stove in the winter. They afterwards anointed it with butter, or the fat of bears, which they had previously boiled with odoriferous herbs, such as sage and lavender. After this unction, they suffered the body to dry; and then repeated the operation, as often as it was necessary, until the whole substance was impregnated with the preparation.—When it was become very light, it was then a certain sign that it was fit, and properly prepared. They then rolled it up in the dried skins of goats; which, when they had a mind to save expense, they suffered to remain with the hair still growing upon them. Purchas assures us, that he has seen mummies of this kind in London : and mentions the name of a gentleman who had seen several of them in the island of Teneriff, which were supposed to have been two thousand years old; but without any certain proofs of such great antiquity. This people, who probably came first from the coasts of Africa, might have learned this art from the Egyptians, as there was a traffic carried on from thence into the most internal parts of Africa.

Father Acosta, and Garcilasso de la Vega, make no doubt but that the Peruvians understood the art of preserving their dead for a very long space of time. They assert their having seen the bodies of several Incas, that were perfectly preserved. They still preserved their hair, and their eye-brows; but they had eyes, made of gold, put in the places of those taken out. They were clothed in their usual habits, and seated in the manner of the Indians, their arms placed on their breasts. Garcilasso touched one of their fingers, and found it apparently as hard as wood; and the whole body was not heavy enough to overburthen a weak man, who should attempt to carry it away. Acosta presumes, that these bodies were embalmed with a bitumen, of which the Indians knew the properties. Garcilasso, however, is of a different opinion, as he saw nothing bituminous about them; but he confesses that he did not examine them very particularly; and he regrets his not having enquired into the methods used for that purpose. He adds, that, being a Peruvian, his countrymen would not have scrupled to inform him of the secret, if they really had it still among them.

Garcilasso, thus being ignorant of the secret,

makes use of some inductions to throw light upon
the subject. He asserts, that the air is so dry
and so cold at Cusco, that flesh dries there like
wood, without corrupting; and he is of opinion,
that they dried the body in snow, before they
applied the bitumen. He adds, that in the times
of the Incas, they usually dried the flesh which was
designed for the army; and that when they had
lost their humidity, they might be kept without salt,
or any other preparation.

It is said, that at Spitsbergen, which lies within
the arctic circle, and, consequently, in the coldest
climate, bodies never corrupt, nor suffer any
apparent alteration, even though buried for thirty
years. Nothing corrupts or putrifies in that
climate; the wood which has been employed in
building those houses where the train-oil is separated, appears as fresh as the day they were first
cut.

If excessive cold, therefore, be thus capable of
preserving bodies from corruption, it is not less
certain, that a great degree of dryness, produced
by heat, produces the same effect. It is well
known, that the men and animals that are buried
in the sands of Arabia, quickly dry up, and
continue in preservation for several ages, as if
they had been actually embalmed. It has often
happened, that whole caravans have perished in
crossing those deserts, either by the burning winds
that infest them, or by the sands which are raised
by the tempest, and overwhelm every creature in
certain ruin. The bodies of those persons are
preserved entire; and they are often found in this
condition by some accidental passenger. Many

authors, both ancient and modern, make mention
of such mummies as these ; and Shaw says, that he
has been assured that numbers of men, as well
as other animals, have been thus preserved, for
times immemorial in the burning sands of Saibah,
which is a place, he supposes, situate between
Rasem and Egypt.

The corruption of dead bodies, being entirely
caused by the fermentation of the humours, whatever is capable of hindering or retarding this
fermentation, will contribute to their preservation.
Both heat and cold, though so contrary in themselves, produce similar effects in this particular,
by drying up the humours. The cold in condensing
and thickening them, and the heat in evaporating
them before they have time to act upon the solids.
But it is necessary that these extremes should
be constant; for if they succeed each other so
as that cold shall follow heat, or dryness humidity,
it must then necessarily happen, that corruption
must ensue. However, in temperate climates,
there are natural causes capable of preserving
dead bodies ; among which we may reckon the
quality of the earth in which they are buried.
If the earth be drying and astringent, it will
imbibe the humidity of the body ; and it may probably be for this reason that the bodies buried in
the monastery of the Cordeliers, at Thoulouse,
do not putrefy, but dry in such a manner, that
they may be lifted up by one arm.

The gums, resins, and bitumens, with which
dead bodies are embalmed, keep off the impressions which they would else receive from the
alteration of the temperature of the air ; and still

more, if a body thus prepared be placed in a dry
or burning sand, the most powerful means will be
united for its preservation. We are not to be surprised, therefore, at what we are told by Chardin, of
the country of Chorosan, in Persia. The bodies
which have been previously embalmed, and buried
in the sands of that country, as he assures us, are
found to petrify, or, in other words, to become
extremely hard, and are preserved for several ages.
It is asserted that some of them have continued
for a thousand years.

... The Egyptians, as has been mentioned above,
swathed the body with linen bands, and enclosed
it in a coffin; however, it is probable that, with
all these precautions, they would not have continued till now, if the tombs, or pits, in which they
were placed, had not been dug in a dry chalky
soil, which was not susceptible of humidity; and
which was, besides, covered over with a dry sand
of several feet thickness.

The sepulchres of the ancient Egyptians subsist
to this day. Most travellers who have been in
Egypt, have described those of ancient mummies,
and have seen the mummies interred there. These
catacombs are within two leagues of the ruins of
this city, nine leagues from Grand Cairo, and
about two miles from the village of Zaccara. They
extend from thence to the pyramids of Pharaoh,
which are about eight miles distant. These sepulchres lie in a field, covered with a fine running sand,
of a yellowish colour. The country is dry and
hilly; the entrance of the tomb is choaked up with
sand; there are many open, but several more that
are still concealed. The inhabitants of the neigh-

bouring village have no other commerce, or method
of subsisting, but by seeking out mummies, and
selling them to such strangers as happen to be at
Grand Cairo. " This commerce, some years ago,
was not only a very common, but a very gainful
one. A complete mummy was often sold for
twenty pounds : but it must not be supposed that
it was bought at such a high price from a mere
passion for antiquity ; there were much more
powerful motives for this traffic. Mummy, at that
time, made a considerable article in medicine ; and
a thousand imaginary virtues were ascribed to it,
for the cure of most disorders, particularly of the
paralytic kind. There was no shop, therefore,
without mummy in it ; and no physician thought
he had properly treated his patient, without adding
this to his prescription. Induced by the general
repute, in which this supposed drug was at that
time, several Jews, both of Italy and France, found
out the art of imitating mummy so exactly, that
they, for a long time, deceived all Europe. This
they did by drying dead bodies in ovens, after
having prepared them with myrrh, aloes, and
bitumen. Still, however, the request for mummies
continued, and a variety of cures were daily ascribed
to them. At length, Paræus wrote a treatise on
their total inefficacy in physic ; and showed
their abuse in loading the stomach, to the exclu-
sion of more efficacious medicines. From that
time, their reputation began to decline ; the Jews
discontinued their counterfeits, and the trade returned entire to the Egyptians, when it was no
longer of value. The industry of seeking after
mummies is now totally relaxed, their price merely

arbitrary, and just what the curious are willing to give."

In seeking for mummies, they first clear away the sand, which they may do for weeks together, without finding what is wanted. Upon coming to a little square opening, of about eighteen feet in depth, they descend into it, by holes for the feet, placed at proper intervals; and there are sure of finding what they seek for. These caves, or wells, as they call them, are hollowed out of a white free-stone, which is found in all this country a few feet below the covering of sand. When one gets to the bottom of these, which are sometimes forty feet below the surface, there are several square openings, on each side, into passages of ten or fifteen feet wide, and these lead to chambers of fifteen or twenty feet square. These are all hewn out of the rock; and in each of the catacombs are to be found several of these apartments, communicating with each other. They extend a great way under ground, so as to be under the city of Memphis, and in a manner to undermine its environs.

In some of the chambers, the walls are adorned with figures and hieroglyphics; in others, the mummies are found in tombs, round the apartment hollowed out in the rock. These tombs are upright, and cut into the shape of a man, with his arms stretched out. There are others found, and these in the greatest number, in wooden coffins, or in cloths covered with bitumen. These coffins, or wrappers, are covered all over with a variety of ornaments. There are some of them painted, and adorned with figures, such as that of death, and the leaden seals, on which several characters are engraven. Some of these coffins are carved into the human shape; but the head alone is distinguishable; the rest of the body is all of a piece, and terminated by a pedestal, while there are some with their arms hanging down; and it is by these marks that the bodies of persons of rank are distinguished from those of the meaner order. These are generally found lying on the floor, without any profusion of ornaments; and in some chambers the mummies are found indiscriminately piled upon each other, and buried in the sand.

Many mummies are found lying on their backs; their heads turned to the north, and their hands placed on the belly. The bands of linen, with which these were swathed, are found to be more than a thousand yards long; and, of consequence, the number of circumvolutions they make about the body must have been amazing. These were performed by beginning at the head, and ending at the feet; but they contrived it so as to avoid covering the face. However, when the face is entirely uncovered, it moulders into dust immediately upon the admission of the air. When, therefore, it is preserved entire, a slight covering of cloth is so disposed over it, that the shape of the eye, the nose, and the mouth, are seen under it. Some mummies have been found with a long beard, and hair that reached down to the mid-leg, nails of a surprising length, and some gilt, or at least painted of a gold colour. Some are found with bands upon the breast, covered with hieroglyphics, in gold, silver, or in green; and some with tutelary idols, and other figures of jasper, within their body. A piece of gold, also, has often been found under their tongues, of about two pistoles value; and, for this reason, the Arabians spoil all the mummies they meet with, in order to get at the gold.

But, although art, or accident, has thus been found to preserve dead bodies entire, it must by no means be supposed that it is capable of preserving the exact form and lineaments of the deceased person. Those bodies which are found dried away in the deserts, or in some particular church-yards, are totally deformed, and scarcely any lineaments remain of their external structure. Nor are the mummies preserved by embalming, in a better condition. The flesh is dried away, hardened, and hidden under a variety of bandages; the bowels, as we have seen, are totally removed; and from hence, in the most perfect of them, we see only a shapeless mass of skin discoloured; and even the features scarcely distinguishable. The art is, therefore, an effort rather of preserving the substance than the likeness of the deceased; and has, consequently, not been brought to its highest pitch of perfection. It appears from a mummy, not long since dug up in France, that the art of embalming was more completely understood in the western world than even in Egypt. This mummy, which was dug up at Auvergne, was an amazing instance of their skill, and is one of the most curious reliques in the art of preservation. As some peasants, in that part of the world, where digging in a field near Rion, within about twenty-six paces of the highway, between that and the river Artiers, they discovered a tomb, about a foot and a half beneath the surface. It was composed only of two stones;

one of which formed the body of the sepulchre,
and the other the cover. This tomb was of free-
stone; seven feet and a half long, three feet and a
half broad, and about three feet high. It was of
rude workmanship; the cover had been polished,
but was without figure or inscription : within this
tomb was placed a leaden coffin, four feet seven
inches long, fourteen inches broad, and fifteen
high. It was not made in the form of a coffin,
but oblong, like a box, equally broad at both ends,
and covered with a lid that fitted on like a snuff-
box, without a hinge. This cover had two holes
in it, each of about two inches long, and very
narrow, filled with a substance resembling butter;
but for what purpose intended, remains unknown.
Within this coffin was a mummy, in the highest
and most perfect preservation. The internal sides
of the coffin were filled with an aromatic substance,
mingled with clay. Round the mummy was
wrapped a coarse cloth, in form of a napkin, under
this were two shirts, or shrouds, of the most exquisite
texture; beneath these a bandage, which covered
all parts of the body, like an infant in swaddling
clothes; still, under this general bandage there
was another, which went particularly round the
extremities, the hands, and the legs. The head
was covered with two caps; the feet and hands
were without any particular bandages; and the
whole body was covered with an aromatic substance, an inch thick. When these were removed,
and the body exposed naked to view, nothing could
be more astonishing than the preservation of the
whole, and the exact resemblance it bore to a body
that had been dead a day or two before. It ap-

peared well proportioned, except that the head was rather large, and the feet small. The skin had all the pliancy and colour of a body lately dead; the visage, however, was of a brownish hue. The belly yielded to the touch; all the joints were flexible, except those of the legs and feet; the fingers stretched forth of themselves when bent inwards. The nails still continued entire; and all the marks of the joints, both in the fingers, the palms of the hands, and the soles of the feet, remained perfectly visible. The bones of the arms and legs were soft and pliant; but, on the contrary, those of the skull preserved their rigidity; the hair, which only covered the back of the head, was of a chesnut colour, and about two inches long. The pericranium at top was separated from the skull, by an incision, in order to open it for the introducing proper aromatics in the place of the brain, where they were found mixed with clay. The teeth, the tongue, and the ears, were all preserved in perfect form. The intestines were not taken out of the body, but remained pliant and entire, as in a fresh subject; and the breast was made to rise and fall like a pair of bellows; the embalming preparation had a very strong and pungent smell, which the body preserved for more than a month after it was exposed to the air. This odour was perceived wherever the mummy was laid; although it remained there but a very short time, it was even pretended that the peasants of the neighbouring villages were incommoded by it. If one touched either the mummy, or any part of the preparation, the hands smelled of it for several hours after, although washed with water, spirit of wine, or vinegar. This mummy, having remained exposed for some months to the curiosity of the public, began to suffer some mutilations. A part of the skin of the forehead was cut off; the teeth were drawn out, and some attempts were made to pull away the tongue. It was, therefore, put into a glass case, and shortly after transmitted to the King of France's cabinet, at Paris.

There are many reasons to believe this to be the body of a person of the highest distinction; however, no marks remain to assure us either of the quality of the person, or the time of his decease. There only are to be seen some irregular figures on the coffin; one of which represents a kind of star. There were also some singular characters upon the bandages, which were totally defaced by those who had torn them away. However, it should seem that it had remained for several ages in this state, since the first years immediately succeeding the interment, are usually those in which the body is most liable to decay. It appears also to be a much more perfect method of embalming than that of the Egyptians; as in this the flesh continues with its elasticity and colour, the bowels remain entire, and the joints have almost the pliancy which they had when the person was alive. Upon the whole, it is probable that a much less tedious preparation than that used by the Egyptians would have sufficed to keep the body from putrefaction; and that an injection of petreoleum inwardly, and a layer of asphaltum without, would have sufficed to have made a mummy; and it is remarkable that Auvergne, where this was found, affords these two substances in sufficient plenty. This art, therefore,

†

might be brought to greater perfection than it has arrived at hitherto, were the art worth preserving. But mankind have long since grown wiser in this respect, and think it unnecessary to keep by them a deformed carcase, which, instead of aiding their magnificence, must only serve to mortify their pride.

CHAP. IX.

Of Animals.

LEAVING man, we now descend to the lower ranks of animated nature, and prepare to examine the life, manners, and characters of these our humble partners in the creation. But, in such a wonderful variety as is diffused around us, where shall we begin? The number of beings endued with life as well as we, seems, at first view, infinite. Not only the forest, the waters, the air, teem with animals of various kinds; but almost every vegetable, every leaf, has millions of minute inhabitants, each of which fill up the circle of its allotted life, and some are found objects of the greatest curiosity. In this seeming exuberance of animals, it is natural for ignorance to lie down in hopeless uncertainty, and to declare what requires labour to particularize to be utterly inscrutable. It is otherwise, however, with the active and searching mind; no way intimidated with the immense variety, it begins the task of numbering, grouping, and classing all the various kinds that fall within its notice; finds every day new relations between the several parts of the creation, acquires the art of considering several at a time under one point of view; and, at last, begins to find that the variety is neither so great nor so inscrutable as was at first imagined. As in a clear night, the number of the stars seems infinite; yet, if we sedulously attend to each in its place, and regularly class them, they will soon be found to diminish, and come within a very scanty computation.

Method is one of the principal helps in natural history, and without it very little progress can be made in this science. It is by that alone we can hope to dissipate the glare, if I may so express it, which arises from a multiplicity of objects at once presenting themselves to the view. It is method that fixes the attention to one point, and leads it, by slow and certain degrees, to leave no part of nature unobserved.

All naturalists, therefore, have been very careful in adopting some method of classing or grouping the several parts of nature; and some have written books of natural history with no other view. These methodical divisions some have treated with contempt,* not considering that books, in general, are written with opposite views: some to be read, and some only to be occasionally consulted. The methodists, in natural history, seem to be content with the latter advantage, and have sacrificed to order alone, all the delights of the subject, all the arts of heightening, awakening, or continuing curiosity. But they certainly have

* M. Buffon in his Introduction, &c.

the same use in science that a dictionary has in
language; but with this difference, that in a dictionary we proceed from the name to the definition; in a system of natural history, we proceed
from the definition to find out the thing. Without
the aid of system, nature must still have lain
undistinguished like furniture in a lumber-room;
every thing we wish for is there, indeed, but we
know not where to find it. If, for instance, in a
morning excursion, I find a plant, or an insect,
the name of which I desire to learn; or, perhaps,
am curious to know whether already known; in
this inquiry I can expect information only from
one of these systems, which, being couched in a
methodical form, quickly directs me to what I
seek for. Thus we will suppose that our inquirer
has met with a spider, and that he has never seen
such an insect before. He is taught by the writer
of a system* to examine whether it has wings,
and he finds that it has none. He, therefore, is
to look for it among the wingless insects, or the
Aptera, as Linnæus calls them; he then is to see
whether the head and breast make one part of the
body, or are disunited: he finds they make one:
he is then to reckon the number of feet and eyes;
and he finds that it has eight of each. The
insect, therefore, must be either a scorpion or a
spider; but he lastly examines its feelers, which
he finds clavated, or clubbed; and, by all these
marks, he at last discovers it to be a spider. Of
spiders there are many sorts; and, by reading the
description of each, the inquirer will learn the

* Linnæus.

K 2

name of that which he desires to know. With
the name of the insect he is also directed to those
authors that have given any account of it, and
the page where that account is to be found; by
this means he may know at once what has been
said of that animal by others, and what there is of
novelty in the result of his own researches.

. Hence it will appear how useful those systems
in natural history are to the inquirer; but, having
given them all their merit, it would be wrong not
to observe, that they have in general been very
much abused. Their authors, in general, seem to
think that they are improvers of natural history,
when in reality they are but guides; they seem to
boast that they are adding to our knowledge,
while they are only arranging it. These authors,
also, seem to think that the reading of their
works and systems is the best method to attain a
knowledge of nature. But, setting aside the impossibility of getting through whole volumes of a
dry, long catalogue, the multiplicity of whose
contents is too great for even the strongest
memory; such works rather tell us the names than
the history of the creature we desire to inquire
after. In these dreary pages, every insect, or
plant, that has a name, makes as distinguished a
figure as the most wonderful, or the most useful.
The true end of studying nature is to make a just
selection, to find those parts of it that most conduce
to our pleasure or convenience, and to leave the
rest in neglect. But these systems, employing
the same degree of attention upon all, give us no
opportunities of knowing which most deserves
attention; and he who has made his knowledge

from such systems only, has his memory crowded with a number of trifling, or minute particulars, which it should be his business and his labour to forget. These books, as was said before, are useful to be consulted, but they are very unnecessary to be read; no inquirer into nature should be without one of them; and without any doubt Linnæus deserves the preference.

One fault more, in almost all these systematic writers, and that which leads me to the subject of the present chapter, is, that seeing the necessity of methodical distribution in some parts of nature, they have introduced it into all. Finding the utility of arranging plants, birds, or insects, they have arranged quadrupeds also with the same assiduity; and although the number of these is so few as not to exceed two hundred,* they have darkened the subject with distinctions and divisions, which only serve to puzzle and perplex. All method is only useful in giving perspicuity, where the subject is either dark or copious: but with regard to quadrupeds, the number is but few; many of them we are well acquainted with by habit; and the rest may very readily be known without any method. In treating of such, therefore, it would be useless to confound the reader with a multiplicity of divisions; as quadrupeds are conspicuous enough to obtain the second rank in nature, it becomes us to be acquainted with, at least, the names of them all. However, as there are naturalists who have gained a name from,

* In Dr. Shaw's General Zoology, the number of quadrupeds, not including the cetaceous and seal tribes, amount to five hundred and twelve, besides their varieties.

the excellence of their methods, in classing these animals, some readers may desire to have a knowledge of what has been laboriously invented for their instruction. I will just take leave, therefore, to mention the most applauded methods of classing animals, as adopted by Ray, Klein, and Linnæus; for it often happens, that the terms which have been long used in a science, though frivolous, become, by prescription, a part of the science itself.

Ray, after Aristotle, divides all animals into two kinds; those which have blood and those which are bloodless. In the last class he places all the insect tribes. The former he divides into such as breathe through the lungs, and such as breathe through gills: these last comprehend the fishes. In those which breathe through the lungs, some have the heart composed of two ventricles, and some have it of one. Of the last are all animals of the cetaceous kind, all oviparous quadrupeds, and serpents. Of those that have two ventricles, some are oviparous, which are the birds; and some viviparous, which are quadrupeds. The quadrupeds he divides into such as have a hoof, and such as are claw-footed. Those with the hoof, he divides into such as have it undivided, such as have it cloven, and such as have the hoof divided into more parts, as the rhinoceros, and hippopotamos. Animals with the cloven hoof, he divides into such as chew the cud, as the cow and the sheep; and such as are not ruminant, as the hog. He divides those animals that chew the cud, into four kinds: the first have hollow horns, which they never shed, as the cow; the second is of a less species, and is of the sheep.

kind; the third is of the goat kind; and the last,
which have solid horns, and shed them annually,
are of the deer kind. Coming to the claw-footed
animals, he finds some with large claws, resembling the fingers of the human hand; and these
he makes the ape kind. Of the others, some have
the foot divided in two, and have a claw to each
division; these are the camel kind. The elephant
makes a kind by itself, as its claws are covered
over by a skin. The rest of the numerous tribe
of claw-footed animals, he divides into two kinds;
the analogous, or such as resemble each other;
and the anomalous, which differ from the rest.
The analogous claw-footed animals, are of two
kinds; they have more than two cutting teeth in
each jaw, such as the lion and the dog, which
are carnivorous; or they have but two cutting
teeth in each jaw, and these are chiefly fed upon
vegetables. The carnivorous kinds are divided
into the great and the little. The great carnivorous animals are divided into such as have a short
snout, as the cat and the lion; and such as have
it long and pointed, as the dog and the wolf.
The little claw-footed carnivorous animals, differ
from the great, in having a proportionably smaller
head, and a slender body, that fits them for
creeping into holes, in pursuit of their prey, like
worms; and they are therefore called the vermin
kind.

We see, from this sketch of division and sub-
division, how a subject, extremely delightful and
amusing in itself, may be darkened, and rendered
disgusting. But, notwithstanding, Ray seems to
be one of the most simple distributors; and his

method is still, and not without reason, adopted by many. Such as have been at the trouble to learn this method, will certainly find it useful; nor would we be thought, in the least, to take from its merits; all we contend for is, that the same information may be obtained by a pleasanter and an easier method.

It was the great success of Ray's method that soon after produced such a variety of attempts in the same manner; but almost all less simple, and more obscure. Mr. Klein's method is briefly as follows: he makes the power of changing place, the characteristic mark of animals in general; and he takes their distinctions from their aptitude and fitness for such a change. Some change place by means of feet, or some similar contrivance; others have wings and feet: some can change place only in water, and have only fins: some go upon earth, without any feet at all; some change place, by moving their shell; and some move only at a certain time of the year. Of such, however, as do not move at all, he takes no notice. The quadrupeds that move chiefly by means of four feet upon land, he divides into two orders. The first are the hoofed kind; and the second the claw kind. Each of these orders is divided into four families. The first family of the hoofed kind are the single hoofed, such as the horse, ass, &c. The second family are such as have the hoof cloven into two parts, such as the cow, &c. The third family have the hoof divided into three parts; and in this family is found only the rhinoceros. The fourth family have the hoof divided into five parts; and in this is only to be found the elephant. With respect to the clawed kind, the first family comprehends those that have but two claws on each foot, as the camel; the second family have three claws; the third, four; and the fourth, five. This method of taking the distinctions of animals from the organs of motion, is ingenious; but it is, at the same time, incomplete: and, besides the divisions into which it must necessarily fall, is inadequate; since, for instance, in his family with two claws, there is but one animal; whereas, in his family with five claws, there are above a hundred.

Brisson, who has laboured this subject with great accuracy, divides animated nature into nine classes: namely, quadrupeds; cetaceous animals, or those of the whale kind; birds; reptiles, or those of the serpent kind; cartilaginous fishes; spinous fishes; shelled animals; insects; and worms. He divides the quadrupeds into eighteen orders; and takes their distinctions from the number and form of their teeth.

But of all those whose systems have been adopted and admired, Linnæus is the foremost; as, with a studied brevity, his system comprehends the greatest variety in the smallest space.

According to him, the first distinction of animals is to be taken from their internal structure. Some have the heart with two ventricles, and hot red blood; namely, quadrupeds and birds. The quadrupeds are viviparous, and the birds oviparous.

Some have the heart with but one ventricle, and cold red blood; namely, amphibia and fishes.

The amphibia are furnished with lungs ; the fishes, with gills.

Some have the heart with one ventricle, and cold white serum ; namely, insects and worms : the insects have feelers ; and the worms, holders.

The distinctions of quadrupeds, or animals with paps, as he calls them, are taken from their teeth. He divides them into seven orders : to which he gives names that are not easy of translation : Primates, or principles, with four cutting teeth in each jaw ; Bruta, or brutes, with no cutting teeth ; Feræ, or wild beasts, with generally six cutting teeth in each jaw ; Glires, or dormice, with two cutting teeth, both above and below ; Pecora, or cattle, with many cutting teeth above, and none below ; Belluæ, or beasts, with the fore teeth blunt ; Cete, or those of the whale kind, with cartilaginous teeth. I have but just sketched out this system, as being, in its own nature, the closest abridgment. It would take volumes to dilate it to its proper length. The names of the different animals, and their classes, alone makes two thick octavo volumes ; and yet nothing is given but the slightest description of each. I have omitted all criticism, also, upon the accuracy of the preceding systems ; this has been done, both by Buffon and Daubenton, not with less truth than humour ; for they had too much good sense not to see the absurdity of multiplying the terms of science to no end ; and disappointing our curiosity rather with a catalogue of nature's varieties than a history of nature.

Instead, therefore, of taxing the memory and teazing the patience with such a variety of divisions and subdivisions, I will take leave to class the productions of nature in the most obvious, though not in the most accurate manner. In natural history, of all other sciences, there is the least danger of obscurity. In morals, or in metaphysics, every definition must be precise, because those sciences are built upon definitions; but it is otherwise in those subjects where the exhibition of the object itself is always capable of correcting the error. Thus it may often happen that in a lax system of natural history, a creature may be ranked among quadrupeds that belongs more properly to the fish or the insect classes. But that can produce very little confusion, and every reader can thus make a system the most agreable to his own imagination. It will be of no manner of consequence whether we call a bird or an insect a quadruped, if we are careful in marking all its distinctions: the uncertainty in reasoning, or thinking, that these approximations of the different kinds of animals produce, is but very small, and happens but very rarely; whereas the labour that naturalists have been at to keep the kinds asunder, has been excessive. This, in general, has given birth to that variety of systems which we have just mentioned; each of which seems to be almost as good as the preceeding.

Taking, therefore, this latitude, and using method only where it contributes to conciseness or perspicuity, we shall divide animated nature into four classes; namely, quadrupeds, birds, fishes, and insects. All these seem in general pretty well distinguished from each other, by nature; yet there are several instances in which we can scarcely tell whether it is a bird or a quadruped that we are about to examine; whether it is a fish or an insect that offers to our curiosity. Nature is varied by imperceptible gradations, so that no line can be drawn between any two classes of its productions, and no definition made to comprehend them all. However, the distinctions between these classes are sufficiently marked, and their encroachments upon each other are so rare, that it will be sufficient particularly to apprize the reader when they happen to be blended.

There are many quadrupeds that we are well acquainted with; and of those we do not know we shall form the most clear and distinct conceptions, by being told wherein they differ, and wherein they resemble those with which we are familiar. Each class of quadrupeds may be ranged under some one of the domestic kinds, that may serve for the model by which we are to form some kind of idea of the rest. Thus we may say that a tiger is of the cat kind, a wolf of the dog kind, because there are some rude resemblances between each; and a person who has never seen the wild animals will have some incomplete knowledge of their figure from the tame ones. On the contrary, I I will not, as some systematic writers have done,* say that the bat is of the human kind, or a hog of the horse kind, merely because there is some resemblance in their teeth, or their paps. For, although this may be striking enough, yet a person who has

* Linnæi Syst.

never seen a bat or a hog, 'will never form any just conception of either, by being told of this minute similitude. In short, the method in classing quadrupeds should be taken from their most striking resemblances; and where these do not offer, we shall not force the similitude, but leave the animal to be described as a solitary species. The number of quadrupeds is so few that, indeed without any method whatever, there is no great danger of confusion.

. All quadrupeds, the number of which, according to Buffon, amounts to but two hundred, may be classed in the following manner.

First, those of the Horse kind. This class contains the Horse, the Ass, and the Zebra. Of these, none have horns; and their hoof is of one solid piece.

The second class are those of the Cow kind; comprehending the Urus, the Buffalo, the Bison, and the Bonassas. These have cloven hoofs, and chew the cud.

The third class is that of the Sheep kind; with cloven hoofs, and chewing the cud like the former: In this is comprehended the Sheep, the Goat, the Lama, the Vigogne, the Gazella, the Guinea-deer, and all of a similar form.

The fourth class is that of the Deer kind; with cloven hoofs, and with solid horns, that are shed every year. ...This class contains the Elk, the Rein-deer, the Stag, the Buck, the Roe-buck, and the Axis.

The fifth class comprehends all those of the Hog kind, the Peccary, and the Babyrouessa.

The sixth class is that numerous one of the Cat kind. This comprehends the Cat, the Lion, the Panther, the Leopard, the Jaguar, the Cougar, the Jaguarette, the Lynx, the Ounce, and the Catamountain. These are all carnivorous, and furnished with crooked claws, which they can sheath and unsheath at pleasure.

The seventh class is that of the Dog kind, carnivorous, and furnished with claws like the former, but which they cannot sheath. This class comprehends the Dog, the Wolf, the Fox, the Jackall, the Isatis, the Hyena, the Civet, the Gibet, and the Genet.

The eighth class is that of the Weasel kind, with a long small body, with five toes, or claws, on each foot; the first of them separated from the rest like a thumb. This comprehends the Weasel, the Martin, the Pole-cat, the Ferret, the Mangoust, the Vansire, the Ermine, with all the varieties of the American Monfettes.

The ninth class is that of the Rabbit kind, with two large cutting teeth in each jaw. This comprehends the Rabbit, the Hare, the Guinea-pig, all the various species of the Squirrel, the Dormouse, the Marmotte, the Rat, the Mouse, Agouti, the Paca, the Aperea, and the Tapati.

The tenth class is that of the Hedge-hog kind, with claw feet, and covered with prickles, comprehending the Hedge-hog and the Porcupine, the Couando, and the Urson.

The eleventh class is that of the Tortoise kind, covered with a shell, or scales. This comprehends the Tortoise, the Pangolin, and the Phatagin.

The twelfth is of the Otter, or amphibious kind, comprehending the Otter, the Beaver, the Desman, the Morse, and the Seal.

The thirteenth class is that of the Ape and Monkey kinds, with hands, and feet resembling hands.

The fourteenth class is that of winged quadrupeds, or the Bat kind, containing the Bat, the Flying Squirrel, and some other varieties.

The animals which seem to approach no other kind, either in nature, or in form, but to make each a distinct species in itself, are the following: the Elephant, the Rhinoceros, the Hippopotamos, the Cameleopard, the Camel, the Bear, the Badger, the Tapir, the Cabrai, the Coati, the Antbear, the Tatou, and lastly the Sloth.

All other quadrupeds, whose names are not set down, will be found among some of the above-mentioned classes, and referred to that which they most resemble. When, therefore, we are at a loss to know the name of any particular animal, by examining which of the known kinds it most resembles, either in shape, or in hoofs, or claws; and then, examining the particular description, we shall be able to discover not only its name, but its history. I have already said that all methods of this kind are merely arbitrary, and that nature makes no exact distinction between her productions. It is hard, for instance, to tell whether we ought to refer the Civet to the dog or the cat kind; but, if we know the exact history of the civet, it is no great matter to which kind we shall judge it to bear the greatest resemblance. It is enough that a distribution of this kind excites in us some rude

outlines of the make, or some marked similitudes
in the nature of these animals ; but, to know them
with any precision, no system, or even description
will serve, since the animal itself, or a good print of
it, must be seen, and its history be read at length,
before it can be said to be known. To pretend to
say that we have an idea of a quadruped, because
we can tell the number, or the make of its teeth, or
its paps, is as absurd as if we should pretend to distinguish men by the buttons of their clothes. Indeed it often happens that the quadruped itself
can be but seldom seen ; that many of the more
rare kinds do not come into Europe above once in
an age, and some of them have never been able to
bear the removal ; in such a case, therefore, there is
no other substitute but a good print of the animal
to give an idea of its figure ; for no description
whatsoever can answer this purpose so well, as I
have just observed. Mr. Locke, with his usual
good sense, has observed, that a drawing of the
animal, taken from the life, is one of the best
methods of advancing natural history ; and yet,
most of our modern systematic writers are content
rather with describing. Descriptions, no doubt, will
go some way towards giving an idea of the figure
of an animal ; but they are certainly much the longest
way about, and, as they are usually managed, much
the most obscure. In a drawing we can, at a
single glance, gather more instruction than by a
day's painful investigation of methodical systems,
where we are told the proportions with great
exactness, and yet remain ignorant of the totality.
In fact, this method of describing all things is a
fault that has infected many of our books, that

treat on the meaner arts, for this last age. They attempt to teach by words what is only to be learnt by practice or inspection. Most of our dictionaries, and bodies of arts and sciences, are guilty of this error. Suppose, for instance, it be requisite to mention the manner of making shoes, it is plain that all the verbal instructions in the world will never give an adequate idea of this humble art, or teach a man to become a shoe-maker. A day or two in a shoe-maker's shop will answer the end better than a whole folio of instruction, which only serves to oppress the learner with the weight of its pretended importance. We have lately seen a laborious work carried on at Paris, with this only intent of teaching all the trades by description: however, the design at first blush seems to be ill considered; and it is probable that very few advantages will be derived from so laborious an undertaking. With regard to the descriptions in natural history, these, without all question, under the direction of good sense, are necessary; but still they should be kept within proper bounds; and, where a thing may be much more easily shown than described, the exhibition should ever precede the account.

CHAP. X.

Of Quadrupeds in general, compared to Man.

UPON comparing the various animals of the globe with each other, we shall find that Quadrupeds demand the rank immediately next ourselves;

and, consequently, come first in consideration. The similitude between the structure of their bodies and ours, those instincts which they enjóy in a superior degree to the rest, their constant services, or their unceasing hostilities, all render them the foremost objects of our curiosity, the most interesting parts of animated nature. These, however, although now so completely subdued, very probably, in the beginning, were nearer upon an equality with us, and disputed the possession of the earth. Man, while yet savage himself, was but ill qualified to civilize the forest. While yet naked, unarmed, and without shelter, every wild beast was a formidable rival: and the destruction of such was the first employment of heroes. But, when he began to multiply, and arts to accumulate, he soon cleared the plains of the most noxious of these his rivals; a part was taken under his protection and care, while the rest found a precarious refuge in the burning desert, or the howling wilderness.

From being rivals, quadrupeds have *now* become the assistants of man; upon them he devolves the most laborious employments, and finds in them patient and humble coadjutors, ready to obey, and content with the smallest retribution. It was not, however, without long and repeated efforts that the independent spirit of these animals was broken ; for the savage freedom, in wild animals, is generally found to pass down through several generations before it is totally subdued. Those cats and dogs that are taken from a state of natural wildness in the forest, still transmit their fierceness to their young: and, however concealed in general, it breaks out upon several occasions. Thus the assiduity and application of man in bringing them up, not only alters their disposition, but their very forms; and the difference between animals in a state of nature and domestic tameness is so considerable, that M. Buffon has taken this as a principal distinction in classing them.

In taking a cursory view of the form of quadrupeds, we may easily perceive that, of all the ranks of animated nature, they bear the nearest resemblance to man. This similitude will be found more striking when, erecting themselves on their hinder feet, they are taught to walk forward in an upright posture. We then see that all their extremities in a manner correspond with ours and present us with a rude imitation of our own. In some of the ape kind the resemblance is so striking, that anatomists are puzzled to find in what part of the human body man's superiority consists; and scarcely any but the metaphysician can draw the line that ultimately divides them.

But, if we compare their internal structure with our own, the likeness will be found still to increase, and we shall perceive many advantages they enjoy in common with us, above the lower tribes of nature. Like us, they are placed above the class of birds, by bringing forth their young alive; like us, they are placed above the class of fishes, by breathing through the lungs; like us, they are placed above the class of insects, by having red blood circulating through their veins; and lastly, like us, they are different from almost all the other classes of animated nature, being either wholly or partly covered with hair. Thus nearly are we represented in point of conformation to the class of animals immediately below us; and this shows what little reason we have to be proud of our persons alone, to the perfection of which quadrupeds make such very near approaches.

The similitude of quadrupeds to man obtains also in the fixedness of their nature, and their being less apt to be changed by the influence of climate or food than the lower ranks of nature.* Birds are found very apt to alter both in colour and size; fishes, likewise, still more; insects may be quickly brought to change and adapt themselves to the climate; and, if we descend to plants, which may be allowed to have a kind of living existence, their kinds may be surprisingly and readily altered, and taught to assume new forms. The figure of every animal may be considered as a kind of drapery, which it may be made to put on or off by human assiduity; in man the drapery is almost invariable; in quadrupeds it admits of some variation; and the variety may be made greater still as we descend to the inferior classes of animal existence.

Quadrupeds, although they are thus strongly marked, and in general divided from the various kinds around them, yet, some of them are often of so equivocal a nature, that it is hard to tell whether they ought to be ranked in the quadruped class, or degraded to those below them. If, for instance, we were to marshal the whole groupe of animals round man, placing the most perfect next him, and those most equivocal near the classes

* Buffon, vol. xviii. p. 179.

they most approach, we should find it difficult,
after the principal had taken their stations near
him, where to place many that lie at the outskirts
of this phalanx. The bat makes a near approach
to the aerial tribe, and might by some be reckoned
among the birds. The porcupine has not less
pretensions to that class, being covered with
quills, and showing that birds are not the only
part of nature that are furnished with such a
defence. The armadillo might be referred to
the tribe of insects, or snails; being, like them,
covered with a shell; the seal and the morse
might be ranked among the fishes, like them being
furnished with fins, and almost constantly residing
in the same element. All these, the farther
they recede from the human figure, become
less perfect, and may be considered as the lowest
kinds of that class to which we have referred
them.

But, although the variety in quadrupeds is thus
great, they all seem well adapted to the stations
in which they are placed. There is scarcely one
of them, how rudely shaped soever, that is not
formed to enjoy a state of happiness fitted to its
nature. All its deformities are only relative to
us, but all its enjoyments are peculiarly its own.
We may superficially suppose the Sloth, that
takes up months in climbing a single tree, or the
Mole, whose eyes are too small for distinct vision,
are wretched and helpless creatures; but it is probable that their life, with respect to themselves,
is a life of luxury; the most pleasing food is easily
obtained; and, as they are abridged in one plea-

sure, it may be doubled in those which remain.
Quadrupeds, and all the lower kinds of animals,
have, at worst, but the torments of immediate
evil to encounter, and this is but transient and
accidental; man has two sources of calamity,—that
which he foresees, as well as that which he feels;
so that, if his reward were to be in this life alone,
then, indeed, would he be of all beings the most
wretched.

The heads of quadrupeds, though differing from
each other, are in general adapted to their way of
living. In some it is sharp, the better to fit the
animal for turning up the earth in which its food
lies. In some it is long, in order to give a greater
room for the olfactory nerves, as in dogs, who
are to hunt and find out their prey by the scent.
In others it is short and thick, as in the lion, to
increase the strength of the jaw, and to fit it the
better for combat. In quadrupeds, that feed upon
grass, they are enabled to hold down their heads
to the ground, by a strong tendinous ligament,
that runs from the head to the middle of the back.
This serves to raise the head, although it has been
held to the ground for several hours, without any
labour, or any assistance from the muscles of the
neck.

The teeth of all animals are entirely fitted to the
nature of their food. Those of such as live upon
flesh differ in every respect from such as live upon
vegetables. In the latter they seem entirely made
for gathering and bruising their simple food, being
edged before, and fitted for cutting; but broad
towards the back of the jaw, and fitted for pounding.

In the carnivorous kinds they are sharp before, and fitted rather for holding than dividing. In the one the teeth serve as grindstones, in the other as weapons of defence; in both, however, the surface of those teeth which serves for grinding are unequal; the cavities and risings fitting those of the opposite so as to tally exactly when the jaws are brought together. These inequalities better serve for comminuting the food; but they become smooth with age; and, for this reason, old animals take a longer time to chew their food than such as are in the vigour of life.

Their legs are not better fitted than their teeth to their respective wants or enjoyments. In some they are made for strength only, and to support a vast unwieldy frame, without much flexibility or beautiful proportion. Thus the legs of the elephant, the rhinoceros, and the sea-horse, resemble pillars; were they made smaller, they would be unfit to support the body; were they endowed with greater flexibility or swiftness, that would be needless, as they do not pursue other animals for food; and, conscious of their own superior strength, there are none that they deign to avoid. Deers, hares, and other creatures, that are to find safety only in flight, have their legs made entirely for speed; they are slender and nervous. Were it not for this advantage, every carnivorous animal would soon make them a prey, and their races would be entirely extinguished. But in the present state of nature, the means of safety are rather superior to those of offence; and the pursuing animal must owe success only to patience, perseverance and industry. The feet of some, that live upon fish alone, are made for swimming. The toes of these animals are joined together with membranes, being web-footed, like a goose or a duck, by which they swim with great rapidity. Those animals that lead a life of hostility, and live upon others, have their feet armed with sharp claws, which some can sheath and unsheath at will. Those, on the contrary, who lead peaceful lives, have generally hoofs, which serve some as weapons of defence; and which in all are better fitted for traversing extensive tracts of rugged country, than the claw foot of their pursuers.

The stomach is generally proportioned to the quality of the animal's food, or the ease with which it is obtained. In those that live upon flesh and such nourishing substances, it is small and glandular, affording such juices as are best adapted to digest its contents; their intestines also are short and without fatness. On the contrary, such animals as feed entirely upon vegetables, have the stomach very large; and those who chew the cud, have no less than four stomachs, all which serve as so many laboratories, to prepare and turn their coarse food into proper nourishment. In Africa, where the plants afford greater nourishment than in our temperate climates, several animals, that with us have four stomachs, have there but two.* However, in all animals the size of the intestines is proportioned to the nature of the food; where that is furnished in large quantities, the stomach

* Buffon.

dilates to answer the increase. In domestic animals that are plentifully supplied, it is large; in
the wild animals, that live precariously, it is much
more contracted, and the intestines are much
shorter.

- In this manner, all animals are fitted by nature
to fill up some peculiar station. The greatest
animals are made for an inoffensive life, to range
the plains and the forest without injuring others; to
live upon the productions of the earth, the grass of
the field, or the tender branches of trees. These,
secure in their own strength, neither fly from any
other quadrupeds nor yet attack them: Nature, to
the greatest strength has added the most gentle and
harmless dispositions; without this those enormous creatures would be more than a match for all
the rest of the creation; for what devastation might
not ensue, were the elephant, or the rhinoceros, or
the buffalo, as fierce and as mischievous as the
tiger or the rat? In order to oppose these larger
animals, and in some measure to prevent their exuberance, there is a species of the carnivorous kind,
of inferior strength indeed, but of greater activity
and cunning. The lion and the tiger generally
watch for the larger kinds of prey, attack them at
some disadvantage, and commonly jump upon
them by surprise. None of the carnivorous kinds,
except the dog alone, will make a voluntary attack,
but with the odds on their side. They are all
cowards by nature, and usually catch their prey by
a bound from some lurking place, seldom attempting to invade them openly; for the larger beasts
are too powerful for them, and the smaller too
swift.

A lion does not willingly attack a horse; and
then only when compelled by the keenest hunger.
The combats between a lion and a horse are frequent enough in Italy; where they are both inclosed in a kind of amphitheatre, fitted for that
purpose. The lion always approaches wheeling
about, while the horse presents his hinder parts to
the enemy. The lion in this manner goes round
and round, still narrowing his circle, till he comes
to the proper distance to make his spring: just at
the time the lion springs, the horse lashes with
both legs from behind, and, in general, the odds
are in his favour; it more often happening that the
lion is stunned and struck motionless by the blow,
than that he effects his jump between the horse's
shoulders. If the lion is stunned, and left sprawl-
ing, the horse escapes without attempting to improve his victory; but if the lion succeeds, he
sticks to his prey, and tears the horse in pieces
in a very short time.

But it is not among the larger animals of the
forest alone, that these hostilities are carried on;
there is a minuter, and still more treacherous contest between the lower rank of quadrupeds. The
panther hunts for the sheep and the goat; the
catamountain for the hare or the rabbit; and the
wild cat for the squirrel or the mouse. In proportion as each carnivorous animal wants strength, it
uses all the assistance of patience, assiduity, and
cunning. However, the arts of these to pursue,
are not so great as the tricks of their prey to
escape; so that the power of destruction in one
class is inferior to the power of safety in the other.
Were this otherwise, the forest would soon be dis-

peopled of the feebler races of animals; and beasts
of prey themselves would want, at one time, that
subsistence which they lavishly destroyed at another.

Few wild animals seek their prey in the day time;
they are then generally deterred by their fears of
man in the inhabited countries, and by the excessive heat of the sun in those extensive forests that
lie towards the south, and in which they reign the
undisputed tyrants. As soon as the morning,
therefore, appears, the carnivorous animals retire
to their dens; and the elephant, the horse, the
deer, and all the hare kinds, those inoffensive
tenants of the plain, make their appearance. But
again, at night fall, the state of hostility begins :
the whole forest then echoes to a variety of different howlings. Nothing can be more terrible than
an African landscape at the close of evening : the
deep-toned roarings of the lion; the shriller yell-
ings of the tiger; the jackall, pursuing, by the
scent, and barking like a dog; the hyæna, with a
note peculiarly solitary and dreadful; but above
all, the hissing of the various kinds of serpents,
that then begin their call, and, as I am assured,
make a much louder symphony than the birds in
our groves in a morning.

Beasts of prey seldom devour each other; nor
can any thing but the greatest degree of hunger
induce them to it. What they chiefly seek after,
is the deer, or the goat; those harmless creatures,
that seem made to embellish nature. These are
either pursued or surprised, and afford the most
agreeable repast to their destroyers. The most
usual method, with even the fiercest animals is to

hide and crouch near some path frequented by their prey; or some water, where cattle come to drink; and seize them at once with a bound. The lion and the tiger leap twenty feet at a spring; and this, rather than their swiftness or strength, is what they have most to depend upon for a supply.. There is scarcely one of the deer or hare kind, that is not very easily capable of escaping them by its swiftness; so that whenever any of these fall a prey, it must be owing to their own inattention.

But there is another class of the carnivorous kind, that hunt by the scent, and which it is much more difficult to escape. It is remarkable, that all animals of this kind pursue in a pack; and encourage each other by their mutual cries. The jackall, the syagush, the wolf, and the dog, are of this kind; they pursue with patience rather than swiftness; their prey flies at first, and leaves them for miles behind; but they keep on with a constant steady pace, and excite each other by a general spirit of industry and emulation, till at last they share the common plunder; though it too often happens, that the larger beasts of prey, when they hear a cry of this kind begun, pursue the pack, and when they have hunted down the animal, come in and monopolize the spoil. This has given rise to the report of the jackall's being the lion's provider; when the reality is, that the jackall hunts for itself, and the lion is an unwelcome intruder upon the fruit of his soil.

Nevertheless, with all the powers which carnivorous animals are possessed of, they generally

lead a life of famine and fatigue. Their prey has
such a variety of methods for escaping, that they
sometimes continue without food for a fortnight
together : but nature has endowed them with a
degree of patience, equal to the severity of their
state; so that, as their subsistence is precarious,
their appetites are complying. They usually seize
their prey with a roar, either of seeming delight,
or perhaps to terrify it from resistance. They
frequently devour it, bones and all, in the most
ravenous manner ; and then retire to their dens,
continuing inactive till the calls of hunger again
excite their courage and industry. But, as all
their methods of pursuit are counteracted by the
arts of evasion, they often continue to range without
success, supporting a state of famine for several
days, nay, sometimes, weeks together. Of their
prey, some find protection in holes, in which nature
has directed them to bury themselves ; some find
safety by swiftness ; and such as are possessed
of neither of these advantages, generally herd together, and endeavour to repel invasion by united
force. The very sheep which to us seem so
defenceless, are by no means so in a state of
nature ; they are furnished with arms of defence,
and a very great degree of swiftness ; but they
are still further assisted by their spirit of mutual
defence: the females fall into the centre ; and the
males, forming a ring round them, oppose their
horns to the assailants. Some animals, that feed
upon fruits which are to be found only at one
time of the year, fill their holes with several sorts
of plants, which enable them to lie concealed during
the hard frosts of the winter, contented with

their prison, since it affords them plenty and protection. These holes are dug with so much art,
that there seems the design of an architect in the
formation. There are usually two apertures, by
one of which the little inhabitant can always
escape, when the enemy is in possession of the
other. Many creatures are equally careful of
avoiding their enemies, by placing a centinel, to
warn them of the approach of danger. These
generally perform this duty by turns; and they
know how to punish such as have neglected their
post, or have been unmindful of the common
safety. Such are a part of the efforts that the
weaker races of quadrupeds exert, to avoid their
invaders; and, in general, they are attended with
success. The arts of instinct are most commonly
found an overmatch for the invasions of instinct.
Man is the only creature against whom all their
little tricks cannot prevail. Wherever he has
spread his dominion, scarcely any flight can save,
or any retreat harbour; wherever he comes, terror
seems to follow, and all society ceases among the
inferior tenants of the plain; their union against
him can yield them no protection, and their
cunning is but weakness. In their fellow-brutes,
they have an enemy whom they can oppose
with an equality of advantage; they can oppose
fraud or swiftness to force; or numbers to invasion: but what can be done against such an
enemy as man, who finds them out though unseen, and though remote destroys them? Wherever
he comes, all the contest among the meaner ranks
seem to be at an end, or is carried on only
by surprise. Such as he has thought proper to

protect, have calmly submitted to his protection; such as he has found it convenient to destroy, carry on an unequal war, and their numbers are every day decreasing.

The wild animal is subject to few alterations; and, in a state of savage nature, continues for ages the same, in size, shape, and colour. But it is otherwise when subdued, and taken under the protection of man; its external form, and even its internal structure, are altered by human assiduity; and this is one of the first and greatest causes of the variety that we see among the several quadrupeds of the same species. Man appears to have changed the very nature of domestic animals, by cultivation and care. A domestic animal is a slave that seems to have few other desires but such as man is willing to allow it. Humble, patient, resigned, and attentive, it fills up the duties of its station; ready for labour, and content with subsistence.

Almost all domestic animals seem to bear the marks of servitude strong upon them. All the varieties in their colour, all the fineness and length of their hair, together with the depending length of their ears, seem to have arisen from a long continuance of domestic slavery. What an immense variety is there to be found in the ordinary race of dogs and horses! the principal differences of which have been effected by the industry of man, so adapting the food, the treatment, the labour, and the climate, that nature seems almost to have forgotten her original design; and the tame animal no longer bears any resemblance to its ancestors in the woods around him.

In this manner, nature is under a kind of constraint, in those animals we have taught to live in a state of servitude near us. The savage animals preserve the marks of their first formation; their colours are generally the same; a rough dusky brown, or a tawny, seem almost their only varieties. But it is otherwise in the tame; their colours are various, and their forms different from each other. The nature of the climate, indeed, operates upon all; but more particularly on these. That nourishment which is prepared by the hand of man, not adapted to their appetites, but to suit his own convenience, that climate the rigours of which he can soften, and that employment to which they are sometimes assigned, produce a number of distinctions that are not to be found among the savage animals. These at first were accidental, but in time became hereditary; and a new race of artificial monsters are propagated, rather to answer the purposes of human pleasure, than their own convenience. In short, their very appetites may be changed; and those that feed only upon grass, may be rendered carnivorous. I have seen a sheep that would eat flesh, and a horse that was fond of oysters.

But not their appetites, or their figure alone, but their very dispositions, and their natural sagacity, are altered by the vicinity of man. In those countries where men have seldom intruded, some animals have been found, established in a kind of civil state of society. Remote from the tyranny of man, they seem to have a spirit of mutual benevolence, and mutual friendship. The beavers, in these distant solitudes, are known to build like architects, and rule like citizens. The habitations that these have been seen to erect, exceed the houses of the human inhabitants of the same country, both in neatness and convenience. But as soon as man intrudes upon their society, they seem impressed with the terrors of their inferior situation, their spirit of society ceases, the bond is dissolved, and every animal looks for safety in solitude, and there tries all its little industry to shift only for itself.

Next to human influence, the climate seems to have the strongest effects both upon the nature and the form of quadrupeds. As in man, we have seen some alterations, produced by the variety of his situation; so, in the lower ranks, that are more subject to variation, the influence of climate is more readily perceived. As these are more nearly attached to the earth, and in a manner connected to the soil; as they have none of the arts of shielding off the inclemency of the weather, or softening the rigours of the sun, they are consequently more changed by its variations. In general, it may be remarked, that the colder the country, the larger and the warmer is the fur of each animal; it being wisely provided by nature, that the inhabitant should be adapted to the rigours of its situation. Thus the fox and wolf, which in temperate climates have but short hair, have a fine long fur in the frozen regions near the pole. On the contrary, those dogs which with us have long hair, when carried to Guinea, or Angola, in a short time cast their thick covering, and assume a lighter dress, and one more adapted to the warmth of the country. The beaver,

and the ermine, which are found in the greatest
plenty in the cold regions, are remarkable for.
the warmth and delicacy of their furs; while
the elephant, and the rhinoceros, that are natives
of the line, have scarcely any hair. Not but
that human industry can, in some measure, co-
operate with, or repress the effects of climate
in this particular. It is well known what alterations are produced by proper care, in the sheep's
fleece, in different parts of our own country; and
the same industry is pursued with a like success
in Syria, where many of their animals are clothed
with a long and beautiful hair, which they take
care to improve, as they work it into that stuff
called camblet, so well known in different parts of
Europe.

The disposition of the animal seems also not
less marked by the climate than the figure. The
same causes that seem to have rendered the
human inhabitants of the rigorous climates savage
and ignorant, have also operated upon their animals. Both at the line and the pole, the wild
quadrupeds are fierce and untameable. In these
latitudes, their savage dispositions having not been
quelled by any efforts from man, and being still
farther stimulated by the severity of the weather,
they continue fierce and untractable. Most of
the attempts which have hitherto been made to
tame the wild beasts brought home from the pole
or the equator, have proved ineffectual. They
are gentle and harmless enough while young;
but as they grow up, they acquire their natural
ferocity, and snap at the hand that feeds them.
It may indeed, in general, be asserted that in all

countries where the men are most barbarous, the
beasts are most fierce and cruel; and this is but
a natural consequence of the struggle between man
and the more savage animals of the forest; for
in proportion as he is weak and timid, they must
be bold and intrusive; in proportion as his dominion is but feebly supported, their rapacity must
be more obnoxious. In the extensive countries,
therefore, lying round the pole, or beneath the
line, the quadrupeds are fierce and formidable.
Africa has ever been remarked for the brutality
of its men, and the fierceness of its animals: its
lions and its leopards are not less terrible than its
crocodiles and its serpents; their dispositions seem
entirely marked with the rigours of the climate;
and being bred in an extreme of heat, they show
a peculiar ferocity, that neither the force of man
can conquer, nor his arts allay. However, it is
happy for the wretched inhabitants of those
climates, that its most formidable animals are all
solitary ones; that they have not learnt the art of
uniting, to oppress mankind; but each depending on its own strength, invades without any
assistant.

The food, also, is another cause in the variety
which we find among quadrupeds of the same
kind. Thus the beasts which feed in the valley
are generally larger than those which glean a
scanty subsistence on the mountain. Such as live
in the warm climates, where the plants are much
larger and more succulent than with us, are equally
remarkable for their bulk. The ox fed in the
plains of Indostan, is very much larger than that
which is more hardily maintained on the side of

the Alps. The deserts of Africa, where the plants are extremely nourishing, produce the largest and fiercest animals; and, perhaps, for a contrary reason, America is found not to produce such large animals as are seen in the ancient continent. But, whatever be the reason, the fact is certain, that while America exceeds us in the size of its reptiles of all kinds, it is far inferior in its quadruped productions. Thus, for instance, the largest animal of that country is the tapir, which can by no means be compared to the elephant of Africa. Its beasts of prey, also, are divested of that strength and courage which is so dangerous in this part of the world. The American lion, tiger, and leopard, if such diminutive creatures deserve these names, are neither so fierce nor so valiant as those of Africa and Asia. The tiger of Bengal has been seen to measure twelve feet in length, without including the tail; whereas the American tiger seldom exceeds three. This difference obtains still more in the other animals of that country, so that some have been of opinion*️ that all quadrupeds in Southern America are of a different species from those most resembling them in the old world; and that there are none which are common to both but such as have entered America by the north; and which, being able to bear the rigours of the frozen pole, have travelled from the ancient continent, by that, passage, into the new. Thus the bear, the wolf, the elk, the stag, the fox, and the beaver are known to the inhabitants as well of North Ame-

* Buffon.

rica as of Russia; while most of the various kinds
to the southward, in both continents, bear no
resemblance to each other. Upon the whole, such
as peculiarly belong to the new continent are
without any marks of the quadruped perfection.
They are almost wholly destitute of the power of
defence; they have neither formidable teeth,
horns, or tail; their figure is awkward, and their
limbs ill proportioned. Some among them, such
as the ant-bear, and the sloth, appear so miserably
formed as scarcely to have the power of moving
and eating. They, seemingly, drag out a miserable
and languid existence in the most desert solitude;
and would quickly have been destroyed in a country
where there were inhabitants, or powerful beasts
to oppose them.

But if the quadrupeds of the new continent be
less, they are found in much greater abundance;
for it is a rule that obtains through nature, that
the smallest animals multiply the fastest. The
goat, imported from Europe to South America,
soon begins to degenerate; but as it grows less it
becomes more prolific; and, instead of one kid a
time, or two at the most, it generally produces
five, and sometimes more. What there is in the
food, or the climate, that produces this change,
we have not been able to learn; we might be apt
to ascribe it to the heat, but that on the African
coast, where it is still hotter, this rule does not
obtain; for the goat, instead of degenerating there,
seems rather to improve.

However, the rule is general among all quadrupeds, that those which are large and formidable
produce but few at a time; while such as are mean

and contemptible are extremely prolific. The lion, or tiger, have seldom above two cubs at a litter; while the cat, that is of a similar nature, is usually seen to have five or six. In this manner, the lower tribes become extremely numerous; and, but for this surprising fecundity, from their natural weakness, they would quickly be extirpated. The breed of mice, for instance, would have long since been blotted from the earth, were the mouse as slow in production as the elephant. But it has been wisely provided that such animals as can make but little resistance, should at least have a means of repairing the destruction, which they must often suffer, by their quick reproduction; that they should increase even among enemies, and multiply under the hand of the destroyer. On the other hand, it has as wisely been ordered by Providence, that the larger kinds should produce but slowly; otherwise, as they require proportional supplies from nature, they would quickly consume their own store; and, of consequence, many of them would soon perish through want; so that life would thus be given without the necessary means of subsistence. In a word, Providence has most wisely balanced the strength of the great against the weakness of the little. Since it was necessary that some should be great and others mean, since it was expedient that some should live upon others, it has assisted the weakness of one by granting it fruitfulness; and diminished the number of the other by infecundity.

In consequence of this provision, the larger creatures, which bring forth few at a time, seldom begin to generate till they have nearly acquired their full growth. On the contrary; those which bring many, reproduce before they have arrived at half their natural size. Thus the horse and the bull are nearly at their best before they begin to breed ; the hog and the rabbit scarce leave the teat before they become parents in turn. Almost all animals likewise continue the time of their pregnancy in proportion to their size. The mare continues eleven months with foal, the cow nine, the wolf five, and the bitch nine weeks. In all, the intermediate litters are the most fruitful; the first and the last generally producing the fewest in number, and the worst of the kind.

Whatever be the natural disposition of animals at other times, they all acquire new courage when they consider themselves as defending their young. No terrors can then, drive them from the post of duty; the mildest begin to exert their little force, and resist the most formidable enemy. Where resistance is hopeless, they then incur every danger in order to rescue their young by flight, and retard their own expedition by providing for their little ones. When the female opossum, an animal of America, is pursued, she instantly takes her young into a false belly, with which nature has supplied her, and carries them off, or dies in the endeavour. I have been lately assured of a she-fox which, when hunted, took her cub in her mouth, and ran for several miles without quitting it, until at last she was forced to leave it behind, upon the approach of a mastiff, as she ran through a farmer's yard. But, if at this period the mildest animals acquire new fierceness, how formidable must those

be that subsist by rapine! At such times, no
obstacles can stop their ravage, nor no threats can
terrify; the lioness then seems more hardy than
even the lion himself. She attacks men and beasts
indiscriminately, and carries all she can overcome
reeking to her cubs, whom she thus early accustoms to slaughter. Milk, in the carnivorous animals, is much more sparing than in others; and it
may be for this reason that all such carry home
their prey alive, that, in feeding their young, its
blood may supply the deficiencies of nature, and
serve instead of that milk, with which they are so
sparingly supplied.

Nature, that has thus given them courage to
defend their young, has given them instinct to
choose the proper times of copulation, so as to bring
forth when the provision suited to each kind is to
be found in the greatest plenty. The wolf, for
instance, couples in December, so that the time of
pregnancy continuing five months, it may have its
young in April. The mare, who goes eleven
months, admits the horse in summer, in order to
foal about the beginning of May. On the contrary those animals which lay up provisions for the
winter, such as the beaver and the marmot,
couple in the latter end of autumn, so as to have
their young about January, against which season
they have provided a very comfortable store.
These seasons for coupling, however, among some
of the domestic kinds, are generally in consequence
of the quantity of provisions with which they are
at any time supplied. Thus we may, by feeding
any of these animals, and keeping off the rigour

of the climate, make them breed whenever we please. In this manner those contrive who produce lambs all the year round.

The choice of situation in bringing forth is also very remarkable. In most of the rapacious kinds, the female takes the utmost precautions to hide the place of her retreat from the male; who otherwise, when pressed by hunger, would be apt to devour her cubs. She seldom, therefore, strays far from the den, and never approaches it while he is in view, nor visits him again till her young are capable of providing for themselves. Such animals as are of tender constitutions take the utmost care to provide a place of warmth as well as safety, for their young; the rapacious kinds bring forth in the thickest woods; those that chew the cud, with the various tribes of the vermin kind, choose some hiding place in the neighbourhood of man. Some dig holes in the ground; some choose the hollow of a tree; and all the amphibious kinds bring up their young near the water, and accustom them betimes to their proper element.

Thus Nature seems kindly careful for the protection of the meanest of her creatures: but there is one class of quadrupeds that seems entirely left to chance, that no parent stands forth to protect, nor no instructor leads, to teach the arts of subsistence. These are the quadrupeds that are brought forth from the egg, such as the lizard, the tortoise, and the crocodile. The fecundity of all other animals compared with these is sterility itself. These bring forth above two hundred at a time; but, as the offspring is more numerous, the parental care is less exerted. Thus the numerous brood of eggs are, without farther solicitude, buried in the warm sands of the shore, and the heat of the sun alone is left to bring them to perfection. To this perfection they arrive almost as soon as disengaged from the shell. Most of them, without any other guide than instinct, immediately make to the water. In their passage thither, they have numberless enemies to fear. The birds of prey that haunt the shore, the beasts that accidentally come there, and even the animals that give them birth, are known, with a strange rapacity, to thin their numbers as well as the rest.

But it is kindly ordered by Providence, that these animals, which are mostly noxious, should thus have many destroyers; were it not for this, by their extreme fecundity, they would soon over-run the earth, and cumber all our plains with deformity.

CHAP. XI.

Of the Horse.*

ANIMALS of the horse kind deserve a place next to man, in a history of nature. Their activity,

---

* As it may happen that, in a description where it is the aim rather to insert what is not usually known, than all that is known, some of the more obvious particulars may be omitted; I will take leave to subjoin in the notes the characteristic marks of each animal, as given us by Linnæus. The horse, with six

their strength, their usefulness, and their beauty,
all contribute to render them the principal objects
of our curiosity and care; a race of creatures
in whose welfare we are interested next to our
own.

Of all the quadruped animals, the horse seems
the most beautiful; the noble largeness of his
form, the glossy smoothness of his skin, the
graceful ease of his motions, and the exact symmetry of his shape, have taught us to regard him as
the first, and as the most perfectly formed ; and yet,
what is extraordinary enough, if we examine him
internally, his structure will be found the most different from that of man of all other quadrupeds

cutting teeth before; and single-hoofed;* a native of Europe
and the East (but I believe rather of Africa) ; a generous, proud,
and strong animal; fit either for the draught, the course, or the
road; he is delighted with woods; he takes care of his hinder
parts; defends himself from the flies with his tail; scratches his
fellow; defends his young; calls by neighing; sleeps after night-
fall; fights by kicking, and by biting also; rolls on the ground
when he sweats; eats the grass closer than the ox; distributes
the seed by dunging; wants a gall bladder; never vomits; the
foal is produced with the feet stretched out; he is injured by
being struck on the ear; upon the stifle; by being caught by
the nose in barnacles; by having his teeth rubbed with tallow;
by the herb padus; by the herb phellandri; by the curculis;
by the conops. His diseases are different in different countries.
A consumption of the ethmoid bones of the nose, called the
glanders, is with us the most infectious and fatal. He eats
hemlock without injury. The mare goes with foal 290 days.
The placenta is not fixed. He acquires not the canine teeth till
the age of five years.

* [In South America is found a horse whose hoofs are divided, like those of
a ruminant quadruped. In its general appearance, size, and colour, it resembles
the ass, but has the voice and ears of a horse, and has no bands crossing the
shoulders. It is very wild, swift, and strong.]

whatsoever. As the ape approaches us the nearest in internal conformation, so the horse is the most remote ;*—a striking proof that there may be oppositions of beauty, and that all grace is not to be referred to one standard.

To have an idea of this noble animal in his native simplicity, we are not to look for him in the pastures, or the stables, to which he has been consigned by man ; but in those wild and extensive plains where he has been *originally* produced, where he ranges without control, and riots in all the variety of luxurious nature. In this state of happy independence, he disdains the assistance of man, which only tends to servitude. In those boundless tracts, where he runs at liberty, he seems no way incommoded with the inconveniences to which he is subject in Europe. The verdure of the fields supplies his wants ; and the climate, that never knows a winter, suits his constitution, which naturally seems adapted to heat. His enemies of the forest are but few, for none but the greater kinds will venture to attack him ; any one of these he is singly able to overcome ; while at the same time he is content to find safety in society ; for the wild horses of those countries always herd together.

In these countries, therefore, the horses are often seen feeding in droves of five or six hundred. As they do not carry on war against any other race of animals, they are satisfied to remain entirely upon the defensive. The pastures on which they live satisfy all their appetites, and all

---

* Histoire Naturelle, Daubenton, vol. vii. p. 374.

other precautions are purely for their security, in
case of a surprise. As' they are never attacked
but at a disadvantage, whenever they sleep in the
forests, they have always one among their number
that stands as centinel, to give notice of any
approaching danger; and this office they take by
turns.* If a man approaches them while they
are feeding by day, their centinel walks up boldly
near him, as if to examine his strength, or to intimidate him from proceeding; but as the man
approaches within pistol shot, the centinel then
thinks it high time to alarm his fellows; this he
does by a loud kind of snorting, upon which
they all take the signal, and fly off with the speed
of the wind; their faithful centinel bringing up
the † rear.‡

* Dictionnaire Universel des Animaux, p. 19.
† Labat. tome vii.
[‡ In the account of the wild horses of Spanish America, by
Don Felix Azara, we are told, " That they are of Spanish origin,
and entirely of the Andalusian breed. They are now become
so numerous as to live in herds, some of which are said to consist
of ten thousand. As soon as they perceive domestic horses
in the fields, they gallop up to them, caress, and by a kind
of grave and prolonged neighing, invite them to run off. The
domestic horses are soon seduced, unite themselves to the independent herd, and depart along with them. It happens not
unfrequently, that travellers are stopped on the road, by the
effect of this desertion. To prevent this, they halt as soon as
they perceive these wanderers, watch their own horses, and
endeavour to frighten away the others. In this case the wild
horses resort to stratagem; some are detached before, and the
rest advance in a close column, which nothing can interrupt.
If they are so alarmed as to be obliged to retire, they change
their direction, but without suffering themselves to be dispersed.
Sometimes they make several turns round those they wish to

It is not easy to say from what country the horse came originally. It should seem that the colder climates do not agree with his constitution; for although he is found almost in them all, yet his form is altered there, and he is found at once diminutive and ill shaped. We have the testimony of the ancients that there were wild horses once in Europe; at present, however, they are totally brought under subjection; and even those which are found in America are of a Spanish breed, which being sent thither upon its first discovery, have since become wild, and have spread over all the south of that vast continent, almost to the Straits of Magellan. These, in general, are a small breed, of about fourteen hands high. They have thick jaws and clumsy joints; their ears and neck also are long; they are easily tamed; for the horse by nature is a gentle complying creature, and resists rather from fear than obstinacy. They are caught by a kind of noose, and then held fast by the legs, and tied to a tree, where they are left for two days, without food or drink. By that time they begin to grow manage-

seduce, in order to frighten them; but they often retire after making one turn. When the inhabitants wish to convert some of these wild horses into domestic ones, which they find not very difficult to be done, persons mounted on horseback attack a troop of them, and when they approach them, they throw ropes with great care round their legs, which prevent them from running away. When brought home, they are tied with a halter to a stake or a tree, without food or drink, for two or three days. After this they are cut, and then broke, in the same manner as the domestic horses. They soon become docile; but if not carefully watched, will again join their friends."]

able; and in some weeks they become as tame
as if they had never been in a state of wildness.
If by any accident they are once more set at
liberty, they never become wild again, but know
their masters, and come to their call. Some of
the buccaneers have often been agreeably surprised,
after a long absence, to see their faithful horses
once more present themselves, with their usual
assiduity; and come up, with fond submission, to
receive the rein.

These American horses, however, cannot properly be ranked among the wild races, since they
were originally bred from such as were tame. It
is not in the new, but the old world, that we are
to look for this animal, in a true state of nature;
in the extensive deserts of Africa, in Arabia, and
those wide-spread countries that separate Tartary
from the more southern nations. Vast droves of
these animals are seen wild among the Tartars:
they are of a small breed, extremely swift, and
very readily evade their pursuers. As they go
together, they will not admit of any strange animals among them, though even of their own kind.
Whenever they find a tame horse attempting to
associate with them, they instantly gather round
him, and soon oblige him to seek safety by flight.
There are vast numbers also of wild horses to the
north of China, but they are of a weak, timid
breed; small of stature, and useless in war.

At the Cape of Good Hope there are numbers
of horses, in a state of nature, but small, vicious,
and untameable. They are found wild, also, in
several other parts of Africa; but the wretched
inhabitants of that country, either want the art

to tame them, or seem ignorant of their uses. It is common with the negroes, who are carried over from thence to America, when they first see a horse, to testify both terror and surprise. These poor men seem not to have any knowledge of such a creature; and though the horse is probably a native of their own country, they have let all the rest of mankind enjoy the benefit of his services, without turning them to any advantage at home. In some parts of Africa, therefore, where the horse runs wild, the natives seem to consider him rather in the light of a dainty, for food, than a useful creature, capable of assisting them either in war or in labour; riding seems a refinement that the natives of Angola, or Caffraria, have not as yet been able to attain to; and whenever they catch a horse, it is only with an intent to eat him.

But of all countries in the world, where the horse runs wild, Arabia produces the most beautiful breed, the most generous, swift, and persevering. They are found, though not in great numbers, in the deserts of that country; and the natives use every stratagem to take them. Although they are active and beautiful, yet they are not so large as those that are bred up tame; they are of a brown colour; their mane and tail very short, and the hair black and tufted.* Their swiftness is incredible; the attempt to pursue them in the usual manner of the chace, with dogs, would be entirely fruitless. Such is the rapidity of their flight, that they are instantly out of view.

* Marm. Descript. de l'Afrique, lib. i. p. 51.

¶

and the dogs themselves give up the vain pursuit. The only method, therefore, of taking them is by traps, hidden in the sand, which entangling their feet, the hunter at length comes up, and either kills them or carries them home alive. If the horse be young, he is considered among the Arabians as a very great delicacy; and they feast upon him while any part is found remaining; but if, from his shape or vigour, he promises to be serviceable in his more noble capacity, they take the usual methods of taming him, by fatigue and hunger, and he soon becomes a useful domestic animal.

The usual manner of trying their swiftness is by hunting the ostrich: the horse is the only animal whose speed is comparable to that of this creature, which is found in the sandy plains, with which those countries abound. The instant the ostrich perceives itself aimed at, it makes to the mountains, while the horseman pursues with all the swiftness possible, and endeavours to cut off its retreat. The chace then continues along the plain, while the ostrich makes use of both legs and wings to assist its motion. However, a horse of the first speed is able to out-run it; so that the poor animal is then obliged to have recourse to art to elude the hunter, by frequently turning: at length, finding all escape hopeless, it hides its head wherever it can, and suffers itself tamely to be taken. If the horse, in a trial of this kind, shows great speed, and is not readily tired, his price becomes proportionably great; and there are some horses valued at a thousand ducats.

But the horses thus caught, or trained in this

manner, are at present but very few; the value of
Arabian horses, all over the world, has in a great
measure thinned the deserts of the wild breed;
and there are very few to be found in those countries, except such as are tame. The Arabians, as
we are told by historians, first began the management of horses in the time of Sheque Ismael.
Before that they wandered wild along the face of
the country, neglected and useless: but the natives
then first began to tame their fierceness, and to
improve their beauty; so that *at present* they
possess a race of the most beautiful horses in the
world, with which they drive a trade, and furnish
the stables of princes at immense prices.

There is scarcely an Arabian, how poor soever,
but his provided with his horse.* They, in general,
make use of mares in their ordinary excursions;
experience having taught them that they support
fatigue, thirst, and hunger, better than the horses
are found to do. They are also less vicious,
of a gentler nature, and are not so apt to neigh.
They are more harmless, also, among themselves, not so apt to kick or hurt each other,
but remain whole days together without the least
mischief. The Turks, on the contrary, are not
fond of mares; and the Arabians sell them such
horses as they do not choose to keep for stallions
at home. They preserve the pedigree of their
horses with great care, and for several ages back.
They know their alliances, and all their genealogy;
they distinguish the races by different names,
and divide them into three classes. The first is

* Buffon.

that of the nobles, the ancient breed, and una-
dulterated on either side : the second is that of
the horses of the ancient race, but adulterated ;
and the third is that of the common and inferior
kind. The last they sell at a low price ; but those
of the first class, and even of the second, amongst
which are found horses of equal value to the
former, are sold extremely dear. They know,
by long experience, the race of a horse by his
appearance; they can tell the name, the surname,
the colour, and the marks properly belonging to
each. When they are not possessed of stallions
of the noble race themselves, for their mares,
they borrow from their neighbours, paying a
proper price as with us, and receive a written
attestation of the whole. In this attestation is contained the name of the horse and the mare, and
their respective genealogies. When the mare has
produced her foal, new witnesses are called, and
a new attestation signed, in which are described
the marks of the foal, and the day noted when
it was brought forth. These attestations increase
the value of the horse; and they are given to the
person who buys him. The most ordinary mare
of this race sells for five hundred crowns ; there
are many that sell for a thousand ; and some of
the very finest kinds for fourteen or fifteen hundred pounds. As the Arabians have no other
house but a tent to live in, this also serves them
for a stable; so that the mare, the foal, the husband, the wife, and the children, lie all together
indiscriminately ; the little children are often seen
upon the body or the neck of the mare, while
these continue inoffensive and harmless, permit-

ting them thus to play with and caress them without
any injury. The Arabians never beat their horses :
they treat them gently ; they speak to them, and
seem to hold a discourse ; they use them as
friends ; they never attempt to increase their
speed by the whip, nor spur them but in cases
of necessity. However, when this happens, they
set off with amazing swiftness ; they leap over
obstacles with as much agility as a buck : and,
if the rider happens to fall, they are so manageable,
that they stand still in the midst of their most
rapid career.* The Arabian horses are of a
middle size, easy in their motions, and rather
inclined to leanness than fat. They are regularly
dressed every morning and evening, and with
such care, that the smallest roughness is not

[* Of the great attachment which the Arabians have for their
mares, M. St. Pierre gives an affecting instance, in his Studies
of Nature.

" The whole stock of a poor Arabian of the desert consisted
of a beautiful mare : this the French consul at Said offered to
purchase, with an intention to send her to Louis the Fourteenth. The Arab, pressed by want, hesitated a long time,
but at length consented, on condition of receiving a very considerable sum of money, which he named. The consul wrote to
France, for permission to close the bargain, and having obtained
it, sent the information immediately to the Arab. The man,
so poor as to possess only a miserable rag, a covering for his
body, arrived with his magnificent courser : he dismounted, and
looking first at the gold, and then steadfastly at his mare, heaved
a sigh. " And to whom is it," he exclaimed, " that I am going
to yield thee up ? To Europeans ! who will tie thee close,
who will beat thee, who will render thee miserable ! Return
with me, my beauty, my jewel ! and rejoice the hearts of my
children." As he pronounced the last words, he sprung upon
her back, and was out of sight almost in a moment."]

left upon their skins. They wash the legs, the
mane, and the tail, which they never cut; and
which they seldom comb, lest they should thin
the hair. They give them nothing to eat during
the day; they only give them to drink once or
twice; and at sun-set they hang a bag to their
heads, in which there is about half a bushel of
clean barley. They continue eating the whole
night, and the bag is again taken away the next
morning. They are turned out to pasture in the
beginning of March, when the grass is pretty
high, and at which time the mares are given to
the stallion. When the spring is past, they take
them again from pasture, and they get neither
grass nor hay during the rest of the year; barley
is their only food, except now and then a little
straw. The mane of the foal is always clipped
when about a year or eighteen months old, in
order to make it stronger and thicker. They begin
to break them at two years old, or two years and
a half at farthest: they never saddle or bridle
them till at that age; and then they are always
kept ready saddled at the door of the tent from
morning till sun-set, in order to be prepared
against any surprise. They at present seem sensible of the great advantage their horses are to
the country; there is a law, therefore, that pro-
hibits the exportation of the mares; and such
stallions as are brought into England are generally purchased on the Eastern shores of Africa,
and come round to us by the Cape of Good Hope.
They are in general less in stature than our own,
being not above fourteen, or fourteen hands and
a half high; their motions are much more grace-

ful and swifter than of our own horses; but
nevertheless their speed is far from being equal;
they run higher from the ground; their stroke is
not so long and close; and they are far inferior
in bottom. Still, however, they must be considered as the first and finest breed in the world;
and that from which all others have derived their
principal qualifications. It is even probable that
Arabia is the original country of horses; since
there, instead of crossing the breed, they take
every precaution to keep it entire. In other
countries they must continually change the races,
or their horses would soon degenerate; but there
the same blood has passed down through a long
succession, without any diminution either of force
or beauty.

The race of Arabian horses has spread itself
into Barbary, among the Moors, and has even
extended across that extensive continent to the
western shores of Africa. Among the Negroes of
Gambia and Senegal, the chiefs of the country
are possessed of horses, which, though little, are
very beautiful and extremely manageable. Instead of barley, they are fed, in those countries,
with maize, bruised and reduced into meal, and
mixed up with milk when they design to fatten
them. These are considered as next to the Arabian horses, both for swiftness and beauty; but
they are rather still smaller than the former. The
Italians have a peculiar sport, in which horses of
this breed run against each other. They have no
riders, but saddles so formed as to flap against the
horses' sides as they move, and thus to spur them
forward. They are set to run in a kind of railed

walk, about a mile long, out of which they never
attempt to escape ; but, when they once set forward, they never .stop, although the walk, from
one end to the other, is covered with a crowd of
spectators, which opens and gives way as the
horses approach; Our horses would scarcely, in
this manner, face a crowd, and continue their
speed, without a rider, through the midst of a
multitude ; and, indeed, it is a little surprising
how, in such a place, the horses find their own
way. However, what our English horses may
want in sagacity, they make up by their swiftness ; and it has been found upon computation
that their speed is nearly one-fourth greater, even
carrying a rider, than that of the swiftest Barb
without one.

The Arabian breed has been diffused into Egypt
as well as Barbary, and into Persia also ; where,
as we are told by Marcus Paulus, there are studs
of ten thousand white mares altogether, very
fleet, and with the hoof so hard that shoeing is
unnecessary. In these countries, they in general
give their horses the same treatment that they
give in Arabia, except that they litter them upon
a bed of their own dung, dried in the sun, and
then reduced to powder. When this, which is
spread under the horse about five inches thick,
is moistened, they dry it again, and spread it as
before. The horses of these countries a good
deal resemble each other. They are usually of a
slender make ; their legs fine, bony, and far apart ;
a thin mane ; a fine crest ; a beautiful head ; the
ear small and well pointed ; the shoulder thin ; the

side rounded, without any unsightly prominence; the croup is a little of the longest, and the tail is generally set high. The race of horses, however, is much degenerated in Numidia; the natives having been discouraged from keeping the breed up by the Turks, who seize upon all the good horses, without paying the owners the smallest gratuity for their care in bringing them up. The Tingitanians and Egyptians have now, therefore, the fame of rearing the finest horses, both for size and beauty. The smallest of these last are usually sixteen hands high; and all of them shaped, as they express it, with the elegance of an antelope.

Next to the Barb, travellers generally rank the Spanish genette. These horses, like the former, are little, but extremely swift and beautiful. The head is something of the largest; the mane thick; the ears long, but well pointed; the eyes filled with fire; the shoulder thickish, and the breast full and large. The croup round and large; the legs beautiful, and without hair; the pastern a little of the longest, as in the Barb, and the hoof rather too high. Nevertheless, they move with great ease, and carry themselves extremely well. Their most usual colour is black, or a dark bay. They seldom or never have white legs, or white snip. The Spaniards, who have a groundless aversion to these marks, never breed from such as have them. They are all branded on the buttock with the owner's name; and those of the province of Andalusia pass for the best. These are said to possess courage, obedience, grace, and spirit, in a greater degree than even the Barb ; and, for this reason, they have been preferred as war-horses to those of any other country.

The Italian horses were once more beautiful than they are at present; for they have greatly neglected the breed. Nevertheless, there are still found some beautiful horses among them, particularly among the Neapolitans, who chiefly use them for the draught. In general they have large heads and thick necks. They are also restive, and consequently unmanageable. These faults, however, are recompensed by the largeness of their size, by their spirit, and the beauty of their motion. They are excellent for show, and have a peculiar aptitude to prance.

The Danish horses are of such an excellent size, and so strong a make, that they are preferred to all others for the draught. There are some of them perfectly well shaped ; but this is but seldom seen, for in general they are found to have a thick neck, heavy shoulders, long and hollow back, and a narrow croup : however, they all move well, and are found excellent both for parade and war. They are of all colours, and often of whimsical ones, some being streaked like the tiger, or mottled like the leopard.

The German horses are originally from Arabian and Barbary stocks ; nevertheless, they appear to be small and ill-shaped; it is said also, that they are weak and washy, with tender hoofs. The Hungarian horses, on the other hand, are excellent for the draught, as well as the saddle. The hussars, who use them in war, usually slit their nostrils ; which is done, as it is said, to prevent their neighing, but, perhaps, without any real foundation.

The Dutch breed is good for the draught, and is generally used for that purpose over Europe: the best come from the province of Friezland. The Flanders horses are much inferior to the former; they have most commonly large heads, flat feet, and swollen legs; which are an essential blemish in horses of this kind.

The French horses are of various kinds; but they have few that are good. The best horses of that country come from Limosin; they have a strong resemblance to the Barb, and, like them, they are excellent for the chace; but they are slow in coming to perfection; they are to be carefully treated while young, and must not be backed till they are eight years old. Normandy furnishes the next best; which, though not so good for the chace, are yet better for war. In general, the French horses have the fault of being heavy-shouldered, which is opposite to the fault of the Barb, which is too thin in the shoulder, and is consequently apt to be shoulder-slipt.

Having mentioned the horses most usually known in Europe, we pass on to those of more distant countries, of whose horses we can only judge by report. We mentioned the wild horses of America. Such as are tame, if we may credit the latest reports,* are admirable. Great numbers of these are bred up to the chace, and are chiefly kept for this purpose, particularly at Quito. The hunters, as Ulloa informs us, are divided into two

* Ulloa's Voyage, vol. i. p. 464.

classes; one part on foot, the other on horseback: the business of the footmen is to rouze the deer; and that of the horsemen, to hunt it down. They all, at break of day, repair to the place appointed, which is generally on the summit of a hill, with every man his greyhound. The horsemen place themselves on the highest peaks; whilst those on foot range the precipices, making a hideous noise, in order to start the deer. Thus the company extend themselves three or four leagues, or more, according to their numbers. On starting any game, the horse which first perceives it sets off, and the rider, being unable to guide or stop him, pursues the chace, sometimes down such a steep slope, that a man on foot, with the greatest care, could hardly keep his legs: from thence he flies up a dangerous ascent, or along the side of a mountain, so that a person not used to this exercise would think it much safer to throw himself out of the saddle, than commit his life to the precipitate ardor of his horse. The other horses, which join in the chace, do not wait for the riders to animate them; they set forward immediately upon seeing another at full speed; and it becomes prudence in the rider to give them their way, and at the same time to let them feel the spur, to carry him over the precipices. These horses are backed and exercised to this method of hunting; and their usual pace is trotting.

There are said to be very good horses in the islands of the Archipelago. Those of Crete were in great reputation among the ancients, for their swiftness and force; however, at present they are but little used, even in the country itself, because

*

of the unevenness of the ground, which is there
very rocky and mountainous. The original horses
of Morocco are much smaller than the Arabian
breed; however, they are very swift and vigorous.
In Turkey there are to be found horses of almost
all races : Arabians, Tartars, Hungarians, and those
natural to the place. The latter are very beautiful
and elegant; they have a great deal of fire, swiftness, and management; but, they are not able to
support fatigue: they eat little; they are easily
heated; and they have skin so sensible, that they
can scarcely bear the rubbing of the stirrup. The
Persian horses are, in general, the most beautiful and
most valuable of all the East. The pastures in the
plains of Media, Persepolis, Ardebil, and Derbent,
are excellent for the purpose of rearing them;
and there were bred in those places vast numbers,
by order of the government of Persia, while that
country was under any government. Pietro della
Valle prefers the horses of Persia to those of Italy;
and informs us, that they are in general of a
middle size; and although some are found even of
the smallest stature, yet that does not impair their
beauty nor their strength: yet, in some places, they
are found of a very good size, and as large as the
English saddle-horses are generally found to be:
they have all a thin head, a fine crest, a narrow
breast, small ears well placed, the legs fine, the
hoof hard, and the croup beautiful; they are docile,
spirited, nimble, hardy, courageous, and capable
of supporting a very great fatigue; they run very
swiftly, without being easily fatigued; they are
strong and easily nourished, being only supplied
with barley and chopped straw; they are put

to grass only for six weeks in the spring; they
have always the tail at full length, and there is no
such thing as geldings among the number; they
are defended from the air, as in England, by
body-cloths; they attend them with the most
punctual exactness; and they are rid generally in
a snaffle, without spurs. Great numbers of these
are every year transported into Turkey, but chiefly
into the East Indies; however, after all, travellers
agree that they are not to be compared to the
Arabian horses, either for courage, force, or beauty;
and that the latter are eagerly sought, even in
Persia.

The horses of India are of a very indifferent
kind, being weak and washy. Those which are
used by the grandees of the country, come from
Persia and Arabia: they are fed with a small
quantity of hay during the day; and at night they
have boiled peas, mixed with sugar and butter,
instead of oats or barley: this nourishment supports
them, and gives them strength; otherwise they
would soon sink and degenerate. Those naturally
belonging to the country are very small and vicious.
Some are so very little, that Taverner reports,
that the young Mogul prince, at the age of seven
or eight, rode one of those little horses, that was
not much larger than a greyhound: and it is not
long since one of these was brought over into this
country, as a present to our Queen, that measures
no more than nine hands high, and is not much
larger than a common mastiff. It would seem
that climates *excessively hot* are unfavourable to
this animal. In this manner, the horses of the
Gold Coast, and of Guinea, are extremely little,

but very manageable. It is a common exercise
with the grandees of that country, who are excellent
horsemen, to dart out the lances before them
upon full gallop, and to catch them again before
they come to the ground. They have a sport also
on horseback, that requires great dexterity in the
rider, and a great share of activity in the horse;
they strike off a ball, with a battledore, while they
are upon a full gallop, and. pursuing it, strike it
again before it comes to the ground; and this they
continue for a mile together, striking sometimes to
the right, and sometimes to the left, with amazing
speed and agility.

The horses of China are as indifferent as those
of India: they are weak, little, ill-shaped, and
cowardly. Those of Corea are not above three
feet high; almost all the breed there are made
geldings, and are so timorous, that they can be
rendered no way serviceable in war; so that it
may be said, that the Tartar horses were properly
the conquerors of China. These, indeed, are very
serviceable in war; and although but of a middle
size, yet they are surprisingly patient, vigorous,
swift, and bold; their hoofs are extremely hard,
though rather too narrow; their heads are fine,
but rather too little; the neck is long and stiff,
the legs of the longest; and yet, with all these
faults, they are found to be an excellent breed.
The Tartars live with their horses pretty much in
the same manner as the Arabians do; they begin
to back them at the age of seven or eight months,
placing their children upon them, who manage
them even at that early age. By these means they
break them, by little and little, till at last, about

the age of six or seven years, they are capable of
enduring amazing hardships. Thus they have
been known to march two or three days without
once stopping; to continue five or six without
eating any thing except a handful of grass at every
eight hours; and, besides, to remain without
drinking for four-and-twenty hours. These horses,
which are so vigorous in their own country, lose
all their strength when they are brought into
China or the Indies; but they thrive pretty well
in Persia and Turkey. The race of little Tartars
towards the north, have also a breed of little
horses, which they set such a value upon, that it
is forbidden to sell them to strangers: these horses
have the very same qualities with those of the larger
kind; which they probably derive from a similar
treatment. There are also very fine horses in
Circassia and Mingrelia. There are some greatly
esteemed in the Ukraine, in Walachia, Poland, and
Sweden; but we have no particular accounts of
their excellencies or defects.

If we consult the ancients on the nature and
qualities of the horses of different countries, we
learn, that the Grecian horses, and particularly
those of Thessaly, had the reputation of being
excellent for war; that those of Achaia were the
largest that were known; that the most beautiful
came from Egypt, which bred great numbers; that
the horses of Ethiopia were not in esteem; that
Arabia and Africa furnished very beautiful horses,
and very fit for the course; that those of Italy, and
particularly of Apulia, were very good; that in
Sicily, Cappadocia, Syria, Armenia, Media, and
Persia, there were excellent horses, equally esteemed

for their speed, and vigour; that those of Sardinia
and Corsica, though small, were sprited and courageous; that those of Spain resembled the Parthian
horses, in being very well adapted for war; that
in Walachia and Transylvania, there were horses
with bushy tails, and manes hanging down to the
ground, which, nevertheless, were extremely swift
and active; that the Danish horses were good
leapers; those of Scandinavia, though little, were
well-shaped, and possessed of great agility; that
the Flanders breed was strong; that the Gaulish
horses were good for carrying burthens; that the
German breeds were so bad, so diminutive, and
ill-shaped, that no use could be made of them;
that the Swiss and Hungarian horses were good;
and, lastly, that those of India were very diminutive and feeble.

Such are the different accounts we have of the
various races of horses in different parts of the
world. I have hitherto omitted making mention
of one particular breed, more excellent than any
that either the ancients or moderns have produced;
and that is our own. It is not without great assiduity, and unceasing application, that the English
horses are now become superior to those of any
other part of the world, for size, strength, swiftness,
and beauty. It was not without great attention
and repeated trials of all the best horses in different parts of the world, that we have been thus
successful in improving the breed of this animal;
so that the English horses are now capable of
performing what no others ever could attain
to. By a judicious mixture of the several kinds,
by the happy difference of our soils, and by our

superior skill in management, we have brought this animal to its highest perfection. An English horse, therefore, is now known to excel the Arabian, in size and swiftness; to be more durable than the Barb, and more hardy than the Persian. An ordinary racer is known to go at the rate of a mile in two minutes: and we had one instance, in the admirable Childers, of still greater rapidity. He has been frequently known to move above eighty-two feet and a half in a second, or almost a-mile in a minute: he has also run round the course of Newmarket, which is very little less than four miles, in six minutes and forty seconds. But what is surprising, few horses have been since found, that ever could equal him; and those of his breed have been remarkably deficient.

However this be, no horses can any way equal our own, either in point of swiftness or strength; and these are the qualifications our horsemen seem chiefly to value. For this reason, when the French, or other foreigners, describe our breed, they all mention, as a fault, the awkward and ungainly motion of our horses; they allow them to be very good indeed, but they will not grant them an easy or an elegant carriage.* But these writers do not consider that this seeming want of grace is entirely the result of our manner of breaking them. We consult only speed and dispatch in this animal's motions: the French, and other nations, are more anxious for parade and spirit. For this reason we always throw our horses forward, while they put them upon their haunches; we give them an easy

---

* See Buffon's account of our horses.

swift gait of going, that covers a great deal of ground: they, on the contrary, throw them back, giving them a more showy appearance indeed, but one infinitely less useful. The fault of our manner of breaking is, that the horse is sometimes apt to fall forward; the French managed horse never falls before, but more usually on one side; and for this reason, the rider wears stiff boots, to guard his legs against such accidents. However, it would be a very easy matter to give our horses all that grace which foreigners are so fond of; but it would certainly take from their swiftness and durability.

But in what degree of contempt soever foreigners might formerly have held our horses, they have for some time perceived their error, and our English hunters are considered as the noblest and the most useful horses in the world. Our geldings are, therefore, sent over to the continent in great numbers, and sell at very great prices; as for our mares and stallions, there is a law prohibiting their exportation; and one similar to this is said to have obtained even as early as the times of Athelstan, who prohibited their exportation, except where designed as presents:

Roger de Belegme, created Earl of Shrewsbury by William the Conqueror,* is the first who is recorded to have made attempts towards the mending our native breed. He introduced Spanish stallions into his estate at Powisland in Wales, from which that part of the country was for many ages

* British Zoology, vol. i. p. 4. To this work I am indebted for several particulars with regard to the native animals of this island.

after famous for a swift and generous race of horses: however, at that time, strength and swiftness were more regarded than beauty; the horses' shapes, in time of action, being entirely hid by a coat of armour, which the knights then usually put upon them, either by way of ornament or defence.

The number of our horses, in London alone, in the time of king Stephen, is said to have amounted to twenty thousand. However, long after, in the times of queen Elizabeth, the whole kingdom could not supply two thousand horses to form our cavalry. At present, the former numbers seem revived; so that, in the late war, we furnished out above thirteen thousand horsemen: and could, if hard pushed, supply above four times that number. How far this great increase of horses among us may be beneficial, or otherwise, is not the proper business of the present page to discuss; but certain it is, that where horses increase in too great a degree, men must diminish proportionably; as that food which goes to supply the one, might very easily be converted into nourishment to serve the other. But, perhaps, it may be speculating too remotely, to argue for the diminution of their numbers upon this principle, since every manufacture we export into other countries, takes up room, and may have occupied that place, which in a state of greater simplicity, might have given birth and subsistence to mankind, and have added to population.

Be this as it will, as we have been at such expense and trouble to procure an excellent breed of horses, it is not now to be expected that we should decline the advantages arising from it, just when in our possession. It may be, therefore, the most prudent measure in our legislature, to encourage the breed, as an useful branch of commerce, and a natural defence to the country. But how far this end is answered by the breeding up of racers, is what most persons, versed in this subject, are very apt to question. They assert, that the running-horse, as the breed has been for a long time refined, is unfit for any other service than that of the course, being too slight either for the road, the chase, or the combat; and his joints so delicately united, as to render him subject to the smallest accidents. They, therefore, conclude, that less encouragement given to racing, would be a means of turning us from breeding rather for swiftness than strength; and that we should thus be again famous for our strong hunters, which they say are wearing out from among us.

How far this may be fact, I will not take upon me to determine, being but little versed in a subject that does not properly come within the compass of natural history. Instead, therefore, of farther expatiating on this well-known animal's qualifications, upon which many volumes might easily be written, I will content myself with just mentioning the description of Camerarius, in which he professes to unite all the perfections which a horse ought to be possessed of. " It must," says he, " have three parts like those of a woman; the breast must be broad, the hips round, and the mane long: it must, in three things, resemble a lion; its countenance must be fierce, its courage

must be great, and its fury irresistible : it must
have three things belonging to the sheep; the
nose, gentleness, and patience : it must have three
of a deer ; head, leg, and skin : it must have three
of a wolf; throat, neck, and hearing : it must
have three of a fox ; ear, tail, and trot : three of
a serpent; memory, sight, and flexibility : and,
lastly, three of a hare ; running, walking, and perseverance."*

CHAP. XII.

Of the Ass.†

ALTHOUGH this animal is very easily distinguished from the horse at first sight, yet, upon a

[* Horses are gregarious, and, in their wild state, inhabit
the most retired deserts and plains. A curious natural fact is
mentioned by Dr. Turton, in his System of Nature, that they
have the singular property of breathing through the nostril
only, and not through the mouth; for in the severest exercise,
the mouth is never seen open, unless the lower jaw be brought
down violently by the force of the bit. This may account for
the great dilatation of the nostrils after hard running.

In those vast desert regions, in the most southern parts of Siberia, is found a horse differing in several particulars from the
common horse already described. It is said to live in small
herds of about twenty each, having the manners of the common wild horse, but far exceeding it in swiftness. Its head is
large, and forehead flat; and its teeth are only thirty-eight in
number. But the most singular mark of difference is, that the
tail is slender, like that of the cow, and destitute of hair for
half its length; the lower part only being covered with a long
ash-coloured hair.]

† Many parts of this account are extracted from Daubenton

closer inspection, the similitude between them is
very striking. They have both a similar outline
in the external parts; the same conformation
within. One would be led, from the great resemblance there is between them, to suppose them of
the same species; and that the ass was only a horse
degenerated; however, they are perfectly distinct,
and there is an inseparable line drawn between
them, for the mule they produce is barren. This
seems to be the barrier between every species of
animals; this keeps them asunder, and preserves
the unities of their form. If the mule, or the
monster bred between two animals whose form
nearly approaches, is no longer fertile, we may
then conclude, that these animals, however resembling, are of different kinds. Nature has provi-
dently stopped the fruitfulness of these ill-formed
productions, in order to preserve the form of every
animal uncontaminated: were it not for this, the
races would quickly be mixed with each other;
no one kind would preserve its original perfection; every creature would quickly degenerate;
and the world would be stocked with imperfection
and deformity.

The horse and the ass, therefore, though so
nearly approaching in form, are of two distinct
kinds, different in their natures; and were there
but one of each kind, both races would then be
extinguished. Their shapes and their habits may,
indeed, be very nearly alike; but there is something in every animal, besides its conformation or

and Buffon; which I mention here, to avoid troubling the reader
with a multiplicity of quotations.

way of life, that determines its specific nature.
Thus there is much greater resemblance between
the horse and the ass, than between the sheep
and the goat; and yet the latter produce an animal that is by no means barren, but which quickly
re-produces an offspring resembling the sheep;
while the mule of the former is marked with certain sterility. The goat and the sheep may be
therefore said to be of one kind, although so much
unlike in figure; while the horse and the ass are
perfectly distinct, though so closely resembling. It
has, indeed, been said by Aristotle, that their male
is sometimes prolific; this, however, has not been
confirmed by any other testimony, although there
has elapsed a period of near two thousand years to
collect the evidence.

But what tends to put the subject out of dispute is, that the two animals are found in a state
of nature entirely different. The onager, or wild
ass, is seen in still greater abundance than the
wild horse; and the peculiarities of its kind are
more distinctly marked than in those of the tame
one. Had it been a horse degenerated, the likeness would be stronger between them, the higher
we went to the original stock from whence both
have been supposed to be sprung. The wild animals of both kinds would, in such a case, resemble
each other, much more than those of the tame
kind, upon whom art has, for a succession of
ages, been exercising all its force, and producing
strange habits and new alterations. The contrary, however, obtains, and the wild ass is even
more asinine, if I may so express it, than that
bred in a state of domestic servitude; and has

even a natural aversion to the horse, as the reader
will shortly learn.

The wild ass has, by some writers, been confounded with the zebra, but very improperly, for
they are of a very different species. The wild ass
is not streaked like the zebra, nor is his shape so
beautiful: his figure is pretty much the same as
that of the common ass, except that he is of a
brighter colour, and has a white list running from
his head to his tail. This animal is found wild in
many islands of the Archipelago, particularly in
that of Cerigo. There are many wild asses in the
deserts of Lybia and Numidia, that run with such
amazing swiftness, scarcely even the coursers of the
country can overtake them. When they see a
man, they set up a horrid braying, and stop short
all together, till he approaches near them; they
then, as if by common consent, fly off with great
speed; and it is upon such occasions that they
generally fall into the traps which are previously
prepared to catch them. The natives take them
chiefly upon account of their flesh, which they
esteem as delicious eating; and for their skins, of
which that kind of leather is made which is called
shagreen.

Olearius relates, that the monarch of Persia invited him on a certain day to be present at an entertainment of a very peculiar nature, which was
exhibited in a small building near the palace, resembling a theatre. After a collation of fruits
and sweetmeats, more than thirty of these wild
asses were driven into the area, among which the
monarch discharged several shot, and some arrows, and in which he was imitated by some of

the rest of his attendants. The asses, finding themselves wounded, and no way of escaping, instantly began to attack each other, biting with great fierceness, and braying terribly. In this manner they continued their mutual animosity, while the arrows were poured in from above, until they were all killed; upon which they were ordered to be taken, and sent to the king's kitchen at Ispahan. The Persians esteem the flesh of this animal so highly, that its delicacy is even become a proverb among them. What may be the taste of the wild ass's flesh, we are unable to say; but certain it is, that the flesh of the tame ass is the worst that can be obtained, being dryer, more tough, and more disagreeable than horse-flesh. Galen even says that it is very unwholesome. Yet we should not judge hastily upon the different tastes of different people, in the preference they give to certain meats. The climate produces very great changes in the tenderness and the savour of several viands: that beef, for instance, which is so juicy and good in England, is extremely tough and dry when killed under the line; on the contrary, that pork which is with us so unpalatable in summer, in the warmer latitudes, where it is always hotter than here, is the finest eating they have, and much preferable to any hog's flesh in Europe.

The ass, like the horse, was originally imported into America by the Spaniards, and afterwards by other nations. That country seems to have been peculiarly favourable to this race of animals; and, where they have run wild, they have multiplied in such numbers, that in some places they are be-

come a nuisance.* In the kingdom of Quito,
the owners of the grounds where they are bred,
suffer all persons to take away as many as they
can, on paying a small acknowledgment, in proportion to the number of days their sport lasts.
They catch them in the following manner: A
number of persons go on horseback, and are attended by Indians on foot: when arrived at the
proper places, they form a circle in order to drive
them into some valley; where at full speed they
throw the noose, and endeavour to halter them.
Those creatures, finding themselves inclosed, make
very furious efforts to escape; and, if only one
forces his way through, they all follow with an irresistible impetuosity. However, when noosed, the
hunters throw them down and secure them with
fetters, and thus leave them till the chace is over.
Then, in order to bring them away with greater
facility, they pair them with tame beasts of the
same kind; but this is not easily performed,—
for they are so remarkably fierce that they often
hurt the persons who undertake to manage them.
They have all the swiftness of horses, and neither
declivities nor precipices can retard their career.
When attacked, they defend themselves with their
heels and mouth with such activity, that without
slackening their pace, they often maim their pursuers. But the most remarkable property in these
creatures is, that after carrying their first load,
their celerity leaves them, their dangerous ferocity
is lost, and they soon contract the stupid look and
dullness peculiar to the asinine species. It is also

* Ulloa, vol. i. p. 316.

observable, that these creatures will not permit a horse to live among them. They always feed together; and, if a horse happens to stray into the place where they graze, they all fall upon him; and without giving him the liberty of flying, they bite and kick him till they leave him for dead upon the spot.

Such is this animal in its natural state, swift, fierce, and formidable; but, in his state of tameness, the ass presents a very different picture; the moment his native liberty is repressed, he seems entirely to give up all claims to freedom; and he assumes a patience and submission even humbler than his situation. He is, in a state of tameness, the most gentle and quiet of all animals. He suffers with constancy, and, perhaps, with courage, all the ill treatment that cruelty and caprice are pleased to inflict. He is temperate with regard to the quantity and the quality of his provision. He is contented with the most neglected weeds; and makes his humble repast upon what the horse and other animals leave behind. If he gives the preference to any vegetable, it is to the plantain; for which he is often seen to neglect every other herb in the pasture: but he is chiefly delicate with respect to his water; he drinks only at the clearest brooks, and chiefly those to which he has been accustomed. He drinks as soberly as he eats; and never, like the horse, dips his nose into the stream. As he is seldom saddled, he frequently rolls himself upon the grass; and lies down, for this purpose, as often as he has an opportunity, without minding what becomes of his burthen.

He never rolls, like the horse, in the mud; he even fears to wet his feet; and turns out of his way to avoid the dirty parts of a road.

When very young, the ass is sprightly, and even tolerably handsome; but he soon loses these qualifications, either by age or bad treatment, and he becomes slow, stupid, and headstrong. He seems to shew no ardour, except for the female, having been often known to die after the covering. The she-ass is not less fond of her young than the male is of her; and we are assured that she will cross fire and water to protect, or rejoin it. This animal is sometimes not less attached to his owner; by whom he is too often abused. He scents him at a distance, and distinguishes him from others in a crowd; he knows the ways he has passed, and the places where he inhabits.

When over-loaded, the ass shews the injustice of his master, by hanging down his head and low-ering his ears; when he is too hard pressed, he opens his mouth and draws back his lips in a very disagreeable manner. If his eyes are covered he will not stir a step; and, if he is laid down in such a manner that one eye is covered with the grass while the other is hidden with a stone, or whatever is next at hand, he will continue fixed in the same situation, and will not so much as attempt to rise to free himself from those slight impediments. He walks, trots, and gallops like a horse; but although he sets out very freely at first, yet he is soon tired; and then no beating will make him mend his pace. It is in vain that his unmerciful rider exerts his whip or his cudgel; the poor little animal bears it

all with patience, and without a groan; and, conscious of his own imbecility, does not offer even to
move.

Notwithstanding the stupid heaviness of his air,
he may be educated with as much ease as any other
animal; and several have been brought up to perform, and exhibited as a show. In general, however, the poor animal is entirely neglected. Man
despises this humble, useful creature, whose efforts
are exerted to please him, and whose services are
too cheaply purchased. The horse is the only
favourite, and upon him alone all expense and
labour are bestowed. He is fed, attended, and
stabled, while the ass is abandoned to the cruelty
of the lowest rustics, or even to the sport of children, and, instead of gaining, by the lessons he
receives, is always a loser. He is conducted along
by blows; he is insulted by unnecessary stripes; he
is overloaded by the lazy; and, being generally the
property of the poor, he shares with them in their
wants and their distresses. Thus this faithful animal, which, were there no horses, would be the first
of the quadruped kind in our esteem, is now considered as nothing; his properties and qualifications being found in a higher degree elsewhere, he
is entirely disregarded; and, from being the second,
he is degraded into one of the most useless of the
domestic quadrupeds.

For this reason, very little care has been taken to
improve the breed; it is suffered to degenerate; and
it is probable, that of all other animals, this alone is
rendered feebler and more diminutive, by being in
a state of domestic servitude. The horse, the cow,
and the sheep, are rendered larger by the assiduity

of man; the ass is suffered to dwindle every generation, and particularly in England, where it is
probable that, but for the medicinal qualities of its
milk, the whole species would have ere now been
extinguished. Nevertheless, we have good reasons
to believe that, were the same care bestowed on
the ass that is spent upon the horse, were the same
industry used in crossing the breed and improving
it, we should see the ass become, from his present
mean state, a very portly and serviceable animal;
we should find him rival the horse in some of his
perfections, and exceed him in others. The ass,
bulk for bulk, is stronger than the horse; is more
sure-footed; and, though more slow in his
motions, he is much less apt to start out of the
way.

The Spaniards, of all people in Europe, seem
alone to be acquainted with the value of the ass.
They take all proper precautions to improve the
breed; and I have seen a jack-ass, from that
country, above fifteen hands high. This animal,
however, seems originally a native of Arabia. A
warm climate is known to produce the largest and
the best; their size and spirit decline in proportion
as they advance into colder regions.

Though now so common in all parts of England,
the ass was entirely lost amongst us during the
reign of queen Elizabeth. Hollingshed informs
us that our land did yield no asses.* However,
there are accounts of their being common in England before that time. In Sweden they are at present a sort of rarity; nor does it appear by the

* British Zoology, vol. i. p. 11.

last history of Norway that they have yet reached that country. It is in the hotter climates alone that we are to look for the original of this service-able creature. In Guinea, they are larger and more beautiful than even the horses of the same country. In Persia, they have two kinds; one of which is used for burthens, being slow and heavy; the other, which is kept for the saddle, being smooth, stately, and nimble. They are managed as horses, only that the rider sits nearer the crup-per, and they are taught to amble like them. They generally cleave their nostrils to give them more room for breathing, and many of these are sold for forty or fifty pounds.

The ass is a much more hardy animal than the horse, and liable to fewer diseases. Of all animals covered with hair, he is the least subject to vermin, for he has no lice, probably owing to the dryness and the hardness of his skin. Like the horse, he is three or four years in coming to per-fection; he lives till twenty or twenty-five; sleeps much less than the horse; and never lies down for that purpose, unless very much tired. The she-ass goes above eleven months with young, and never brings forth more than one at a time. The mule may be engendered either between a horse and a she-ass, or between a jack-ass and a mare. The latter breed is every way preferable, being larger, stronger, and better shaped. It is not yet well known whether the animal called the Gimerro be one of these kinds; or, as is asserted, bred between the ass and the bull. While naturalists affirm the impossibility of this mixture, the natives of the Alpine countries, where this animal is bred, as

strongly insist upon its reality. The common
mule is very healthy, and will live above thirty
years, being found very serviceable in carrying
burthens, particularly in mountainous and stony
places, where horses are not so sure-footed. The
size and strength of our asses is at present greatly
improved by the importation of Spanish jack-asses;
and it is probable we may come in time to equal
the Spaniards in breeding them, where it is not
uncommon to give fifty or sixty guineas for a
mule; and, indeed, in some mountainous countries,
the inhabitants cannot well do without them.
Their manner of going down the precipices of the
Alps, or the Andes, is very extraordinary; and with
it we will conclude their history. In these passages, on one side, are steep eminencies, and, on
the other, frightful abysses; and, as they generally
follow the direction of the mountain, the road,
instead of lying in a level, forms at every little
distance steep declivities, of several hundred yards
downward. These can only be descended by
mules; and the animal itself seems sensible of the
danger, and the caution that is to be used in such
descents. When they come to the edge of one of
these descents, they stop without being checked
by the rider; and, if he inadvertently attempts to
spur them on, they continue immoveable. They
seem all this time ruminating on the danger that
lies before them, and preparing themselves for the
encounter. They not only attentively view the
road, but tremble and snort at the danger. Having
prepared for the descent, they place their fore-feet
in a posture, as if they were stopping themselves;
they then also put their hinder feet together, but

The Zebra.

a little forward, as if they were going to lie down. In this attitude, having taken as it were a survey of the road, they slide down with the swiftness of a meteor. In the mean time, all the rider has to do is to keep himself fast on the saddle without checking the rein, for the least motion is sufficient to disorder the equilibrium of the mule; in which case they both unavoidably perish. But their address, in this rapid descent, is truly wonderful; for, in their swiftest motion, when they seem to have lost all government of themselves, they follow exactly the different windings of the road, as if they had previously settled in their minds the route they were to follow, and taken every precaution for their safety. In this journey the natives, who are placed along the sides of the mountains, and hold by the roots of the trees, animate the beast with shouts, and encourage him to perseverance. Some mules, after being long used to these journeys, acquire a kind of reputation for their safety and skill; and their value rises in proportion to their fame.*

CHAP. XIII.

Of the Zebra.

THERE are but three animals of the horse kind. The horse, which is the most stately and courageous; the ass, which is the most patient and humble; and the zebra, which is the most beautiful, but

* Ulloa, vol. i.

at the same time the wildest animal in nature.
Nothing can exceed the delicate regularity of this
creature's colour, or the lustrous smoothness of its
skin; but, on the other hand, nothing can be more
timid or more untameable.

It is chiefly a native of the southern parts of
Africa; and there are whole herds of them often
seen feeding in those extensive plains that lie
towards the Cape of Good Hope. However, their
watchfulness is such, that they will suffer nothing
to come near them; and their swiftness so great,
that they readily leave every pursuer far behind.
The zebra, in shape, rather resembles the mule,
than the horse, or the ass. It is rather less than
the former, and yet larger than the latter. Its ears
are not so long as those of the ass, and yet not so
small as in the horse kind. Like the ass, its head
is large, its back straight, its legs finely placed, and
its tail tufted at the end; like the horse, its skin is
smooth and close, and its hind quarters round and
fleshy. But its greatest beauty lies in the amazing
regularity and elegance of its colours. In the
male, they are white and brown; in the female,
white and black. These colours are disposed in
alternate stripes over the whole body, and with
such exactness and symmetry, that one would
think Nature had employed the rule and compass
to paint them. These stripes, which, like so many
ribbands, are laid all over its body, are narrow,
parallel, and exactly separated from each other.
It is not here as in other party-coloured animals,
where the tints are blended into each other; every
stripe here is perfectly distinct, and preserves its
colour round the body, or the limb, without any

diminution. In this manner are the head, the body, the thighs, the legs, and even the tail and the ears beautifully streaked, so that at a little distance one would be apt to suppose that the animal was dressed out by art, and not thus admirably adorned by nature.

In the male zebra, the head is striped with fine bands of black and white, which in a manner centre in the forehead. The ears are variegated with a white and dusky brown. The neck has broad stripes of the same, dark brown running round it, leaving narrow white stripes between. The body is striped also across the back with broad bands leaving narrower spaces of white between them, and ending in points at the sides of the belly, which is white, except a black line pectinated on each side, reaching from between the fore-legs along the middle of the belly, two-thirds of its length. There is a line of separation between the trunk of the body and the hinder quarters, on each side; behind which, on the rump, is a plat of narrow stripes, joined together, by a stripe down the middle, to the end of the tail. The colours are different in the female; and in none the stripes seem entirely to agree in form, but in all they are equally distinct; the hair equally smooth and fine; the white shining and unmixed; and the black, or brown, thick and lustrous.

Such is the beauty of this creature, that it seems by nature fitted to satisfy the pride and the pleasure of man; and formed to be taken into his service. Hitherto, however, it appears to have disdained servitude, and neither force nor kindness have been able to wean it from its native independence

and ferocity. But this wildness might, perhaps,
in time, be surmounted; and, it is probable,
the horse and the ass, when *first* taken from
the forest, were equally obstinate, fierce, and
unmanageable. M. Buffon informs us, that the
zebra from which he took his description, could
never be entirely mastered, notwithstanding all the
efforts which were tried to tame it. They continued, indeed, to mount it, but then with such
precautions as evidently showed its fierceness, for
two men were obliged to hold the reins while the
third ventured upon its back; and even then it
attempted to kick whenever it perceived any person
approaching. That which is now in the Queen's
menagerie, at Buckingham-Gate, is even more
vicious than the former; and the keeper who
shows it, takes care to inform the spectators of its
ungovernable nature. Upon my attempting to
approach it, it seemed quite terrified, and was preparing to kick, appearing as wild as if just caught,
although taken extremely young, and used with
the utmost indulgence. Yet still it is most probable that this animal, by time and assiduity, could
be brought under subjection. As it resembles the
horse in form, without all doubt it has a similitude
of nature, and only requires the efforts of an
industrious and skilful nation to be added to the
number of our domestics. It is not *now* known
what were the pains and the dangers which were
first undergone to reclaim the breed of horses from
savage ferocity; these, no doubt, made an equal
opposition; but, by being opposed, by an industrious and enterprising race of mankind, their
spirit was at last subdued, and their freedom

restrained. It is otherwise with regard to the
zebra; it is the native of countries where the
human inhabitants are but little raised above the
quadruped. The natives of Angola, or Cafraria,
have no other idea of advantage from horses but
as they are good for food; neither the fine stature
of the Arabian courser, nor the delicate colourings
of the zebra, have any allurements to a race of
people who only consider the quantity of flesh, and
not its conformation. The delicacy of the zebra's
shape, or the painted elegance of its form, are no
more regarded by such, than by the lion that
makes it his prey. For this reason, therefore, the
zebra may hitherto have continued wild, because
it is the native of a country where there have been
no successive efforts made to reclaim it. All
pursuits that have been hitherto instituted against it,
were rather against its life than its liberty; the
animal has thus been long taught to consider man
as its most mortal enemy; and it is not to be
wondered that it refuses to yield obedience, where it
has so seldom experienced mercy. There is a kind
of knowledge in all animals, that I have often considered with amazement; which is, that they seem
perfectly to know their enemies, and to avoid
them. Instinct, indeed, may teach the deer to fly
from the lion; or the mouse to avoid the cat: but
what is the principle that teaches the dog to attack
the dog-butcher wherever he sees him? In China,
where the killing and dressing dogs is a trade,
whenever one of these people moves out, all the
dogs of the village, or the street, are sure to be
after him. This I should hardly have believed,
but that I have seen more than one instance of it

among ourselves. I have seen a poor fellow who
made a practice of stealing and killing dogs for
their skins, pursued in full cry for three or four
streets together, by all the bolder breed of dogs,
while the weaker flew from his presence with
affright. How these animals could thus find out
their enemy, and pursue him, appears I own
unaccountable, but, such is the fact; and it not
only obtains in dogs, but in several other animals,
though perhaps to a less degree. This very probably may have been, in some measure, a cause
that has hitherto kept the zebra in its state of
natural wildness; and in which it may continue,
till kinder treatment shall have reconciled it to its
pursuers.

It is very likely, therefore, as a more civilized
people are now placed at the Cape of Good Hope,
which is the chief place where this animal is found,
that we may have them tamed and rendered serviceable. Nor is its extraordinary beauty the only
motive we have for wishing this animal among the
number of our dependants: its swiftness is said to
surpass that of all others; so that the speed of a
zebra is become a proverb among the Spaniards
and Portuguese. It stands better upon its legs
also than a horse; and is consequently stronger
in proportion. Thus, if by proper care we improved the breed, as we have in other instances,
we should probably in time to come have a race
as large as the horse, as fleet, as strong, and much
more beautiful.

The zebra, as was said, is chiefly a native of
the Cape of Good Hope. It is also found in the
kingdom of Angola; and, as we are assured by

Lopez, in several provinces also of Barbary. In those boundless forests it has nothing to restrain its liberty; it is too shy to be caught in traps, and therefore seldom taken alive. It would seem, therefore, that none of them have ever been brought into Europe, that were caught sufficiently young, so as to be untinctured by their original state of wildness. The Portuguese, indeed, pretend that they have been able to tame them, and that they have sent four from Africa to Lisbon, which were so far brought under as to draw the king's coach;* they add, that the person who sent them over, had the office of notary conferred upon him for his reward, which was to remain to him and his posterity for ever: but I do not find this confirmed by any person who says he saw them. Of those which were sent to Brazil, not one could be tamed; they would permit one man only to approach them; they were tied up very short; and one of them, which had by some means got loose, actually killed his groom, having bitten him to death.† Notwithstanding this, I believe, were the zebra taken up very young, and properly treated, it might be rendered as tame as any other animal; and Merolla, who saw many of them, asserts, that when tamed, which he speaks of as being common enough, they are not less estimable for their swiftness than their beauty.

This animal, which is neither to be found in Europe, Asia, or America, is nevertheless very easily fed. That which came over into England some years ago, would eat almost any thing, such

* Dapper.   † Pyrard. tom. ii. p. 376.

as bread, meat, and tobacco; that which is now
among us, subsists entirely upon hay. As it so
nearly resembles the horse and the ass in structure,
so it probably brings forth annually as they do.
The noise they make is neither like that of a horse
or an ass, but more resembling the confused
barking of a mastiff dog. In the two which I saw,
there was a circumstance that seems to have
escaped naturalists; which is, that the skin hangs
loose below the jaw upon the neck, in a kind of
dewlap, which takes away much from the general
beauty. But whether this be a natural or accidental blemish, I will not take upon me to
determine.

These animals are often sent as presents to the
princes of the east. We are told, that one of the
governors of Batavia gave a zebra, which had
been sent to him from Africa, to the emperor of
Japan, for which he received as an equivalent,
for the Company, a present to the value of sixty
thousand crowns.* Teller also relates that the
Great Mogul gave two thousand ducats for one
of them; and it is frequent with the African
ambassadors to the court of Constantinople, to bring
some of these animals with them, as presents for
the Grand Seignor.†

* Navendorf.

[† In addition to these species may be mentioned the Quagga.
This animal, which used to be confounded with the zebra, is
now acknowledged to be quite distinct. It inhabits the same
parts of Africa as the zebra, but is always found in separate
herds, never associating with it. It is about the same size as
the zebra, but less elegant in its shape and marks; and is of a
much more docile nature; the Dutch colonists at the Cape,
having been said to tame them, and use them for the draught.

CHAP. XIV.

Of Ruminating Animals.

OF all animals, those that chew the cud are the most harmless, and the most easily tamed. As they live entirely upon vegetables, it is neither their interest nor their pleasure to make war upon the rest of the brute creation ; content with the pastures where they are placed, they seldom desire to change, while they are furnished with a proper supply ; and, fearing nothing from each other, they generally go in herds for their mutual security. All the fiercest of the carnivorous kinds seek their food in gloomy solitude ; these, on the contrary, range together ; the very meanest of them are found to unite in each other's defence ; and the hare itself is a gregarious animal, in those countries where it has no other enemies but the beasts of the forest to guard against.

As the food of ruminant animals is entirely of the vegetable kind, and as this is very easily procured, so these animals seem naturally more indolent and less artful than those of the carnivorous kinds ; and as their appetites are more simple, their instincts seem to be less capable of variation.

and saddle. Its general colour is of a ferruginous tinge, with brown stripes. These stripes, however, are much fewer in number than those of the zebra, and much less elegantly disposed, there being seldom any on the haunches, shoulders, and legs ; and, on the hinder parts, they gradually diminish into spots.]

The fox or the wolf are for ever prowling; their long habits of want give them a degree of sharpness and cunning; their life is a continued scene of stratagem and escape: but the patient ox, or the deer, enjoy the repast that nature has abundantly provided; certain of subsistence, and content with security.

As Nature has furnished these animals with an appetite for such coarse and simple nutriment, so she has enlarged the capacity of the intestines, to take in a greater supply. In the carnivorous kinds, as their food is nourishing and juicy, their stomachs are but small, and their intestines short; but in those whose pasture is coarse, and where much must be accumulated before any quantity of nourishment can be obtained, their stomachs are large and numerous, and their intestines long and muscular. The bowels of a ruminating animal may be considered as an elaboratory, with vessels in it, fitted for various transmutations. It requires a long and tedious process before grass can be transmuted into flesh; and for this purpose, Nature, in general, has furnished such animals as feed upon grass with four stomachs, through which the food successively passes, and undergoes the proper separations.*

[* All quadrupeds that chew the cud have suet instead of the soft fat of other animals; and they have the awkward habit of rising, when in a recumbent posture, upon their hind legs first. A cow, when she rises from the ground, places herself on the fore-knees, and then lifts up the whole binder parts. A horse springs up first on his fore legs, and then rises up his hinder parts. This may be owing to the different conformation of the stomach.]

Of the four stomachs with which ruminant animals are furnished, the first is called the paunch,
which receives the food after it has been slightly
chewed; the second is called the honeycomb, and
is properly nothing more than a continuation of
the former; these two, which are very capacious,
the animal fills as fast as it can, and then lies
down to ruminate, which may be properly considered as a kind of vomiting without effort or
pain. The two stomachs above mentioned being
filled with as much as they can contain, and the
grass, which was slightly chewed, beginning to
swell with the heat of the situation, it dilates the
stomachs, and these again contract upon their
contents. The aliment, thus squeezed, has but
two passages to escape at; one into the third stomach, which is very narrow; and the other back,
by the gullet, into the mouth, which is wider.
The greatest quantity, therefore, is driven back,
through the largest aperture into the mouth, to
be chewed a second time; while a small part, and
that only the most liquid, is driven into the third
stomach, through the orifice which is so small.
The food which is driven to the mouth, and chewed
a second time, is thus rendered more soft and
moist, and becomes at last liquid enough to pass into
the conduit that goes to the third stomach, where
it undergoes a still farther comminution. In this
stomach, which is called the manifold, from the
number of its leaves, all which tend to promote
digestion; the grass has the appearance of boiled
spinach, but not yet sufficiently reduced, so as
to make a part of the animal's nourishment: it
requires the operation of the fourth stomach for

this purpose, where it undergoes a complete maceration, and is separated to be turned into chyle.

But Nature has not been less careful in another respect, in fitting the intestines of these animals for their food. In the carnivorous kinds they are thin and lean; but in ruminating animals they are strong, fleshy, and well covered with fat. Every precaution seems taken that can help their digestion: their stomach is strong and muscular, the more readily to act upon its contents; their intestines are lined with fat, the better to preserve their warmth; and they are extended to a much greater length, so as to extract every part of that nourishment which their vegetable food so scantily supplies.

In this manner are all quadrupeds of the cow, the sheep, or the deer kind, seen to ruminate; being thus furnished with four stomachs, for the macerating of their food. These, therefore, may most properly be called the ruminant kinds; although there are many others that have this quality in a less observable degree. The rhinoceros, the camel, the horse, the rabbit, the marmot, and the squirrel, all chew the cud by intervals, although they are not furnished with stomachs like the former. But not these alone, there are numberless other animals that appear to ruminate; not only birds, but fishes and insects. Among birds are the pelican, the stork, the heron, the pigeon, and the turtle; these have a power of disgorging their food to feed their young. Among fishes are lobsters, crabs, and that fish called the dorado. The salmon also is said to be of this number: and, if we may believe Ovid, the scarus likewise; of which he says :*

> Of all the fish that graze beneath the flood,
> He only ruminates his former food.

Of insects, the ruminating tribe is still larger : the mole, the cricket, the wasp, the drone, the bee, the grasshopper, and the beetle. All these animals either actually chew the cud, or seem at least to ruminate. They have the stomach composed of muscular fibres, by means whereof the food is ground up and down, in the same manner as in those which are particularly distinguished by the appellation of ruminants.

But not these alone; men themselves have been often known to ruminate, and some even with pleasure. The accounts of these calamities, for such I must consider them, incident to our fellow-creatures, are not very pleasant to read; yet I must transcribe a short one, as given us by Slare, in the Philosophical Transactions, as it may in some measure show the satisfaction which the lower tribes of animals enjoy while they ruminate. The man in question was a citizen of Bristol, of about twenty years of age, and, what seemed more extraordinary still, of a ruminating family, for his father was frequently subject to the same infirmity, or amusement, as he himself perhaps would call it. This young man usually began to chew his meat over again within about a quarter of an hour after eating.

---

* At contra herbosa pisces laxantur arena,
  Ut scarus epastas solus qui ruminat escas.

His ruminating after a full meal generally lasted about an hour and a half; nor could he sleep until this task was performed. The victuals, upon the return, tasted even more pleasantly than at first; and returned as if they had been beaten up in a mortar. If he ate a variety of things, that which he ate first came up again first; and if this return was interrupted for any time, it produced sickness and disorder, and he was never well till it returned. Instances of this kind, however, are rare and accidental; and it is happy for mankind that they are so. Of all other animals, we spend the least time in eating; this is one of the great distinctions between us and the brute creation; and eating is a pleasure of so low a kind, that none but such as are nearly allied to the quadruped, desire its prolongation.

CHAP. XV.

Of Quadrupeds of the Cow Kind.*

OF all ruminant animals, those of the cow kind deserve the first rank, both for their size, their beauty, and their services. The horse is more properly an animal belonging to the rich; the sheep chiefly thrives in a flock, and requires attendance; but the cow is more especially the poor man's

[* The animals of this kind have the horns hollow, smooth, turned outwards and forwards, in a semicircular form: in the lower jaw there are eight front teeth, but none in the upper; and there are no tusks in either.]

pride, his riches, and his support. There are many of our peasantry that have no other possession but a cow; and even of the advantages resulting from this most useful creature, the poor are but the nominal possessors. Its flesh they cannot pretend to taste, since then their whole riches are at once destroyed; its calf they are obliged to fatten for sale, since veal is a delicacy they could not make any pretensions to; its very milk is wrought into butter and cheese for the tables of their masters; while they have no share even in their own possession, but the choice of their market. I cannot bear to hear the rich crying out for liberty, while they thus starve their fellow creatures; and feed them up with an imaginary good, while they monopolize the real benefits of nature.

In those countries where the men are under better subordination, this excellent animal is of more general advantage. In Germany, Poland, and Switzerland, every peasant keeps two or three cows, not for the benefit of his master, but for himself. The meanest of the peasants there kills one cow at least for his own table, which he salts and hangs up, and thus preserves as a delicacy all the year round. There is scarcely a cottage in those countries that is not hung round with these marks of hospitality; and which often make the owner better contented with hunger, since he has it in his power to be luxurious when he thinks proper. A piece of beef hung up there, is considered as an elegant piece of furniture, which, though seldom touched, at least argues the possessor's opulence and ease. But it is very different, for some years past, in this country, where our lower rustics at

Q

least are utterly unable to purchase meat any part
of the year, and by them even butter is considered
as an article of extravagance.

The climate and pasture of Great Britain, however, are excellently adapted to this animal's moderate nature ; and the verdure and the fertility of
our plains are perfectly suited to the manner of its
feeding ; for wanting the upper fore teeth, it loves
to graze on a high rich pasture. This animal
seems but little regardful of the quality of its food,
provided it be supplied in sufficient abundance.;
it makes no particular distinction in the choice of
its herbage, but indiscriminately and hastily devours
the proper quantity. For this reason, in our pastures, where the grass is rather high than succulent,
more flourishing than nutritious, the cow thrives
admirably; and there is no part of Europe where
the tame animal grows larger, yields more milk, or
more readily fattens, than with us.

Our pastures supply them with abundance, and
they in return enrich the pasture ; for, of all animals, the cow seems to give back more than it
takes from the soil. The horse and the sheep are
known, in a course of years, to impoverish the
ground. The land where they have fed becomes
weedy, and the vegetables coarse and unpalatable :
on the contrary, the pasture where the cow has
been bred, acquires a finer, softer surface, and becomes every year more beautiful and even. The
reason is, that the horse being furnished with fore
teeth in the upper jaw, nips the grass closely, and,
therefore, only chooses that which is the most delicate and tender ; the sheep also, though, with respect to its teeth, formed like the cow, only bites

the most succulent parts of the herbage: these
animals, therefore, leave all the high weeds standing;
and while they cut the finer grass too closely,
suffer the ranker herbage to vegetate and over-run
the pasture. But it is otherwise with the cow; as
its teeth cannot come so close to the ground as
those of the horse, nor so readily as those of the
sheep, which are less, it is obliged to feed upon
the tallest vegetables that offer; thus it eats them
all down, and, in time, levels the surface of the
pasture.

The age of the cow is known by the teeth and
horns. This animal is furnished with eight cutting
teeth in the lower jaw; at the age of ten months,
the two middlemost of these fall out, and are
replaced by others, that are not so white, but
broader; at the age of sixteen months, the two
next milk-white teeth fall out likewise, and others
come up in their room: thus, at the end of every
six months, the creature loses and gains, till, at the
age of three years, all the cutting teeth are renewed;
and then they are long, pretty white and equal;
but in proportion as the animal advances in years,
they become irregular and black, their inequalities
become smoother, and the animal less capable of
chewing its food. Thus the cow often declines
from this single cause; for, as it is obliged to eat
a great deal to support life, and as the smoothness
of the teeth makes the difficulty of chewing great,
a sufficient quantity of food cannot be supplied to
the stomach. Thus the poor animal sinks in the
midst of plenty, and every year grows leaner and
leaner, till it dies.

The horns are another, and a surer method of

determining this animal's age. At three years old, it sheds its horns, and new ones arise in their place, which continue as long as it lives. At four years of age, the cow has small pointed neat smooth horns, thickest near the head; at five the horns become larger, and are marked round with the former year's growth. Thus, while the animal continues to live, the horns continue to lengthen; and every year a new ring is added at the root; so that, allowing three years before their appearance, and then reckoning the number of rings, we have, in both together, the animal's age exactly.*

As we have, indisputably, the best breed of horned cattle of any in Europe, so it was not without the same assiduity that we came to excel in these, as in our horses. The breed of cows has been entirely improved by a foreign mixture, properly adapted to supply the imperfections of our own. Such as are purely British, are far inferior in size to those on many parts of the continent; but those which we have thus improved, by far excel all others. Our Lincolnshire kind derive their size from the Holstein breed; and the large hornless cattle that are bred in some parts of England came originally from Poland. We

[* How the Count de Buffon should have fallen into the extraordinary error, that the bull and cow cast their horns at the age of three years, which are replaced by others, it is hard to conjecture. However, in his sixth supplementary volume, this mistake is very candidly and handsomely acknowledged and corrected. It is in part explained by an observation communicated by Dr. Forster, namely, that, at the age of three years, the horns are not cast, but the animal rubs off a very slight external shell coating, scarcely thicker than writing paper.]

were once famous for a wild breed of these animals, but these have long since been worn out; and perhaps no kingdom in Europe can furnish so few wild animals of all kinds, as our own. Cultivation and agriculture are sure to banish these, wherever they are found; and every addition a country receives from art, drives away those animals that are only fitted for a state of nature.

Of all quadrupeds, the cow seems most liable to alteration from its pasture. In the different parts of our own country, we easily perceive the great varieties produced among these animals, by the richness or poverty of the soil. In some they grow to a great bulk; and I have seen an ox sixteen hands high, which is taller than the general run of our horses. In others they appear as diminutive; being not so large as an ass. The breed of the Isle of Man, and most parts of Scotland, is much less in general than in England or Ireland; they are differently shaped also, the dewlap being much smaller, and, as the expression is, the beast has more of the ewe neck. This, till some years ago, was considered in cattle as a deformity; and the cow was chosen, according to Virgil's direction, with a large dewlap; however, at present it is the universal opinion, that the cow wants in udder what it has in neck, and the larger the dewlap, the smaller is the quantity of its milk. Our graziers, now, therefore, endeavour to mix the two breeds, the large Holstein with the small northern; and from both results that fine milch breed, which excels the cattle of any other part of the world.

Q 2

This difference, arising from pasture, is more observable in other countries than in our own. The cow kind is to be found in almost every part of the world, large in proportion to the richness of the pasture; and small, as the animal is stinted in its food. Thus Africa is remarkable for the largest and the smallest cattle of this kind; as is also India, Poland, Switzerland, and several other parts of Europe. Among the Eluth Tartars, where the pastures are remarkably rich and nourishing, the cow becomes so large, that he must be a tall man who can reach the tip of its shoulder. On the contrary, in France, where the animal is stinted in its food, and driven from the most flourishing pastures, it greatly degenerates.

But the differences in the size of this animal are not so remarkable as those which are found in its form, its hair, and its horns. The difference is so very extraordinary in many of them, that they have been even considered as a different kind of creature, and names have been given them as a distinct species, when in reality they are all the same.* In this manner the urus and the bison have been considered, from the variety in their make, to be distinct in their production; but they are all in fact the descendants of one common stock, as they have that certain mark of unity, they breed and propagate among each other. Naturalists have therefore laboured under an obvious error, when, because of the extreme bulk of the urus, or because of the hump upon the

* Buffon, vol. xxiii. p. 78.

back of the bison, they assigned them different places in the creation, and separated a class of animals which was really united. It is true, the horse and the ass do not differ so much in form, as the cow and the bison; nevertheless, the former are distinct animals, as their breed is marked with sterility;—the latter are animals of the same kind, as their breed is fruitful, and a race of animals is produced, in which the hump belonging to the bison is soon worn away. The differences, therefore, between the cow, the urus, and the bison, are merely accidental. The same caprice in nature that has given horns to some cows, and denied them to others, may also have given the bison a hump, or increased the bulk of the urus; it may have given the one a mane, or denied a sufficiency of hair to the other.

But before we proceed farther, it may be proper to describe these varieties, which have been thus taken for distinct kinds.* The urus, or wild bull, is chiefly to be met with in the province of Lithuania; and grows to a size, that scarcely any other animal, except the elephant, is found to equal. It is quite black, except a stripe mixed with white, that runs from the neck to the tail, along the top of the back; the horns are short, thick, and strong; the eyes are fierce and fiery; the forehead is adorned with a kind of garland of black curled hair, and some of them are found to have beards of the same; the neck is short and strong, and the skin has an odour of musk. The female, though not so big as the

* This description is chiefly taken from Klein.

male, exceeds the largest of our bulls in size; nevertheless, her udder and teats are so small, that they can scarcely be perceived. Upon the whole, however, this animal resembles the tame one very exactly, except in some trifling varieties, which his state of wildness, or the richness of the pastures where he is found, may easily have produced.*

[* In Lord Tankerville's park, at Chillingham, near Berwick-upon-Tweed, there is yet left a breed of wild cattle; probably the only remains of the true and genuine breed of that species at present to be found in this kingdom.

Their colour is invariably white, with the muzzle black; and the whole inside of the ear, and about one-third part of the outside, from the hip downwards, red. Their horns are white, with black tips, very fine, and bent downwards. The weight of the bulls is from thirty-five to forty-five stone; and of the cows, from twenty-five to thirty-five.

At the first appearance of any person near them, they set off in full gallop, and at the distance of two or three hundred yards, wheel round, and come boldly up again, tossing their heads in a menacing manner; on a sudden they make a full stop, at the distance of forty or fifty yards, and look wildly at the object of their surprise; but, on the least motion, they all turn round, and gallop off again with equal speed, but not to the same distance, forming a smaller circle; and again returning with a bolder and more threatening aspect than before, they approach much nearer, probably within thirty yards, when they make another stand, and again gallop off. This they do several times, shortening their distance, and advancing nearer, till they come within a few yards, when most people think it prudent to leave them, not choosing to provoke them further, as it is probable that in a few turns more they would make an attack. When the cow calves, they hide their young for a week or ten days, in some sequestered retreat, and go to suckle them two or three times a day. If any persons come near the calves, they clap their heads down close to the ground, and lie like a hare in form, to hide themselves. This seems a proof of their native wildness,

7

De Seve del.   Wörner sc.

The Bison.

The bison, which is another variety of the cow
kind, differs from the rest, in having a lump
between its shoulders. These animals are of
various kinds; some very large, others as diminu-
tively little. In general, to regard this animal's
fore parts, he has somewhat the look of a lion, with
a long shaggy mane, and a beard under his chin;
his head is little, his eyes red and fiery, with a
furious look; the forehead is large, and the horns
so big, and so far asunder, that three men might
often sit between them. On the middle of the
back there grows a bunch almost as high as that
of a camel, covered with hair, and which is considered as a great delicacy by those that hunt him.
There is no pursuing him with safety, except
in forests where there are trees large enough
to hide the hunters. He is generally taken by
pit-falls; the inhabitants of those countries where
he is found wild, digging holes in the ground,
and covering them over with boughs of trees and
grass; then provoking the bison to pursue them,

and it is corroborated by the following circumstance, that happened to Dr. Tuller, the author of the history of Berwick, who
found a hidden calf two days old, very lean and weak. On his
stroking its head, it got up, pawed two or three times, like an
old bull, bellowed very loud, went back a few steps, and bolted
at his legs with all its force; it then began to paw again, bellowed, stepped back, and bolted as before. But being aware
of its intentions, he moved aside, and it missed its aim, fell, and
was so weak, that, though it made several efforts, it was not able
to rise. It, however, had done enough, the whole herd was
alarmed, and coming to its rescue, they obliged him to return.
When any one of them happens to be wounded, or is grown
weak and feeble through age or sickness, the rest of the herd
set upon and gore it to death.]   *Bewick's Quadrupeds.*

they get on the opposite side of the pit-fall, while the furious animal, running head foremost, falls into the pit prepared for him, and is there quickly overcome and slain.

Besides these real distinctions in the cow kind, there have been many others made, that appear to be in name only. Thus the bonasus, of which naturalists have given us long descriptions, is supposed by Klein and Buffon to be no more than another name for the bison, as the descriptions given of them by the ancients coincide. The bubalus also of the ancients, which some have supposed to belong to the cow kind, Buffon places among the lower class of ruminant quadrupeds, as it most resembles them in size, shape, and the figure of its horns. Of all the varieties, therefore, of the cow kind, there are but two that are really distinct; namely, the cow and the buffalo; these two are separated by Nature; they seem to bear an antipathy to each other; they avoid each other, and may be considered as much removed as the horse is from the ass or the zebra. When, therefore, we have described the varieties of the cow kind, we shall pass on to the buffalo, which being a different animal, requires a separate history.

There is scarcely a part of the world, as was said before, in which the cow is not found in some one of its varieties; either large, like the urus, or humped as the bison; with strait horns, or bending, inverted backwards, or turning sideways to the cheek, like those of the ram; and, in many countries, they are found without any horns whatsoever. But to be more particular, beginning at the north, the few kine which subsist in Iceland are without horns, although of the same race originally with ours. The size of these is rather relative to the goodness of the pasture, than the warmth or coldness of the climate. The Dutch frequently bring great quantities of lean cattle from Denmark, which they fatten on their own rich grounds. These are in general of a larger size than their own natural breed, and they fatten very easily. The cattle of the Ukraine, where the pasture is excellent, become very fat, and are considered as one of the largest breeds of Europe. In Switzerland, where the mountains are covered with rich nourishing herbage, which is entirely reserved for their kine, these animals grow to a very large size. On the contrary, in France, where they get no other grass but what is thought unfit for horses, they dwindle, and grow lean. In some parts of Spain, the cow grows to a good size; those wild bulls, however, which they pride themselves so much in combating, are a very mean despicable little animal, and somewhat shaped like one of our cows, with nothing of that peculiar sternness of aspect for which our bulls are remarkable. In Barbary, and the provinces of Africa, where the ground is dry, and the pasturage short, the cows are of a very small breed, and give milk in proportion. On the contrary, in Ethiopia, they are of a prodigious bigness. The same holds in Persia and Tartary; where, in some places, they are very small, and in others, of an amazing stature. It is thus, in almost every part of the world, this animal is found to correspond in size to the quantity of its provision.

If we examine the form of these animals, as they
are found tame, in different regions, we shall find,
that the breed of the urus, or those without a
hump, chiefly occupies the cold and the temperate
zones, and is not so much dispersed towards the
south. On the contrary, the breed of the bison,
or the animal with a hump, is found in all the
southern parts of the world; throughout the vast
continent of India; throughout Africa, from Mount
Atlas to the Cape of Good Hope. In all these countries, the bison seems chiefly to prevail; where they
are found to have a smooth soft hair, are very nimble of foot, and in some measure supply the want
of horses. The bison breed is also more expert
and docile than ours; many of them, when they
carry burthens, bend their knees to take them up,
or set them down: they are treated, therefore, by
the natives of those countries, with a degree of
tenderness and care equal to their utility; and the
respect for them in India has degenerated even into
blind adoration. But it is among the Hottentots
where these animals are chiefly esteemed, as being
more than commonly serviceable. They are their
fellow-domestics, the companions of their pleasures
and fatigues; the cow is at once the Hottentot's
protector and servant, assists him in attending his
flocks, and guarding them against every invader;
while the sheep are grazing, the faithful backely,
as this kind of cow is called, stands or grazes
beside them: still, however, attentive to the looks
of its master, the backely flies round the field,
herds in the sheep that are straying, obliges them
to keep within proper limits, and shows no mercy
to robbers, or even strangers, who attempt to plun-

der. But it is not the plunderers of the flock alone, but even the enemies of the nation, that these backelies are taught to combat. Every army of Hottentots is furnished with a proper herd of these, which are let loose against the enemy, when the occasion is most convenient. Being thus sent forward, they overturn all before them; they strike every opposer down with their horns, and trample upon them with their feet; and thus often procure their masters an easy victory, even before they have attempted to strike a blow. An animal so serviceable, it may be supposed, is not without its reward. The backely lives in the same cottage with its master, and, by long habit, gains an affection for him; and in proportion as the man approaches to the brute, so the brute seems to attain even to some share of human sagacity. The Hottentot and his backely thus mutually assist each other; and when the latter happens to die, a new one is chosen to succeed him, by a council of the old men of the village. The new backely is then joined with one of the veterans of his own kind, from whom he learns his art, becomes social and diligent, and is taken for life into human friendship and protection.

The bisons, or cows with a hump, are found to differ very much from each other, in the several parts of the world where they are found. The wild ones of this kind, as with us, are much larger than the tame. Some have horns, and some are without any; some have them depressed, and some raised in such a manner that they are used as weapons of annoyance or defence; some are extremely large; and others among them, such as

†

the zebu, or Barbary cow, are very small. They are all, however, equally docile and gentle when tamed; and, in general, furnished with a fine lustrous soft hair, more beautiful than that of our own breed; their hump is also of different sizes, in some weighing from forty to fifty pounds, in others less; it is not, however, to be considered as a part necessarily belonging to the animal; and probably it might be cut away without much injury: it resembles a gristly fat; and, as I am assured, cuts and tastes somewhat like a dressed udder. The bisons of Malabar, Abyssinia, and Madagascar, are of the great kind, as the pastures there are plentiful. Those of Arabia Petræa, and most parts of Africa, are small, and of the zebu or little kind.: In America, especially towards the north, the bison is well known. The American bison, however, is found to be rather less than that of the ancient continent; its hair is longer and thicker, its beard more remarkable, and its hide more lustrous and soft. There are many of them brought up tame in Carolina; however, their wild dispositions still seem to continue, for they break through all fences to get into the corn-fields, and lead the whole tame herd after them, wherever they penetrate. They breed also with the tame kinds originally brought over from Europe; and thus produce a race peculiar to that country.

From all this it appears,* that naturalists have given various names to animals in reality the same; and only differing in some few accidental circumstances. The wild cow and the tame, the animal

* Buffon, vol. xxiii. p. 130.

belonging to Europe, and that of Asia, Africa, and
America, the bonasus and the urus, the bison and
the zebu, are all one and the same, propagate
among each other, and, in the course of a few
generations, the hump wears away, and scarcely
any vestiges of savage fierceness are found to re-.
main. Of all animals, therefore, except man alone,
the cow seems most extensively propagated. Its
nature seems equally capable of the rigours of heat
and cold. It is an inhabitant as well of the frozen
fields of Iceland, as the burning deserts of Lybia.
It seems an ancient inmate in every climate,
domestic and tame in those countries which have
been civilized, savage and wild in the countries
which are less peopled, but capable of being made
useful in all; able to defend itself in a state of
nature against the most powerful enemy of the
forest; and only subordinate to man, whose force
it has experienced, and whose aid it at last seems
to require. However wild the calves are which
are taken from the dam in a savage state, either in
Africa or Asia, they soon become humble, patient,
and familiar; and man may be considered, in
those countries, as almost helpless without their
assistance. Other animals preserve their nature or
their form with inflexible perseverance; but these,
in every respect, suit themselves to the appetites
and conveniencies of mankind; and as their shapes
are found to alter, so also does their nature;
in no animal is there seen a greater variety of
kinds, and in none a more humble and pliant disposition.*

[* Mr. Pennant, in his Arctic Zoology, has lately brought to
our knowledge a singular species, differing in its habits and

The Buffalo.

If we should compare the shape of our common
cow with that of the bison, the difference will ap-

appearance very considerably from others of its kind: he calls it
the Musk Ox. It is found chiefly in the most rocky and barren
mountains of North America. In size it is not quite so high as
the deer, but it is larger or thicker in the body. Its horns are
set close together at the base, and though they are only two feet
long, measure two feet in girth near the base: a pair of them,
when separated from the head, weigh frequently sixty pounds.
The body is clothed with an extremely fine hair, so long as to
trail on the ground, giving the animal the appearance of a shapeless mass: in the ox it is of a dusky red colour, but in the cow
of a fine glossy black ; beneath which is an extremely fine wool,
more beautiful than silk when manufactured into stockings and
other articles. They delight most in rocky and barren mountains, seldom frequenting the woods or plains ; run very nimbly, and climb the rocks with great facility. Their flesh tastes
so strongly of musk, as to be hardly eatable. Of the tail the
Esquimaux of the north-west side of Hudson's Bay, make a cap
of the most horrible appearance; for the hairs fall all round
their heads, and cover their faces ; yet it is highly serviceable, in
keeping off the moschetoes, which would otherwise be intolerable.

Captain Turner has likewise, in his account of an embassy to
Tibet, described what he calls the Yak of Tartary, or bushy-tailed
bull of Tibet. In common appearance and size it resembles the
English bull, but it has a hunch on its back, and is covered all
over with a thick coat of long hair, which is manufactured into
tents and ropes. But the greatest singularity about their tails,
which is composed of a prodigious quantity of long, flowing,
glossy hair, which is furnished in such abundance, that not a
joint of the tail is perceptible ; but it has much the appearance
of a large cluster of hair artificially set on. Throughout the
East these tails are in universal use, under the denomination of

pear very great. The shaggy main of the latter,
the beard, the curled forehead, the inverted horns,
the broad breast, and the narrow hinder parts, give
it the appearance rather of a lion than a cow; and
fit it more for a state of war with mankind, than a
state of servitude. Yet, notwithstanding these
appearances, both animals are found to be the
same; or at least so nearly allied, that they breed
among each other, and propagate a race that continues the kind.

On the other hand, if we compare the buffalo
with our common cow, no two animals can be
more nearly alike, either in their form or their
nature; both equally submissive to the yoke, both
often living under the same roof, and employed in
the same domestic services; the make and the
turn of their bodies so much alike, that it requires
a close attention to distinguish them: and yet, after
all this, no two animals can be more distinct, or
seem to have stronger antipathies to each other.*
Were there but one of each kind remaining, it is
probable the race of both would shortly be extinct.
However, such is the fixed aversion formed between these creatures, that the cow refuses to
breed with the buffalo, which it nearly resembles;
while it is known to propogate with the bison, to

chowries, for driving away moschetoes, flies, and other insects
from the face and person.

These animals have a downcast, heavy look, and appear sullen
and suspicious, discovering much impatience at the near approach of strangers. They do not low loud like other cattle,
but make a grunting noise, scarcely audible, when under some
impression of uneasiness.]

* Buffon.

which it has, in point of form, but a very distant similitude.

. The buffalo is, upon the whole, by no means so beautiful a creature as the cow; his figure is more clumsy and awkward; his air is wilder; and he carries his head lower, and nearer the ground; his limbs are less fleshy, and his tail more naked of hair; his body is shorter and thicker than that of the cow kind; his legs are higher; his head smaller; his horns not so round, black, and compressed, with a bunch of curled hair hanging down between them; his skin is also harder and thicker, more black and less furnished with hair; his flesh, which is hard and blackish, is not only disagreeable to the taste, but likewise to the smell. The milk of the female is by no means so good as that of the cow; it is however produced in great abundance. In the warm countries, almost all their cheese is made of the milk of the buffalo; and they supply butter also in large quantities. The veal of the young buffalo is not better eating than the beef of the old. The hide of this animal seems to be the most valuable thing he furnishes. The leather made of it is well known for its thickness, softness, and impenetrability. As these animals are, in general, larger and stronger than the cow, they are usefully employed in agriculture. They are used in drawing burthens, and sometimes in carrying them; being guided by a ring, which is thrust through their nose. Two buffaloes yoked in a waggon are said to draw more than four strong horses; as their heads and necks are naturally bent downward, they are thus better fitted for the draught, and the whole weight of their bodies is applied to the carriage that is to be drawn forward.

From the size and bulk of the buffalo, we may be easily led to conclude that he is a native of the warmer climates. The largest quadrupeds are generally found in the torrid zone; and the buffalo is inferior, in point of size, only to the elephant, the rhinoceros, or the hippopotamos. The cameleopard, or the camel, may, indeed, be taller, but they are neither so long, nor near so corpulent. Accordingly, we find this animal wild in many parts of India; and tamed also wherever the natives have occasion for his services. The wild buffaloes are very dangerous animals, and are often found to gore travellers to death, and then trample them with their feet, until they have entirely mangled the whole body: however, in the woods they are not so much to be feared as in the plains, because in the violence of their pursuit their large horns are apt to be entangled in the branches of the trees, which gives those who have been surprised by them time to escape the danger. There is scarcely any other method of avoiding their pursuit; they run with great swiftness; they overturn a tree of moderate growth; and are such swimmers, as to cross the largest rivers without any difficulty. In this manner, like all other large animals of the torrid zone, they are very fond of the water; and, in the midst of their pursuit, often plunge in, in order to cool themselves. The Negroes of Guinea, and the Indians of Malabar, where buffaloes are in great abundance, take great delight in hunting and destroying them; however, they never attempt to face the buffalo openly, but, generally climbing up the tree, shoot at him from thence, and do not come down till they find they have effectually dispatched him. When they are tamed, no animal can be more patient or humble; and though by no means so docile as the cow kind, yet they go through domestic drudgeries with more strength and perseverance.

- Although these animals be chiefly found in the torrid zone, yet they are bred in several parts of Europe, particularly in Italy, where they make the food and the riches of the poor. The female produces but one at a time, in the same manner as the cow; but they are very different in the times of gestation; for the cow, as we know, goes but nine months; whereas the buffalo continues pregnant for twelve. They are all afraid of fire; and, perhaps in consequence of this, have an aversion to red colours, that resemble the colour of flame: it is said, that in those countries where they are found in plenty, no person dares to dress in scarlet. In general they are inoffensive animals, if undisturbed; as indeed all those which feed upon grass are found to be; but when they are wounded, or when even but fired at, nothing then can stop their fury; they then turn up the ground with their fore feet, bellow much louder and more terribly than the bull, and make at the object of their resentment with ungovernable rage. It is happy, in such circumstances, if the person they pursue has a wall to escape over, or some such obstacle, otherwise they soon overtake, and instantly destroy him. It is remarkable, however, that although their horns are so very formidable, they in general make more use of their feet in combat, and rather tread their enemies to death than gore them.*

Having thus gone through the history of these animals, it may be proper to observe, that no names have been more indiscriminately used than those of the bull, the urus, the bison, and the buffalo. It therefore becomes such as would have distinct ideas of each, to be careful in separating the kinds, the one from the other, allowing the cow for the standard of all. The urus, whether of the large enormous kind of Lithuania, or the smaller race of Spain, whether with long or short horns, whether with or without long hair in the forehead, is every way the same with what our common breed was before they were taken from the forest, and reduced to a state of servitude. The bison, and all its varieties, which are known by a hump between the shoulders, is also to be ranked in the same class. This animal, whether with crooked or straight horns, whether they be turned towards the cheek, or totally wanting, whether it be large or diminutive, whatever be its colour, or whatever the length of its hair, whether called the bonasus by some, or the

[* In Malabar, and the islands of Borneo, and Ceylon, this animal is said to be remarkably dangerous and treacherous. He hides himself among the trees, and lies concealed there, till some animal or man passes near him, when he suddenly starts out, and sometimes catches him. Not content with throwing down his prey, and instantly destroying it, he gets the unfortunate man or animal under him, tramples upon his body, rubs him with his knees, tears him with his horns and feet, and literally fleas him by stripping off the skin with licking him. This cruelty he does not exercise without some interval; he goes away from time to time to a certain distance, and then returns and begins again.]

bubalus by others, is but a variety of the cow kind, with whom it breeds, and with whom of consequence it has the closest connexion. Lastly, the buffalo, though shaped much more like the cow, is a distinct kind by itself, that never mixes with any of the former; that goes twelve months with young, whereas the cow goes but nine; that testifies an aversion to the latter; and, though bred under the same roof, or feeding in the same pasture, has always kept separate; and makes a distinct race in all parts of the world. These two kinds are supposed to be the only real varieties in the cow kind, of which naturalists have given so many varieties. With respect to some circumstances mentioned by travellers, such as that of many kinds defending themselves by voiding their dung against their pursuers; this is a practice which they have in common with other timid creatures when pursued, and arises rather from fear than a desire of defence. The musky smell, also, by which some have been distinguished, is found common to many of these kinds, in a state of nature; and does not properly make the characteristic marks of any. The particular kind of noise also which some of them are known to make, which rather resembles grunting than bellowing or lowing, is but a savage variety, which many wild animals have, and yet lose when brought into a state of tameness. For these reasons M. Buffon, whom I have followed in this description, is of opinion, that the zebu, or little African cow, and the grunting, or Siberian cow, are but different races of the bison; as the shape of the horns, or the length of the hair, are

8

De Seve del.   Waner sc.

The Zebu.

never properly characteristic marks of any animal, but are found to vary with climate, food, and cultivation.

In this manner the number of animals of the cow kind, which naturalists have extended to eight or ten sorts, are reduced to two; and as the utmost deference is paid to the opinion of M. Buffon in this particular, I have taken him for my guide. Nevertheless, there is an animal of the cow kind, which neither he, nor any other naturalist that I know of, has hitherto described, yet which makes a very distinct class, and may be added as a third species.

This animal was shown some years ago in London, and seemed to unite many of the characteristics of the cow and the hog; having the head, the horns, and the tail of the former, with the bristles, the colour, and the grunting of the latter. It was about the size of an ass, but broader and thicker; the colour resembling that of a hog, and the hair bristly, as in that animal. The hair upon the body was thin, as in the hog; and a row of bristles ran along the spine, rather shorter and softer than in the hog kind. The head was rather larger than that of a cow; the teeth were entirely resembling those of that animal, and the tongue was rough in like manner. It fed upon hay; and, consequently its internal conformation must have resembled that of the cow kind more than the hog, whose food is always chosen of a kind more succulent. The eyes were placed in the head as with the cow, and were pretty nearly of the same colour; the horns were black and flattish, but bent rather backwards to the

neck, as in the goat kind; the neck was short
and thick, and the back rather rising in the middle;
it was cloven-footed, like the cow, without those
hinder claws that are found in the hog kinds.
But the greatest variety of all in this extraordinary
creature, which was a female, was, that it had
but two teats, and, consequently, in that respect,
resembled neither of the kinds to which, in
other circumstances, it bore so strong a similitude.   Whether this animal was a distinct kind,
or a monster, I will not pretend to say.   It was
shown under the name of a bonasus; and it
was said, by the person who showed it, to have
come from India; but no credit is to be given to
interested ignorance; the person only wanted to
make the animal appear as extraordinary as possible;
and I believe would scarcely scruple a lie or two,
to increase that wonder in us, by which he found
the means of living.

CHAP. XVI.

Of Animals of the Sheep and Goat Kind.*

As no two animals are found entirely the same,
so it is not to be expected that any two races of

[* In the sheep kind the horns are hollow, wrinkled, peren-
nial, bent backwards and outwards, into a circular or spiral
form, and generally placed at the sides of the head; in the lower
jaw there are eight front teeth, but none in the upper; there are
no canine teeth in either.   In the goat the horns are hollow,
rough, compressed, and rise somewhat erect from the top of the
head, and bend backwards; there are eight front teeth in the
lower jaw, none in the upper, and no canine teeth in either;
the chin is bearded.]

§

animals should exactly correspond in every particular. The goat and the sheep are apparently
different, in the form of their bodies, in their covering, and in their horns. They may from hence
be considered as two different kinds, with regard
to all common and domestic purposes. But if we
come to examine them closer, and observe their
internal conformation, no two animals can be more
alike; their feet, their four stomachs, their suet,
their appetites, all are entirely the same, and show
the similitude between them; but what makes a
much stronger connexion is, that they propagate
with each other. The buck goat is found to produce with the ewe an animal that in two or three
generations returns to the sheep, and seems to
retain no marks of its ancient progenitor.* The
sheep and the goat, therefore, may be considered as
belonging to one family; and were the whole races
reduced to one of each, they would quickly replenish
the earth with their kind.

If we examine the sheep and goat internally,
we shall find, as was said, that their conformation
is entirely the same; nor is their structure very
remote from that of the cow kind, which they
resemble in their hoofs, and in their chewing the
cud. Indeed, all ruminant animals are internally
very much alike. The goat, the sheep, or the
deer, exhibit to the eye of the anatomist the same
parts in miniature, which the cow or the bison
exhibited in the great. But the differences between
those animals are, nevertheless, sufficiently apparent.
Nature has obviously marked the distinctions be-

* Buffon, passim.

tween the cow and the sheep kind, by their form
and size; and they are also distinguished from
those of the deer kind, by never shedding their
horns. Indeed, the form and figure of these animals, if there were nothing else, would seldom
fail of guiding us to the kind; and we might
almost, upon sight, tell which belongs to the
deer kind, and which are to be degraded into that
of the goat. However, the annually shedding
the horns in the deer, and the permanence in the
sheep, draws a pretty exact line between the
kinds; so that we may hold to this distinction
only, and define the sheep and goat kind as ruminant animals of a smaller size, that never shed their
horns.

If we consider these harmless and useful animals in one point of view, we shall find that both
have been long reclaimed, and brought into a
state of domestic servitude. Both seem to require
protection from man; and are, in some measure,
pleased with his society. The sheep, indeed, is
the more serviceable creature of the two; but
the goat has more sensibility and attachment.
The attending upon both was once the employment of the wisest and the best of men; and
those have been ever supposed the happiest times,
in which these harmless creatures were considered
as the chief objects of human attention. In the
earliest ages, the goat seemed rather the greater
favourite; and, indeed, it continues such, in some
countries, to this day among the poor. However,
the sheep has long since become the principal object of human care; while the goat is disregarded
by the generality of mankind, or become the pos-

session only of the lowest of the people. The sheep, therefore, and its varieties, may be considered first; and the goat, with all those of its kind, will then properly follow.

The Sheep.

Those animals that take refuge under the protection of man, in a few generations become indolent and helpless. Having lost the habit of self-defence, they seem to lose also the instincts of nature. The sheep, in its present domestic state, is of all animals the most defenceless and inoffensive. With its liberty it seems to have been deprived of its swiftness and cunning; and what in the ass might rather be called patience, in the sheep appears to be stupidity. With no one quality to fit it for self-preservation, it makes vain efforts at all. Without swiftness, it endeavours to fly; and without strength, sometimes offers to oppose. But these feeble attempts rather incite than repress the insults of every enemy; and the dog follows the flock with greater delight upon seeing them fly, and attacks them with more fierceness upon their unsupported attempts at resistance. Indeed they run together in flocks, rather with the hopes of losing their single danger in the crowd, than of uniting to repress the attack by numbers. The sheep, therefore, were it exposed in its present state to struggle with its natural enemies of the forest, would soon be extirpated. Loaded with a heavy fleece, deprived of the defence of its horns, and rendered heavy,

slow, and feeble, it can have no other safety than
what it finds from man. This animal is now,
therefore, obliged to rely solely upon that art for
protection, to which it originally owes its degra-
dation.

But we are not to impute to Nature the formation of an animal so utterly unprovided against
its enemies, and so unfit for defence. The
moufflon, which is the sheep in a savage state, is a
bold, fleet creature, able to escape from the greater
animals by its swiftness, or to oppose the smaller
kinds with the arms it has received from Nature.
It is by human art alone that the sheep is become
the tardy, defenceless creature we find it. Every
race of quadrupeds might easily be corrupted by
the same allurements by which the sheep has been
thus debilitated and depressed. While undisturbed, and properly supplied, none are found to
set any bounds to their appetite. They all pursue
their food while able, and continue to graze, till
they often die of disorders occasioned by too much
fatness. But it is very different with them in a
state of nature: they are in the forest surrounded
by dangers, and alarmed with unceasing hostilities; they are pursued every hour from one tract
of country to another; and spend a great part
of their time in attempts to avoid their enemies.
Thus constantly exercised, and continually prac-
tising all the arts of defence and escape, the animal
at once preserves its life and native independence,
together with its swiftness, and the slender agility
of its form.

The sheep, in its servile state, seems to be
divested of all inclinations of its own; and of all

animals it appears the most stupid. Every quadruped has a peculiar turn of countenance, a physiognomy, if we may so call it, that generally marks its nature. The sheep seems to have none of those traits that betoken either courage or cunning; its large eyes, separated from each other, its ears sticking out on each side, and its narrow nostrils, all testify the extreme simplicity of this creature; and the position of its horns, also, shows that Nature designed the sheep rather for flight than combat. It appears a large mass of flesh, supported upon four small straight legs, ill fitted for carrying such a burthen; its motions are awkward, it is easily fatigued, and often sinks under the weight of its own corpulency. In proportion as these marks of human transformation are more numerous, the animal becomes more helpless and stupid. Those which live upon a more fertile pasture, and grow fat, become entirely feeble; those that want horns, are found more dull and heavy than the rest;* those whose fleeces are longest and finest, are most subject to a variety of disorders; and, in short, whatever changes have been wrought in this animal by the industry of man, are entirely calculated for human advantage, and not for that of the creature itself. It might require a succession of ages, before the sheep could be restored to its primitive state of activity, so as to become a match for its pursuers of the forest.

The goat, which it resembles in so many other respects, is much its superior. The one has its

* Daubenton upon the Sheep.

particular attachments, sees danger, and generally
contrives to escape it; but the other is timid
without a cause, and secure when real danger
approaches. Nor is the sheep, when bred up tame
in the house, and familiarized with its keepers, less
obstinately absurd: from being dull and timid, it
then acquires a degree of pert familiarity; butts
with its head, becomes mischievous, and shows
itself every way unworthy of being singled out
from the rest of the flock. Thus it seems rather
formed for slavery than friendship; and framed
more for the necessities than the amusements of
mankind. There is but one instance in which the
sheep shows any attachment to its keeper; and
that is seen rather on the continent than among
us in Great Britain. What I allude to is, their
following the sound of the shepherd's pipe.
Before I had seen them trained in this manner, I
had no conception of those descriptions in the old
pastoral poets, of the shepherd leading his flock
from one country to another. As I had been
used only to see these harmless creatures driven
before their keepers, I supposed that all the rest
was but invention: but in many parts of the
Alps, and even some provinces of France, the
shepherd and his pipe are still continued, with
true antique simplicity. The flock is regularly
penned every evening, to preserve them from the
wolf; and the shepherd returns homeward at
sun-set, with his sheep following him, and seemingly
pleased with the sound of the pipe, which is blown
with a reed, and resembles the chanter of a bag-
pipe. In this manner, in those countries that still
continue poor, the Arcadian life is preserved in

all its former purity: but in countries where a greater inequality of conditions prevail, the shepherd is generally some poor wretch who attends a flock from which he is to derive no benefits, and only guards those luxuries which he is not fated to share.

It does not appear, from early writers, that the sheep was bred in Britain; and it was not till several ages after this animal was cultivated, that the woollen manufacture was carried on among us.* That valuable branch of business lay for a considerable time in foreign hands; and we were obliged to import the cloth, manufactured from our own materials. There were, notwithstanding, many unavailing efforts among our kings to introduce and preserve the manufactory at home. Henry the Second, by a patent granted to the weavers in London, directed, that if any cloth was found made of a mixture of Spanish wool, it should be burned by the mayor. Such edicts, at length, although but slowly, operated towards the establishing this trade among us. The Flemings, who, at the revival of arts, possessed the art of cloth-working in a superior degree, were invited to settle here; and, soon after, foreign cloth was prohibited from being worn in England. In the times of queen Elizabeth, this manufacture received every encouragement; and many of the inhabitants of the Netherlands being then forced, by the tyranny of Spain, to take refuge in this country, they improved us in those arts, in which we at present excel the rest of the world. Every

* British Zoology, vol. i. p. 29.

art, however, has its rise, its meridian, and its
decline; and it is supposed by many, that the
woollen manufacture has for some time been
decaying amongst us. The cloth now made is
thought to be much worse than that of some years
past; being neither so firm nor so fine, neither so
much courted abroad, nor so serviceable at home.

No country, however, produces such sheep as
England; either with larger fleeces, or better
adapted for the business of clothing. Those of
Spain, indeed, are finer, and we generally require
some of their wool to work up with our own;
but the weight of a Spanish fleece is no way comparable to one of Lincoln or Warwickshire; and,
in those counties, it is no uncommon thing to give
fifty guineas for a ram.

The sheep without horns are counted the best
sort, because a great part of the animal's nourishment is supposed to go up into the horns.* Sheep,
like other ruminant animals, want the upper fore
teeth; but have eight in the lower jaw: two of
these drop, and are replaced at two years old; four
of them are replaced at three years old; and
all at four. The new teeth are easily known from
the rest, by their freshness and whiteness. There
are some breeds, however, in England, that never
change their teeth at all; these the shepherds call
the leather-mouthed cattle; and, as their teeth
are thus longer wearing, they are generally supposed to grow old a year or two before the rest.†
The sheep brings forth one or two at a time; and
sometimes three or four. The first lamb of an ewe

* Lisle's Husbandry, vol. ii. p. 155.   † Ibid.

is generally pot-bellied, short and thick, and of
less value than those of a second or third production ; the third being supposed the best of all.
They bear their young five months; and, by
being housed, they bring forth at any time of the
year.

But this animal, in its domestic state, is too
well known to require a detail of its peculiar
habits, or of the arts which have been used to
improve the breed.   Indeed, in the eye of an
observer of Nature, every art which tends to render
the creature more helpless and useless to itself,
may be considered rather as an injury than an
improvement; and if we are to look for this animal
in its noblest state, we must seek for it in the
African desert, or the extensive plains of Siberia.
Among the degenerate descendants of the wild
sheep, there have been so many changes wrought,
as entirely to disguise the kind, and often to mislead
the observer.   The variety is so great, that scarcely
any two countries have their sheep of the same
kind; but there is found a manifest difference
in all, either in the size, the covering, the shape,
or the horns.

The woolly sheep,* as it is seen among us, is
found only in Europe, and some of the temperate
provinces of Asia.   When transported into warmer
countries, either into Florida or Guinea, it loses
its wool, and assumes a covering fitted to the
climate, becoming hairy and rough ; it there also
loses its fertility, and its flesh no longer has the
same flavour.   In the same manner, in the very

* Buffon, vol. xxiii. p. 168.

cold countries, it seems equally helpless and a stranger; it still requires the unceasing attention of mankind for its preservation; and although it is found to subsist as well in Greenland as in Guinea,* yet it seems a natural inhabitant of neither.

Of the domestic kinds to be found in the different parts of the world, besides our own, which is common in Europe, the first variety is to be seen in Iceland, Muscovy, and the coldest climates of the north. This, which may be called the Iceland sheep, resembles our breed, in the form of the body and the tail; but differs in a very extraordinary manner in the number of the horns; being generally found to have four, and sometimes even eight, growing from different parts of the forehead. These are large and formidable; and the animal seems thus fitted by Nature for a state of war; however, it is of the nature of the rest of its kind, being mild, gentle, and timid. Its wool is very different, also, from that of the common sheep, being long, smooth, and hairy. Its colour is of a dark brown; and under its outward coat of hair, it has an internal covering, that rather resembles fur than wool, being fine, short, and soft.

The second variety to be found in this animal, is that of the broad-tailed sheep, so common in Tartary, Arabia, Persia, Barbary, Syria, and Egypt. This sheep is only remarkable for its large and heavy tail, which is often found to weigh from twenty to thirty pounds. It sometimes grows a

* Krantz.

foot broad, and is obliged to be supported by a
small kind of board, that goes upon wheels. This
tail is not covered underneath with wool, like the
upper part, but is bare ; and the natives, who consider it as a very great delicacy, are very careful
in attending and preserving it from injury. M.
Buffon supposes that the fat which falls into the
caul in our sheep, goes in these to furnish the tail;
and that the rest of the body is from thence
deprived of fat in proportion. With regard to their
fleeces in the temperate climates, they are, in our
own breed, soft and woolly; but in the warmer
latitudes, they are hairy : yet in both they preserve
the enormous size of their tails.

The third observable variety is that of the sheep
called strepsicheros. This animal is a native of the
islands of the Archipelago, and only differs from
our sheep, in having straight horns, surrounded with
a spiral furrow.

The last variety is that of the Guinea sheep,
which is generally found in all the tropical climates,
both of Africa and the East Indies. They are
of a large size, with a rough hairy skin, short horns,
and ears hanging down, with a kind of dewlap
under the chin. They differ greatly in form from
the rest ; and might be considered as animals of
another kind, were they not known to breed with
other sheep. These, of all the domestic kinds,
seem to approach the nearest to the state of nature.
They are larger, stronger, and swifter than the
common race ; and, consequently, better fitted for
a precarious forest life. However, they seem to rely,
like the rest, on man for support ; being entirely

of a domestic nature, and subsisting only in the warmer climates.

Such are the varieties of this animal, which have been reduced into a state of domestic servitude. These are all capable of producing among each other ; all the peculiarities of their form have been made by climate and human cultivation : and none of them seem sufficiently independent, to live in a state of savage nature. They are, therefore, to be considered as a degenerate race, formed by the hand of man, and propagated merely for his benefit. At the same time, while man thus cultivates the domestic kinds, he drives away and destroys the savage race, which are less beneficial, and more headstrong. These, therefore, are to be found in but a very small number, in the most uncultivated countries, where they have been able to subsist by their native swiftness and strength. It is in the more uncultivated parts of Greece, Sardinia, Corsica, and particularly in the deserts of Tartary, that the moufflon is to be found, that bears all the marks of being the primitive race ; and that has been actually known to breed with the domestic animal.

The moufflon, or musmon, though covered with hair, bears a stronger similitude to the ram than to any other animal ; like the ram, it has the eyes placed near the horns ; and its ears are shorter than those of the goat : it also resembles the ram in its horns, and in all the particular contours of its form. The horns also are alike ; they are of a yellow colour ; they have three sides, as in the ram, and bend backwards in the same manner

De Sève del.

The Mouttlon.

behind the ears. The muzzle, and the inside of the ears, are of a whitish colour, tinctured with yellow ; the other parts of the face are of a brownish grey. The general colour of the hair over the body is of a brown, approaching to that of the red deer. The inside of the thighs and the belly are of a white tinctured with yellow. The form, upon the whole, seems more made for agility and strength than that of the common sheep ; and the moufflon is actually found to live in a savage state, and maintain itself, either by force or swiftness, against all the animals that live by rapine. Such is its extreme speed, that many have been inclined rather to rank it among the deer kind, than the sheep. But in this they are deceived, as the musmon has a mark that entirely distinguishes it from that species, being known never to shed its horns. In some these are seen to grow to a surprising size; many of them measuring, in their convolutions, above two ells long. They are of a yellow colour, as was said ; but the older the animal grows, the darker the horns become : with these they often maintain very furious battles between each other ; and sometimes they are found broken off in such a manner, that the small animals of the forest creep into the cavity for shelter.* When, the musmon is seen standing on the plain, his fore legs are always straight, while his hinder legs seem bent under him ; but in cases of more active necessity, this seeming deformity is removed, and he moves with great swiftness and agility ; the female very much resembles the male of this species, but

* Gmelin, as quoted by Buffon.

s 2

that she is less, and her horns also are never seen
to grow to that prodigious size they are of in the
wild ram. Such is the sheep in its savage state;
a bold, noble, and even beautiful animal; but it is
not the most beautiful creatures that are always
found most useful to man. Human industry
has therefore destroyed its grace, to improve its
utility.*

The Goat,

And its numerous Varieties.

There are some domestic animals that seem
as auxiliaries to the more useful sorts; and, that
by ceasing to be the first, are considered as nothing.
We have seen the services of the ass slighted,
because inferior to those of the horse; and, in
the same manner, those of the goat are held cheap,
because the sheep so far exceeds it. Were the
horse or the sheep removed from nature, the inferior
kinds would then be invaluable; and the same

[* In Barbary, Ethiopia, and Tartary, a singularly awkward
variety of sheep occurs, called the Broad-tailed Sheep. In its
general appaerance, except the tail, it does not much differ from
that of Europe. The tail of this animal acquires a bulk greatly
disproportionable to its body, being so large, long, and heavy,
as to trail along the ground, and to weigh from fifteen to fifty
pounds. It is composed of a substance between marrow and fat,
and is considered in the East as a great delicacy: to prevent the
incobvenience of this incumbrance in grazing, the shepherds are
often obliged to place a board under the tail, furnished with
small wheels. The fleece is of exquisite fineness, and in Thibet
is worked into shawls.]

arts would probably be bestowed in perfecting
their kinds, that the higher order of animals have
experienced. But in their present neglected state,
they vary but little from the wild animals of the
same kind; man has left them their primitive habits
and forms: and the less they owe to his assiduity,
the more they receive from nature.

The goat seems, in every respect, more fitted
for a life of savage liberty than the sheep.* It is
naturally more lively, and more possessed with
animal instinct. It easily attaches itself to man, and
seems sensible of his caresses. It is also stronger
and swifter, more courageous, and more playful,
lively, capricious, and vagrant: it is not easily
confined to its flock, but chooses its own pastures,
and loves to stray remote from the rest. It chiefly
delights in climbing precipices; in going to the
very edge of danger: it is often seen suspended
upon an eminence hanging over the sea, upon a
very little base, and even sleeps there in security.
Nature has, in some measure, fitted it for traversing
these declivities with ease; the hoof is hollow
underneath, with sharp edges, so that it walks as
securely on the ridge of a house, as on the level
ground. It is a hardy animal, and very easily
sustained; for which reason it is chiefly the property of the poor, who have no pastures with
which to supply it. Happily, however, it seems
better pleased with the neglected wild, than the
cultivated fields of art; it chooses the heathy mountain, or the shrubby rock; its favourite food is the
tops of boughs, or the tender bark of young trees:

* Buffon.

it seems less afraid of immoderate heat, and bears the warm climates better than the sheep : it sleeps exposed to the sun ; and seems to enjoy its warmest fervours ; neither is it terrified at the storm, or incommoded by the rain: immoderate cold alone seems to affect it, and is said to produce a vertigo, with which this animal is sometimes incommoded. The inconstancy of its nature is perceivable in the irregularity of its gait ; it goes forward, stops, runs, approaches, flies, merely from caprice, and with no other seeming reason than the extreme vivacity of its disposition.

There are proofs of this animal's being naturally the friend of man ; and that the goat seldom resumes its primeval wildness, when once reduced into a state of servitude. In the year 1698, an English vessel happening to touch at the islands of Bonavista, two Negroes came, and offered the sailors as many goats as they chose to take away. Upon the captain's expressing his astonishment at this offer, the Negroes assured him that there were but twelve persons in the island, and that the goats were multiplied in such a manner as even to become a nuisance : they added, that instead of giving any trouble to catch them, they followed the few inhabitants that were left with a sort of obstinacy, and rather became importunate with their tameness.

The goat produces but two at a time ; and three at the most. But in the warmer climates, although the animal degenerates, and grows less, yet it becomes more fruitful, being generally found to bring forth three, four, and five at a single delivery. The buck is capable of propagating at the age of

one year, and the female at seven months : however, the fruits of this premature generation are
weak and defective; and their best breeding-time
is generally delayed till the age of two years, or
eighteen months at least. One buck is sufficient
for a hundred and fifty goats; his appetites are
excessive: but this ardour brings on a speedy
decay, so that he is enervated in four years at most,
and even becomes old before he reaches his seventh
year. The goat, like the sheep, continues five
months with young; and, in some places, bears
twice a year.

The milk of the goat is sweet, nourishing, and
medicinal; not so apt to curdle upon the stomach
as that of the cow; and, therefore, preferable to
those whose digestion is but weak. The peculiarity of this animal's food gives the milk a flavour
different from that either of the cow or the sheep;
for as it generally feeds upon shrubby pastures, and
heathy mountains, there is an agreeable mildness in
the taste, very pleasing to such as are fond of that
aliment. In several parts of Ireland, and the highlands of Scotland, the goat makes the chief possession of the inhabitants. On those mountains,
where no other useful animal could find subsistence,
the goat continues to glean a sufficient living; and
supplies the hardy natives with what they consider
as varied luxury. They lie upon beds made of
their skins, which are soft, clean, and wholesome;
they live upon their milk, with oat bread; they
convert a part of it into butter, and some into
cheese; the flesh, indeed, they seldom taste of, as
it is a delicacy which they find too expensive;
however, the kid is considered, even by the city

epicûre, as a great rarity ; and the flesh of the goat, when properly prepared, is ranked by some as no way inferior to venison. In this manner, even in the wildest solitudes, the poor find comforts of which the rich do not think it worth their while to dispossess them ; in these mountainous retreats, where the landscape presents only a scene of rocks, heaths, and shrubs, that speak the wretchedness of the soil, these simple people have their feasts, and their pleasures ; their faithful flock of goats attends them to these awful solitudes; and furnishes them with all the necessaries of life ; while their remote situation happily keeps them ignorant of greater luxury.

As these animals are apt to stray from the flock, no man can attend above fifty of them at a time. They are fattened in the same manner as sheep ; but, taking every precaution, their flesh is never so good, or so sweet, in our climate, as that of mutton. It is otherwise between the tropics. The mutton there becomes flabby and lean, while the flesh of the goat rather seems to improve ; and in some places the latter is cultivated in preference to the former. We, therefore, find this animal in almost every part of the world, as it seems fitted for the necessities of man in both extremes. Towards the north, where the pasture is coarse and barren, the goat is fitted to find a scanty subsistence : between the tropics, where the heat is excessive, the goat is fitted to bear the climate, and its flesh is found to improve.

One of the most remarkable varieties we find in the goat is in that of Natolia. The Natolian goat, or, as M. Buffon calls it, the goat of Angora, has the ears longer than ours, and broader in proportion. The male has horns of about the same length with the goat of Europe, but black, and turned very differently, going out horizontally on each side of the head, and twisted round in the manner of a cork-screw. The horns of the female are shorter, and encircle the ear somewhat like those of the ram. They are of a dazzling white colour, and in all the hair is very long, thick, fine, and glossy; which, indeed, is the case with almost all the animals of Syria. There are a great number of these animals about Angora, where the inhabitants drive a trade with their hair, which is sent, either raw or manufactured, into all parts of Europe. Nothing can exceed the beauty of the stuffs which are made from the hair of almost all the animals of that country. These are well known among us by the name of camlet.

A second variety is the Assyrian goat of Gesner, which is somewhat larger than ours, with ears almost hanging down to the ground, and broad in proportion.* The horns, on the contrary, are not above two inches and a half long, black, and bending a little backwards. The hair is of a fox colour, and under the throat there are two excrescences, like the gills of a cock. These animals are chiefly kept round Aleppo, for the sake of their milk. They are driven through the streets, and their milk is sold to the inhabitants as they pass along.

[* M. Sonnini assures us, that though the ears of this variety are much longer than those of the common goat, they never reach so low as the ground, nor, as has been reported, are they ever cropped.]

In the third variety may be reckoned the little goat of Africa, which is of the size of a kid, but the hair is as long as that of the ordinary breed. The horns, which do not exceed the length of a man's finger, are thick, and bend downwards so close to the head, that they almost enter the skin.

There is an animal of this kind at the Cape of Good Hope, called the blue goat, which may be ranked as the fourth variety. It is in shape like the domestic, but much larger, being nearly of the size of a stag. Its hair is very short, and of a delightful blue; but it loses a great deal of its beauty when the animal is dead. It has a very long beard; but the horns are not so long in proportion as in other goats, being turned spirally, in the manner of a cork-screw. It has very long legs, but well proportioned; and the flesh is very well tasted, but lean. For this reason, in that plentiful country, it is chiefly killed upon account of its skin. It is a very shy animal, and seldom comes near the Dutch settlements; but they are found in great abundance in the more uncultivated parts of the country. Besides these, they are found in this extensive region of various colours, and many of them are spotted beautifully, with red, white, and brown.*

In fine, the Juda goat resembles ours in most parts, except in size, it being much smaller. This animal is common in Guinea, Angola, and all along the coasts of Africa: it is not much larger

[* This species is now known to be of the antelope tribe, and is, by all modern zoological writers, called the Blue Antelope.]

than a hare, but it is extremely fat, and its flesh
admirably tasted. It is in that country universally
preferred to mutton.

These animals seem all of one kind, with very
trifling distinctions between them. It is true that
they differ in some respects; such as having neither the same colour, hair, ears, or horns. But
it ought to be considered as a rule in natural history, that neither the horns, the colour, the fineness, or the length of the hair, or the position of
the ears, are to be considered as making an actual
distinction in the kinds. These are accidental
varieties, produced by climate and food, which are
known to change even in the same animal, and
give it a seeming difference of form. When we
see the shapes, the inclinations, and the internal
conformation of seemingly different creatures
nearly the same; and, above all, when we see
them producing among each other, we then have
no hesitation in pronouncing the species, and
asserting that these are of the goat kind, with
which they are so materially connected.

But, although these are evidently known to belong to the goat kind, there are others nearly resembling the goat, of whose kindred we cannot
be equally certain. These are such as, being found
in a state of nature, have not as yet been sufficiently
subjected to human observation. Hence it is impossible to determine with precision to which class
they belong; whether they be animals of a particular kind, or merely the goat in its state of
savage freedom. Were there but one of these
wild animals, the inquiry would soon be ended;
and we might readily allow it for the parent

stock ; but in the present case, there are two kinds
that have almost equal pretensions to this honour ;
and the claims of which it has been found difficult
to determine. The animals in question are the
chamois and the ibex. These both bear very near
approaches to the goat in figure ; have horns that
never shed ; and, at the same time, are more different from each other than from the animal in question. From which of these two sources our
domestic goat is derived, is not easy to settle. Instead, therefore, of entering into the discussion,
I will content myself with the result of M. Buffon's inquiries. He is of opinion that the ibex
is the principal source, that our domestic goat is
the immediate descendant, and that the chamois
is but a variety from that stock, a sort of collateral
branch of the same family. His principal reason
for giving the preference to the ibex, is its having
a more masculine figure, large horns, and a large
beard ; whereas the chamois wants these marks of
primitive strength and wildness. He supposes,
therefore, in their original savage state, that our
goat has taken after the male of the parent stock,
and the chamois after the female ; and that this
has produced a variety in these animals, even before
they underwent human cultivation.*

[* The ibex, or steinboc, is now considered as the original
stock, from which the common goat is derived ; the chamois is
a species of antelope. Mr. Coxe says of the former, that it is
very strong, and when close pressed, will sometimes turn upon
the incautious huntsman, and tumble him down the precipices,
unless he has time to lie down, and let the animal pass over
him. It is said, also, that when it cannot otherwise avoid the
hunter, it will sometimes throw itself down the steepest pre-

However this be, the two animals in question seem both well fitted for their precarious life, being extremely swift, and capable of running with ease along the ledges of precipices, where even the wolf or the fox, though instigated by hunger, dares not pursue them. They are both natives of the Alps, the Pyrenees, and the mountains of Greece; there they propagate in vast numbers, and continue to exist, in spite of the hunter and every beast of prey that is found incessantly to pursue them.

The ibex resembles the goat in the shape of its body; but differs in the horns, which are much larger. They are bent backward, full of knots; and it is generally asserted that there is a knot added every year. There are some of these found, if we may believe Bellonius, at least two yards long. The ibex has a large black beard, is of a brown colour, with a thick warm coat of hair. There is a streak of black runs along the top of the back; and the belly and back of the thighs are of a fawn colour.

The chamois,* though a wild animal, is very easily tamed, and docile; and to be found only in rocky and mountainous places. . It is about the size of a domestic goat, and resembles one in many respects. It is most agreeably lively, and

cipices, and fall on its horns in such a manner as to escape unhurt. It is certain, that they are often found with only one horn, the other being probably broken off in some fall. It is even pretended, that to get out of the reach of huntsmen, they will hang by their horns over the precipices, by a projecting tree, and remain suspended till the danger is over.]

* M. Peroud's Account, as quoted by Buffon.

active beyond expression. The chamois's hair is short, like that of the doe; in spring it is of an ash colour, in autumn a dun colour, inclining to black, and in winter of a blackish brown. This animal is found in great plenty in the mountains of Dauphiny, of Piedmont, Savoy, Switzerland, and Germany. They are peaceful, gentle creatures, and live in society with each other. They are found in flocks of from four to fourscore, and even a hundred, dispersed upon the crags of the mountains. The large males are seen feeding detached from the rest, except in rutting time, when they approach the females, and drive away the young. The time of their coupling is from the beginning of October to the end of November; and they bring forth in March and April. The young keeps with the dam about five months, and sometimes longer, if the hunters and the wolves do not separate them. It is asserted that they live between twenty and thirty years. Their flesh is good to eat; and they are found to have ten or twelve pounds of suet, which far surpasses that of the goat in hardness and goodness. The chamois has scarcely any cry, as most animals are known to have; if it has any, it is a kind of feeble bleat, by which the parent calls its young. But in cases of danger, and when it is to warn the rest of the flock, it uses a hissing noise, which is heard at a great distance. For it is to be observed that this creature is extremely vigilant, and has an eye the quickest and most piercing in nature. Its smell also is not less distinguishing. When it sees its enemy distinctly, it stops for a moment; and then if the person be

near, in an instant after it flies off. In the same
manner, by its smell, it can discover a man at
half a league distance, and gives the earliest
notice. Upon any alarm, therefore, or any apprehension of danger, the chamois begins his hissing
note with such force, that the rocks and the
forests re-echo to the sound. The first hiss continues as long as the time of one inspiration.
In the beginning it is very sharp, and deeper
towards the close. The animal having, after
this first alarm, reposed a moment, again looks
round, and, perceiving the reality of its fears,
continues to hiss by intervals, until it has spread
the alarm to a very great distance. During
this time, it seems in the most violent agitation ;
it strikes the ground with its fore-foot, and
sometimes with both ; it bounds from rock to
rock ; it turns and looks round ; it runs to the
edge of the precipice ; and, still perceiving the
enemy, flies with all its speed. The hissing of
the male is much louder and sharper than that of
the female ; it is performed through the nose ;
and is properly no more than a very strong breath,
driven violently through a small aperture. The
chamois feeds upon the best herbage, and chooses
the most delicate parts of the plants, the flower,
and the tender buds. It is not less delicate
with regard to several aromatic herbs, which
grow upon the sides of the mountains. It drinks
but very little while it feeds upon the succulent
herbage, and chews the cud in the intervals of
feeding. This animal is greatly admired for the
beauty of its eyes, which are round and sparkling,
and which mark the warmth of its constitution.

†

Its head is furnished with two small horns, of about half a foot long, of a beautiful black, and rising from the forehead, almost betwixt the eyes. These, contrary to what they are found in other animals, instead of going backwards, or sideways, jet out forward, and bend a little, at their extremities, backward, in a small circle, and end in a very sharp point. The ears are placed in a very elegant manner, near the horns; and there are two stripes of black on each side of the face, the rest being of a whitish yellow, which never changes. The horn of this animal is often used as the head of a cane. Those of the female are less, and not so much bent; and some farriers are seen to bleed cattle with them. These animals are so much incommoded by heat, that they are never found in summer, except in the caverns of rocks, amidst fragments of unmelted ice, under the shade of high and spreading trees, or of rough and hanging precipices, that face the north, and which keep off entirely the rays of the sun. They go to pasture both morning and evening, and seldom during the heat of the day. They run along the rocks with great ease and seeming indifference, and leap from one to another, so that no dogs are able to pursue them. There is nothing more extraordinary than to see them climbing and descending precipices, that to all other quadrupeds are inaccessible. They always mount or descend in an oblique direction; and throw themselves down a rock of thirty feet, and light with great security upon some excrescence, or fragment, on the side of the precipice, which is just large enough to place their feet upon; they strike the rock, however, in their descent, with their feet, three or four times, to stop the velocity of their motion; and, when they have got upon their base below, they at once seem fixed and secure. In fact, to see them jump in this manner, they seem rather to have wings than legs; some, indeed, pretend to say that they use their horns for climbing, but this wants confirmation. Certain it is that their legs alone are formed for this arduous employment, the hinder being rather longer than the former, and bending in such a manner that, when they descend upon them, they break the force of the fall. It is also asserted, that when they feed, one of them always stands as centinel; but how far this may be true is questionable. For certain, while they feed, there are some of them that keep continually gazing round the rest; but this is practised among all gregarious animals; so that, when they see any danger, they warn the rest of the herd of its approach. During the rigours of winter, the chamois sleeps in the thicker forests, and feeds upon the shrubs and the buds of the pine-tree. It sometimes turns up the snow with its foot to look for herbage; and, where it is green, makes a delicious repast. The more craggy and uneven the forest, the more this animal is pleased with the abode, which thus adds to its security. The hunting the chamois is very laborious, and extremely difficult. The most usual way is to hide behind the clefts of the rocks and shoot them. This, however, must be done with great precaution; the sportsman must creep for a vast way upon his belly, in silence, and take also the advantage of the wind, which if it blow from

him they would instantly perceive. When arrived
at a proper distance, he then advances his piece,
which is to be rifle-barrelled, and to carry one ball,
and tries his fortune among them. Some also
pursue this animal as they do the stag, by placing
proper persons at all the passages of a glade, or
valley, and then sending in others to rouse the
game. Dogs are quite useless in this chase, as
they rather alarm than overtake. Nor is it without
danger even to the men; for it often happens
that when the animal finds itself over-pressed, it
drives at the hunter with its head, and often
tumbles him down the neighbouring precipice.
This animal cannot go upon ice when smooth; but
if there be the least inequalities on its surface, it
then bounds along in security, and quickly evades
all pursuit.

The skin of the chamois was once famous, when
tanned, for its softness and warmth; at present,
however, since the art of tanning has been brought
to greater perfection, the leather called chamois or
chammoy is made also from those of the tame goat,
the sheep, and the deer. Many medicinal virtues
also were said to reside in the blood, fat, gall, and
the concretion sometimes found in the stomach of
this animal called the German bezoar. The fat,
mixed with milk, was said to be good in ulcers of
the lungs. The gall was said to be useful in
strengthening the sight; the stone, which is generally about the size of a walnut, and blackish, was
formerly in great request for having the same virtues
with oriental bezoar. However, in the present
enlightened state of physic, all these medicines are
quite out of repute; and, although we have the virtues

of several medicines procurable from quadrupeds,
yet, except the musk or hartshorn alone, I know
of none in any degree of reputation. It is true, the
fat, the urine, the beak, and even the dung of
various animals, may be found efficacious, where
better remedies are not to be had; but they are far
surpassed by many at present in use, whose operation we know, and whose virtues are confirmed
by repeated experience.

Such are the quadrupeds that more peculiarly
belong to the goat kind. Each of these, in all
probability, can engender and breed with the
other; and were the whole race extinguished,
except any two, these would be sufficient to replenish the world, and continue the kind. Nature,
however, proceeds in her variations by slow and
insensible degrees, and scarcely draws a firm,
distinguished line between any two neighbouring
races of animals whatsoever. Thus it is hard to
discover where the sheep ends and the goat begins;
and we shall find it still harder to fix precisely the
boundaries between the goat kind and the deer.
In all transitions from one kind to the other, there
are to be found a middle race of animals, that seem
to partake of the nature of both, and that can
precisely be referred to neither. That race of
quadrupeds, called the gazelles, are of this kind;
they are properly neither goat nor deer, and yet
they have many of the marks of both; they make
the shade between these two kinds, and fill up the
chasm in nature.

The Gazelles.*

The gazelles, of which there are several kinds, can, with propriety, be referred neither to the goat

[* This tribe goes now under the common denomination of Antelope. Their horns are hollow, seated on a long core, they grow upwards, are annulated or wreathed, and permanent. They have eight front teeth in the lower jaw, and no canine ones. In Dr. Shaw's General Zoology; thirty distinct species are enumerated and described. Their general habits are thus described by Mr. Pennant, " They inhabit, except two or three species, the hottest part of the globe; or at least, those parts of the temperate zone that lie so near the tropics as to form a doubtful climate. None, therefore, except the saiga and the chamois, are to be met with in Europe; and, notwithstanding the warmth of South America is suited to their nature, not a single species has yet been discovered in any part of the New World. Their proper climates seem, therefore, to be those of Asia and Africa, where the species are very numerous.

. " As there appears a general agreement in the nature of the species that form this great genus, it will prevent needless repetition to observe, the antelopes are animals generally of a most elegant and active make, of a restless and timid disposition, extremely watchful, of great vivacity, remarkably swift and agile, and most of their boundings so light, so elastic, as to strike the spectator with astonishment. What is very singular is, that they will stop in the midst of their course, gaze a moment at their pursuers, and then resume their flight.

" As the chase of these animals is a favourite amusement with the eastern nations, from that may be collected proofs of the rapid speed of the antelope tribe. The grey-hound, the fleetest of dogs, is usually unequal in the course; and the sportsman is obliged to call in the aid of the falcon, trained for the purpose of seizing on the animal, and impeding its motions, in order to give the dogs an opportunity of taking it. In India and Persia, a species of leopard is made use of in the chase: this being an or the deer; and yet they partake of both natures. Like the goat, they have hollow horns that never fall, which is otherwise in the deer. They have a gall-bladder, which is found in the goat and not in the deer; and, like that animal, they feed rather upon shrubs than grassy pastures. On the other hand, they resemble the roe-buck in size and deli-

animal that takes its prey, not by swiftness of foot, but by the greatness of its spring, by motions similar to those of the antelope: but should the leopard fail in its first essay, the game escapes.

" The fleetness of the Antelope was proverbial in the country it inhabited, even in the earliest times: the speed of Asahel, (2 Sam. 11, 18,) is beautifully compared to that of the tzebi, and the Gadites were said to be as swift as the antelopes upon the mountains. The sacred writers took their similes from such objects as were before the eyes of the people to whom they addressed themselves. There is another instance drawn from the same subject: the disciple raised to life at Joppa was supposed to have been called Tabitha, i. e. Dorcas or the Antelope, from the beauty of her eyes; and to this day, one of the highest compliments that can be paid to female beauty, in the eastern regions, is, you have the eyes of an antelope.

" Some species of antelopes form herds of two or three thousand, while others keep in troops of five or six. They generally reside in hilly countries, though some inhabit plains: they often browse like the goat, and feed on the tender shoots of trees, which gives their flesh an excellent flavour. This is to be understood of those which are taken in the chase; for those which are fattened in houses are far less delicious. The flesh of some species is said to taste of musk, which perhaps depends upon the quality of the plants they feed upon.

" This preface was thought necessary, to point out the difference in nature, between this and the goat kind, with which most systematic writers have classed the antelope: but the antelope forms an intermediate genus and link between the goat and deer; agreeing with the former in the texture of the horns, which have a core in them, and are never cast; and with the latter in elegance of form, and swiftness."]

cacy of form; they have deep pits under the eyes
like that animal; they resemble the roe-buck in the
colour and nature of their hair; they resemble him
in the bunches upon their legs, which only differ in
being upon the fore legs in these, and on the hind
legs in the other. They seem, therefore, to be of
a middle nature between these two kinds; or, to
speak with greater truth and precision, they form a
distinct kind by themselves.

The distinguishing marks of this tribe of animals,
by which they differ both from the goat and deer,
are these: their horns are made differently, being
annulated or ringed round, at the same time that
there are longitudinal depressions running from
the bottom to the point. They have bunches of
hair upon their fore-legs; they have a streak of
black, red, or brown, running along the lower part
of their sides, and three streaks of whitish hair in
the internal side of the ear. These are characters
that none of them are without; besides these, there
are others which, in general, they are found to
have, and which are more obvious to the beholder.
Of all animals in the world, the gazelle has the
most beautiful eye, extremely brilliant, and yet so
meek, that all the eastern poets compare the eyes
of their mistresses to those of this animal. A
gazelle-eyed beauty is considered as the highest
compliment that a lover can pay; and, indeed, the
Greeks themselves thought it no inelegant piece of
flattery to resemble the eyes of a beautiful woman
to those of a cow. The gazelle, for the most part,
is more delicately and finely limbed than even the
roe-buck; its hair is as short, but finer and more
glossy. Its hinder legs are longer than those

before, as in the hare, which gives it greater security
in ascending or descending steep places. Their
swiftness is equal, if not superior to that of the roe;
but as the latter bounds forward, so these run
along in an even uninterrupted course. Most of
them are brown upon the back, white under the
belly, with a black stripe, separating those colours
between. Their tail is of various lengths, but is
all covered with pretty long hair; and their ears
are beautiful, well placed, and terminating in a
point. They all have a cloven hoof, like the
sheep; they all have permanent horns; and the
female has them smaller than the male.

Of these animals, M. Buffon makes twelve
varieties: which, however, is much fewer than
what other naturalists have made them. The first
is the Gazella, properly so called, which is of the
size of the roe-buck, and very much resembling it in
all the proportions of its body, but entirely differing,
as was said, in the nature and fashion of the horns,
which are black and hollow, like those of the ram,
or the goat, and never fall. The second he calls
the Kevel, which is rather less than the former;
its eyes also seem larger; and its horns, instead of
being round, are flatted on the sides, as well in the
male as the female. The third he calls the Corin,
which very much resembles the two former, but
that it is still less than either. Its horns also are
smaller in proportion, smoother than those of the
other two, and the annular prominencies belonging
to the kind are scarcely discernible, and may rather
be called wrinkles than prominencies. Some of
these animals are often seen streaked like the tiger.
These three are supposed to be of the same species.

The fourth he calls the Zeiran, the horns only of
which he has seen ; which, from their size, and the
description of travellers, he supposes to belong to
a larger kind of the gazelle, found in India and
Persia, under that denomination.

The fifth he calls the Koba, and the sixth the
Kob; these two differ from each other only in size,
the former being much larger than the latter.   The
muzzle of these animals is much longer than those
of the ordinary gazelle ;   the head is differently
shaped, and they have no depressions under the
eyes.   The seventh he calls after its Egyptian
name, the Algazel; which is shaped pretty much
like the ordinary gazelle, except that the horns
are much longer, being generally three feet
from the point to the insertion :   whereas, in the
common gazelle, they are not above a foot ; they
are smaller, also, and straighter, till near the extremities, when they turn short, with a very sharp
flexure ;   they are black and smooth, and the
annular prominencies. are scarcely observable.
The eighth is called the Pazan ;   or, by some, the
Bezoar Goat, which greatly resembles the former,
except a small variety in their horns; and also
with this difference, that as the algazel feeds upon
the plains, this is only found in the mountains.
They are both inhabitants of the same countries
and climate; being found in Egypt, Arabia, and
Persia.   This last is the animal famous for that
concretion in the intestines or stomach, called the
Oriental Bezoar, which was once in such repute all
over the world for its medicinal virtues.   The
word bezoar is supposed to take its name either
from the pazan or pazar, which is the animal that

produces it; or from a word in the Arabic language, which signifies antidote, or counter-poison. It is a stone of a glazed blackish colour, found in the stomach, or the intestines of some animal, and brought over to us from the East Indies. Like all other animal concretions, it is found to have a kind of nucleus, or hard substance within, upon which the external coatings were formed; for, upon being sawed through, it is seen to have layer over layer, as in an onion. This nucleus is of various kinds; sometimes the buds of a shrub, sometimes a piece of stone, and sometimes a marcasite. This stone is from the size of an acorn to that of a pigeon's egg; the larger the stone, the more valuable it is held; its price increasing like that of a diamond. There was a time when a stone of four ounces sold in Europe for above two hundred pounds; but, at present, the price is greatly fallen, and they are in very little esteem. The bezoar is of various colours; sometimes of a blood colour, sometimes of a pale yellow, and of all the shades between these two. It is generally glossy, smooth, and has a fragrant smell, like that of ambergrise, probably arising from the aromatic vegetables upon which the animal that produces it feeds. It has been given in vertigoes, epilepsies, palpitations of the heart, colic, jaundice, and, in those places where the dearness and not the value of medicines is consulted, in almost every disorder incident to man. In all, perhaps, it is equally efficacious, acting only as an absorbent powder, and possessing virtues equal to common chalk, or crab's claws. Judicious physicians have therefore discarded it; and this celebrated medicine is now chiefly consumed in countries where the knowledge of nature has been but little advanced. When this medicine was in its highest reputation, many arts were used to adulterate it; and many countries endeavoured to find out a bezoar of their own. Thus we had occidental bezoar, brought from America; German bezoar, which has been mentioned before; cow bezoar, and monkey bezoar. In fact, there is scarcely an animal, except of the carnivorous kinds, that does not produce some of these concretions in the stomach, intestines, kidnies, bladder, and even in the heart. To these ignorance may impute virtues that they do not possess: experience has found but few cures wrought by their efficacy; but it is well known, that they often prove fatal to the animal that bears them. These concretions are generally found in cows, by their practice of licking off their hair, which gathers in the stomach into the shape of a ball, acquires a surprising degree of hardness, and sometimes a polish like leather. They are often as large as a goose-egg; and, when become too large to pass, block up the passage of the food, and the animal dies. The substance of these balls, however, is different from the bezoar mentioned above; being rather a concretion of hair than of stone. There is a bezoar found in the gall-bladder of a boar, and thence called hog bezoar, in very great esteem; but perhaps with as little justice as any of the former. In short, as we have already observed, there is scarcely an animal, or scarcely a part of their bodies, in which concretions are not formed; and it is more than probable, as M. Buffon justly remarks, that the bezoar so much in use formerly,

was not the production of the pazar, or any one
animal only, but that of the whole gazelle kind;
who, feeding upon odoriferous herbs and plants,
gave this admirable fragrance to the accidental
concretions which they were found to produce.
As this medicine, however, is but little used at
present, our curiosity is much abated, as to the
cause of its formation. To return, therefore, to
the varieties in the gazelle tribe, the ninth is called
the Ranguer, and is a native of Senegal. This
differs somewhat in shape and colour from the
rest; but particularly in the shape of its horns,
which are straight to near the points, where they
crook forward pretty much in the same manner
as in the chamois they crook backward. The
tenth variety of the gazelle is the Antelope, so
well known to the English, who have given it the
name. This animal is of the size of a roe-buck,
and resembles the gazelle in many particulars, but
differs in others: it has deeper eye-pits than the
former; the horns are formed differently also,
being about sixteen inches long, almost touching
each other at the bottom, and spreading as they
rise, so as at their tips to be sixteen inches asunder.
They have the annular prominences of their kind,
but not so distinguishable as in the gazelle: however, they have a double flexure, which is very
remarkable, and serves to distinguish them from
all others of their kind. At the root they have a
tuft of hair, which is longer than that of any part
of the body. Like others of the same kind, the
antelope is brown on the back, and white under
the belly; but these colours are not seperated by
the black streak which is to be found in all the

rest of the gazelle kinds. There are different
sorts of this animal, some with larger horns than
others, and others with less. The one which
makes the eleventh variety in the gazelle kind,
M. Buffon calls the Lidme, which has very long
horns; and the other, which is the twelfth and
last, he calls the Indian Antelope, the horns of
which are very small.

To these may be added three or four varieties
more, which it is not easy to tell whether to refer
to the goat or the gazelle, as they equally resemble
both. The first of these is the Bubalus; an
animal that seems to partake of the mixed natures
of the cow, the goat, and the deer. It resembles
the stag in the size and the figure of its body, and
particularly in the shape of its legs. But it has
permanent horns, like the goat; and made entirely
like those of the gazelle kind. It also resembles
that animal in its way of living; however, it differs
in the make of its head, being exactly like the
cow in the length of its muzzle, and in the disposition of the bones of its skull; from which similitude
it has taken its name. This animal has a narrow,
long head: the eyes are placed very high; the
forehead short and narrow; the horns permanent,
about a foot long, black, thick, annulated, and
the rings of the gazelle kind, remarkably large;
its shoulders are very high, and it has a kind
of bunch on them, that terminates at the neck;
the tail is about a foot long, and tufted with hair
at the extremity. The hair of this animal is
remarkable in being thicker at the middle than at
the root; in all other quadrupeds, except the elk
and this, the hair tapers off from the bottom

to the point; but in these, each hair seems to swell in the middle like a nine-pin. The bubalus also resembles the elk in size, and the colour of its skin; but these are the only similitudes between them: as the one has a very large branching head of solid horns that are annually deciduous, the other has black, unbranching, hollow horns, that never fall. The bubalus is common enough in Barbary, and has often been called by the name of the Barbary Cow, from which animal it differs so widely. It partakes pretty much of the nature of the antelope; like that having the hair short, the hide black, the ears pointed, and the flesh good for food.

The second anomalous animal of the goat kind, M. Buffon calls the Condoma. It is supposed to be equal in size to the largest stag, but with hollow horns, like those of the goat kind, and with varied flexures, like those of the antelope. They are above three feet long; and, at their extremities about two feet asunder. All along the back there runs a white list, which ends at the insertion of the tail; another of the same colour crosses this, at the bottom of the neck, which it entirely surrounds: there are two more of the same kind running round the body, one behind the fore legs; and the other running parallel to it before the hinder. The colour of the rest of the body is greyish, except the belly, which is white: it has also a long grey beard; and its legs, though long, are well proportioned.

The third that may be mentioned, he calls the Guiba. It resembles the gazelles in every particular, except in the colour of the belly, which, as

we have seen, is white in them, but in this is of a
deep brown. Its horns, also, are not marked with
annular prominencies, but are smooth and polished.
It is also remarkable for white lists, on a brown
ground, that are disposed along the animal's body,
as if it were covered with a harness. Like the
former, it is a native of Africa.

The African Wild Goat of Grimmius is the
fourth. It is of a dark ash colour; and in the
middle of the head is a hairy tuft, standing upright;
on both sides, between the eyes and the nose,
there are very deep cavities, greater than those
of the other kinds, which contain a yellow, oily
liquor, coagulating into a black substance, that
has a smell between musk and civet. This being
taken away, the liquor again runs out, and
coagulates as before. These cavities have no communication with the eyes, and consequently, this
oozing substance can have nothing of the nature
of tears.

To this we may add the Chevrotin, or little
Guinea Deer, which is the least of all cloven-footed
quadrupeds, and perhaps the most beautiful; its
legs, at the smallest part, are not much thicker
than the shank of a tobacco pipe; it is about seven
inches high, and about twelve from the point of
the nose to the insertion of the tail. It is the
most delicately shaped animal in the world, being
completely formed like a stag in miniature; except
that its horns, when it has any, are more of the
gazelle kind, being hollow and annulated in the
same manner. It has two canine teeth in the upper
jaw; in which respect it differs from all other
animals of the goat or deer kind, and thus makes

a species entirely distinct by itself. This wonderful animal's colour is not less pleasing; the hair, which is short and glossy, being in some of a beautiful yellow, except on the neck and belly, which is white. They are natives of India, Guinea, and the warm climates between the tropics; and are found in great plenty. But though they are amazingly swift for their size, yet the negroes often overtake them in the pursuit, and knock them down with their sticks. They may be easily tamed, and then they become familiar and pleasing; but they are of such delicate constitutions, that they can bear no climate but the hottest; and they always perish with the rigours of ours, when they are brought over. The male in Guinea has horns; the female is without any; as are all the kinds of this animal, to be found either in Java or Ceylon, where they chiefly abound.*

Such is the list of the gazelles; all which pretty nearly resemble the deer in form, and delicacy of

[* The author here has confounded together two animals very distinct in their formation and manners: the pigmy antelope, and the pigmy musk. The former is a native of the hottest parts of Africa, and, like all others of its tribe, is furnished with horns, and wants the canine teeth. It is in height about nine inches, and is said to be so remarkably active in its native regions, as to be able to leap over a wall twelve feet high. Its general colour is a bright bay; the horns are straight, short, strong, pointed, and quite black; the legs are hardly thicker than a quill.

The pigmy musk is a native of many parts of the East Indies. It has no horns, and in the upper jaw there are a pair of projecting tusks or canine teeth; but the most remarkable characteristic by which it may be distinguished from the pigmy antelope, is, that it has no appendicular or false hoofs. In size it is smaller than a domestic cat, and its general colour is a bright bay.]

shape; but have the horns hollow, single, and permanent, like those of the goat. They properly fill up, as has been already observed, the interval between these two kinds of animals: so that it is difficult to tell where the goat ends, and the deer may be said to begin. If we compare the gazelles with each other, we shall find but very slight distinctions between them. The turn or the magnitude of the horns, the different spots on the skin, or a difference of size in each, are chiefly the marks by which their varieties are to be known; but their way of living, their nature, and their peculiar swiftness, all come under one description.

The gazelles are, in general, inhabitants of the warmer climates; and contribute, among other embellishments, to add beauty to those forests that are for ever green. They are often seen feeding in herds, on the sides of the mountains, or in the shade of the woods; and fly all together, upon the smallest approaches of danger. They bound with such swiftness, and are so very shy, that dogs or men vainly attempt to pursue them. They traverse those precipices with ease and safety, which to every quadruped else are quite impracticable; nor can any animals, but of the winged kind, overtake them. Accordingly, in all those countries where they are chiefly found, they are pursued by falcons; and this admirable manner of hunting makes one of the principal amusements of the upper ranks of people all over the East.

The Arabians, Persians, and Turks, breed up for this purpose that kind of hawk called the Falcon Gentle, with which, when properly trained, they go forth on horseback among the forests and the mountains, the falcon perching upon the hand of the hunter. Their expedition is conducted with profound silence; their dogs are taught to hang behind; while the men, on the fleetest coursers, look round for the game. Whenever they spy a gazelle at the proper distance, they point the falcon to its object, and encourage it to pursue. The falcon, with the swiftness of an arrow, flies to the animal; that, knowing its danger, endeavours, but too late, to escape. The falcon soon coming up with its prey, fixes its talons, one into the animal's cheek, the other in its throat, and deeply wounds it. On the other hand, the gazelle attempts to escape, but is generally wounded too deeply to run far. The falcon clings with the utmost perseverance, nor ever leaves its prey till it falls; upon which the hunters from behind approaching, take up both, and reward the falcon with the blood of the spoil. They also teach the young ones, by applying them to the dead animal's throat, and accustoming them betimes to fix upon that particular part; for if it should happen that the falcon fixed upon any other part of the gazelle, either its back or its haunches, the animal would easily escape among the mountains, and the hunter would also lose his falcon.

They sometimes also hunt these animals with the ounce. This carnivorous and fierce creature being made tame and domestic, generally sits on horseback behind the hunter, and remains there with the utmost composure, until the gazelle is shown; it is then that it exerts all its arts and fierceness; it does not at once fly at its prey, but

approaches slily, turning and winding about until it
comes within the proper distance, when all at once
it bounds upon the heedless animal, and instantly
kills it, and sucks its blood.   If, on the other
hand, it misses its aim, it rests in its place, without attempting to pursue any farther, but seems
ashamed of its own inability.

There is still another way of taking the gazelle,
which seems not so certain nor so amusing as
either of the former.   A tame gazelle is bred up
for this purpose, who is taught to join those of its
kind, wherever it perceives them.   When the
hunter, therefore, perceives a herd of these together, he fixes a noose round the horns of the tame
gazelle, in such a manner, that if the rest but touch
it, they are entangled; and thus prepared he sends
his gazelle among the rest.   The tame animal no
sooner approaches, but the males of the herd instantly sally forth to oppose him; and, in butting
with their horns, are caught in the noose.   In
this, both struggling for some time, fall together
to the ground; and, at last, the hunter coming up,
disengages the one, and kills the other.   Upon
the whole, however, these animals, whatever be
the arts used to pursue them, are very difficult to
be taken.   As they are continually subject to
alarms from carnivorous beasts, or from man, they
keep chiefly in the most solitary and inaccessible
places, and find their only protection from situations of the greatest danger.

The Musk.

CHAP. XVII.

Of the Musk Animal.

.THE more we search into Nature, the more we shall find how little she is known; and we shall more than once have occasion to find, that protracted inquiry is more apt to teach us modesty, than to produce information. Although the number and nature of quadrupeds at first glance seems very well known; yet, when we come to examine closer, we find some with which we are very partially acquainted, and others that are utterly unknown. There is scarcely a cabinet of the curious but what has the spoils of animals, or the horns or the hoofs of quadrupeds, which do not come within former descriptions. There is scarcely a person whose trade is to dress or improve furs, but knows several creatures by their skins; which no naturalist has hitherto had notice of. But of all quadrupeds, there is none so justly the reproach of natural historians, as that which bears the musk. This perfume, so well known to the elegant, and so very useful in the hands of the physician, a medicine that has for more than a century been imported from the East in great quantities, and during all that time has been improving in its reputation, is, nevertheless, so very little understood, that it remains a doubt whether the animal that produces it be a hog, an ox, a goat, or a deer. When an animal with which we are so nearly connected, is so

utterly unknown, how little must we know of
many that are more remote and unserviceable!
Yet naturalists proceed in the same train, enlarg-
ing their catalogues and their names, without endeavouring to find out the nature, and fix the
precise history of those with which we are very
partially acquainted. It is the spirit of the scholars of the present age, to be fonder of increasing
the bulk of our knowledge than its utility; of extending their conquests than of improving their
empire.*

The musk which comes to Europe is brought
over in small bags, about the size of a pigeon's
egg, which, when cut open, appear to contain a
kind of dusky reddish substance, like coagulated
blood, and which, in large quantities, has a very
strong smell; but when mixed and diffused, becomes a very agreeable perfume. Indeed, no substance now known in the world has a stronger or a

[* The musk is a family of quadrupeds, whose form and
manner have, till lately, remained in much obscurity. The
number of species already known, amounts to seven. They inhabit warm climates, and, like other mountain quadrupeds, wander
in places the most difficult of access, are possessed of powers of
great activity, and when pursued take refuge among the highest
summits. The well-known perfume called musk is contained in
an oval receptacle, hardly as large as an egg, hanging from the
middle of the abdomen, and is peculiar to the male. The species
from which this is procured, is the musk of Thibet, an animal
about the size of a small roe-buck, measuring about three feet
three inches in length, and about two feet three inches in height.
The tail is so short, as to be hardly visible. The general colour
is a deep iron grey. The ears are large, and the upper jaw is
considerably longer than the lower, and is furnished on each side
with an incurved tusk, extending nearly two inches beyond the
mouth; these tusks are sharp-edged on their inner side.]

more permanent smell. A grain of musk perfumes a whole room; and its odour continues for some days, without diminution. But in a larger quantity it continues for years together; and seems scarcely wasted in its weight, although it has filled the atmosphere to a great distance with its parts. It is particularly used in medicine, in nervous and hysteric disorders; and is found, in such cases, to be the most powerful remedy now in use: however, the animal that furnishes this admirable medicine has been very variously described, and is known but very imperfectly.

The description given of this animal by Grew, is as follows. The musk animal is properly neither of the goat nor deer kind, for it has no horns, and it is uncertain whether it ruminates or not; however, it wants the four teeth in the upper jaw, in the same manner as in ruminating animals; but, at the same time, it has tusks like those of a hog. It is three feet six inches in length, from the head to the tail; and the head is above half a foot long. The fore part of the head is like that of a greyhound; and the ears are three inches long, and erect, like those of a rabbit; but the tail is not above two inches. It is cloven-footed, like beasts of the goat kind; the hair on the head and legs is half an inch long, on the belly an inch and a half, and on the back and buttocks three inches, and proportionably thicker than in any other animal. It is brown and white alternately, from the root to the point; on the head and thighs it is brown, but under the belly and tail white, and a little curled, especially on the back and belly. On each side of the lower jaw, under the corners of the mouth, there is a tuft of thick hair, which is short and hard, and about three quarters of an inch long. The hair, in general, of this animal, is remarkable for its softness and fine texture; but what distinguishes it particularly are the tusks, which are an inch and a half long, and turn back in the form of a hook; and more particularly the bag which contains the musk, which is three inches long, two broad, and stands out from the belly an inch and a half. It is a very fearful animal, and, therefore, it has long ears; and the sense of hearing is so quick, that it can discover an enemy at a great distance.

After so long and circumstantial a description of this animal, its nature is but very little known; nor has any anatomist as yet examined its internal structure, or been able to inform us whether it be a ruminant animal, or one of the hog kind; how the musk is formed, or whether those bags in which it comes to us be really belonging to the animal, or are only the sophistications of the venders. Indeed, when we consider the immense quantities of this substance which are consumed in Europe alone, not to mention the East, where it is in still greater repute than here, we can hardly suppose that any one animal can furnish the supply; and particularly when it must be killed before the bag can be obtained. We are told, it is true, that the musk is often deposited by the animal upon trees and stones, against which it rubs itself when the quantity becomes uneasy; but it is not in that form which we receive it; but always in what seems to be its own natural bladder. Of these, Taverner brought home near two thousand in one year; and

as the animal is wild, so many must, during that
space, have been hunted and taken. But as the
creature is represented very shy, and as it is found
but in some particular provinces of the East, the
wonder is how its bag should be so cheap, and furnished in such great plenty. The bag in common
does not cost (if I do not forget) above a crown
by retail, and yet this is supposed the only one belonging to the animal; and for the obtaining of
which, it must have been hunted and killed. The
only way of solving this difficulty, is to suppose
that these bags are, in a great measure, counterfeit,
taken from some other animal, or from some part
of the same, filled with its blood, and a very little
of the perfume, but enough to impregnate the rest
with a strong and permanent odour. It comes to
us from different parts of the East; from China,
Tonquin, Bengal, and often from Muscovy: that
of Thibet is reckoned the best, and sells for fourteen shillings an ounce; that of Muscovy the
worst, and sells but for three; the odour of this,
though very strong at first, being quickly found
to evaporate.

Musk was some years ago in the highest request
as a perfume, and but little regarded as a medicine;
but at present its reputation is totally changed;
and having been found of great benefit in physic,
it is but little regarded for the purposes of elegance. It is thus that things which become necessary, cease to continue pleasing; and the con-
sciousness of their use, destroys their power of
administering delight.

CHAP. XVIII.

Animals of the Deer Kind.*

IF we compare the stag and the bull, as to shape
·and form, no two animals can be more unlike; and
yet, if we examine their internal structure, we shall
find a striking similitude between them. Indeed,
their differences, except to a nice observer, will
scarcely be perceivable. All of the deer kind want
the gall-bladder; their kidneys are formed differently; their spleen is also proportionably larger;
their tail is shorter; and their horns, which are
solid, are renewed every year. Such are the slight
·internal discriminations between two animals, one
of which is among the swiftest, and the other the
heaviest of the brute creation.

The stag is one of those innocent and peaceable
animals that seem made to embellish the forest, and
animate the solitudes of nature. The easy elegance of his form, the lightness of his motions,
those large branches that seem made rather for the

[* The quadrupeds of this tribe have horns which are solid
and branched: they are renewed every year, and when young
are clothed with a fine velvety vascular skin, which falls off
when the horns have attained their full size. In the lower jaw
they have eight front teeth; and are generally destitute of canine
teeth: but sometimes a single one is found on each side in the
upper jaw. There are about fourteen distinct species. They
are all extremely active, inhabiting chiefly woods and neglected
situations; and in fighting not only make use of their horns, but
stamp furiously with the fore feet.]

ornament of his head than its defence, the size, the
strength, and the swiftness of this beautiful creature,
all sufficiently rank him among the first of quadrupeds, among the most noted objects of human
curiosity.

The Stag, or Hart, whose female is called a
hind, and the young a *calf*, differs in size and
in horns from a fallow-deer. He is much larger,
and his horns are round; whereas, in the fallow
kind they are broad and palmated. By these the
animal's age is known. The first year, the stag
has no horns, but a horny excrescence, which is
short, rough, and covered with a thin hairy skin.
The next year the horns are single and straight;
the third year they have two antlers, three the
fourth, four the fifth, and five the sixth; this
number is not always certain, for sometimes there
are more, and often less. When arrived at the
sixth year, the antlers do not always increase;
and, although the number may amount to six or
seven on each side, yet the animal's age is then
estimated rather from the size of the antlers, and
the thickness of the branch which sustains them,
than from their variety.

These horns, large as they seem, are, notwithstanding, shed every year, and new ones come in
their place. The old horns are of a firm, solid
texture, and usually employed in making handles
for knives and other domestic utensils. But, while
young, nothing can be more soft or tender; and
the animal, as if conscious of his own imbecility,
at those times, instantly upon shedding his former
horns, retires from the rest of his fellows, and
hides himself in solitudes and thickets, never ven-

turing out to pasture, except by night. During
this time, which most usually happens in the
spring, the new horns are very painful, and have
a quick sensibility of any external impression.
The flies also are extremely troublesome to him.
When the old horn is fallen off, the new does not
begin immediately to appear; but the bones of
the skull are seen covered only with a transparent
periosteum, or skin, which, as anatomists teach
us, covers the bones of all animals. After a short
time, however, this skin begins to swell, and to
form a soft tumour, which contains a great deal
of blood, and which begins to be covered with a
downy substance that has the feel of velvet, and
appears nearly of the same colour with the rest of
the animal's hair. This tumour every day buds
forward from the point like the graft of a tree;
and, rising by degrees from the head, shoots out
the antlers on either side, so that, in a few days,
in proportion as the animal is in condition, the
whole head is completed. However, as was said
above, in the beginning, its consistence is very
soft, and has a sort of bark, which is no more
than a continuation of the integument of the skull.
It is velveted and downy, and every where furnished with blood-vessels, that supply the growing
horns with nourishment. As they creep along
the sides of the branches, the print is marked
over the whole surface; and the larger the blood-
vessels, the deeper these marks are found to be:
from hence arises the inequality of the surface of
the deer's horns; which, as we see, are furrowed
all along the sides, the impressions diminishing
towards the point, where the substance is as smooth

and as solid as ivory. But it ought to be observed, that this substance, of which the horns are composed, begins to harden at the bottom while the upper part remains soft, and still continues growing; from whence it appears that the horns grow differently in deer from those of sheep or cows; in which they are always seen to increase from the bottom. However, when the whole head has received its full growth, the extremities then begin to acquire their solidity; the velvet covering or bark, with its blood-vessels, dry up, and then begin to fall; and this the animal hastens, by rubbing its antlers against every tree it meets. In this manner, the whole external surface being stripped off by degrees, at length the whole head acquires its complete hardness, expansion, and beauty.

It would be a vain task to inquire into the cause of the animal production of these horns; it is sufficient to observe, that if a stag be castrated when its horns are fallen off, they will never grow again; and, on the contrary, if the same operation is performed when they are on, they will never fall off. If only one of his testicles is taken out, he will want the horn on that side; if one of the testicles only be tied up, he will want the horn of the opposite side. The increase of their provision also tends to facilitate the growth and the expansion of the horns; and M. Buffon thinks it possible to retard their growth entirely, by greatly retrenching their food.* As a proof of this, nothing can be more obvious than the difference

* Buffon, vol. xi. p. 115.

between a stag bred in fertile pastures and undisturbed by the hunter, and one often pursued and
ill nourished. The former has his head expanded,
his antlers numerous, and the branches thick;
the latter has but few antlers, the traces of the
blood-vessels upon them are but slight, and the
expansion but little. The beauty and size of their
horns, therefore, mark their strength and their
vigour; such of them as are sickly, or have been
wounded, never shooting out that magnificent
profusion so much admired in this animal. Thus
the horns may, in every respect, be resembled to
a vegetable substance, grafted upon the head of
an animal. Like a vegetable they grow from the
extremities; like a vegetable they are for a while
covered with a bark that nourishes them; like a
vegetable they have their annual production and
decay; and a strong imagination might suppose
that the leafy productions on which the animal
feeds, go once more to vegetate in his horns.*

The stag is usually a twelvemonth old before
the horns begin to appear, and then a single
branch is all that is seen for the year ensuing.
About the beginning of spring, all of this kind
are seen to shed their horns, which fall off of
themselves; though sometimes the animal assists
the efforts of nature, by rubbing them against a
tree. It seldom happens that the branches on
both sides fall off at the same time, there often
being two or three days between the dropping of
the one and the other. The old stags usually

---

* M. Buffon has supposed something like this. Vid.
passim.

shed their horns first: which generally happens
towards the latter end of February, or the beginning of March; those of the second head, (namely,
such as are between five and six years old,) shed
their horns about the middle or latter end of
March; those still younger, in the month of
April; and the youngest of all, not till the middle,
or the latter end of May; they generally shed
them in pools of water, whither they retire
from the heat: and this has given rise to the opinion of their always hiding their horns. These
rules, though true in general, are yet subject
to many variations; and universally it is known
that a severe winter retards the shedding of the
horns.

The horns of the stag generally increase in
thickness, and in height from the second year of
its age to the eighth. In this state of perfection
they continue during the vigour of life: but as
the animal grows old, the horns feel the impressions
of age, and shrink like the rest of the body.
No branch bears more than twenty or twenty-two
antlers, even in the highest state of vigour;
and the number is subject to great variety; for
it happens that the stag at one year has either
less or more than the year preceding, in proportion
to the goodness of his pasture, or the continuance
of his security, as these animals seldom thrive
when often roused by the hunters. The horns
are also found to partake of the nature of the soil;
in the more fertile pastures they are large and
tender; on the contrary, in the barren soil they
are hard, stunted, and brittle.

As soon as the stags have shed their horns, they

separate from each other, and seek the plainer
parts of the country, remote from every other
animal, which they are utterly unable to oppose.
They then walk with their heads stooping down,
to keep their horns from striking against the
branches of the trees above. In this state of imbecility they continue near three months before
their heads have acquired their full growth and
solidity; and then, by rubbing them against the
branches of every thicket, they at length clear
them of the skin which had contributed to their
growth and nourishment. It is said by some that
the horn takes the colour of the sap of the tree
against which it is rubbed; and that some thus
become red, when rubbed against the heath; and
others brown, by rubbing against the oak; this,
however, is a mistake, since stags kept in parks
where there are no trees, have a variety in the
colour of their horns, which can be ascribed to
nothing but nature.

A short time after they have furnished their
horns, they begin to feel the impressions of the
rut, or the desire of copulation. The old ones
are the most forward; and about the end of
August, or the beginning of September, they quit
their thickets, and return to the mountain in order
to seek the hind, to whom they call with a
loud tremulous note. At this time their neck is
swollen; they appear bold and furious; fly from
country to country; strike with their horns against
the trees and other obstacles, and continue restless and fierce until they have found the female;
who at first flies from them, but is at last compelled and overtaken. When two stags contend

for the same female, how timorous soever they
may appear at other times, they then seem agitated
with an uncommon degree of ardour. They
paw up the earth, menace each other with their
horns, bellow with all their force, and striking in
a desperate manner against each other, seem determined upon death or victory. This combat
continues till one of them is defeated or flies; and
it often happens that the victor is obliged to fight
several of those battles before it remains undisputed master of the field. The old ones are
generally the conquerors upon these occasions, as
they have more strength and greater courage : and
these are also preferred by the hind to the young
ones, as the latter are more feeble and less ardent.
However, they are all equally inconstant, keeping
to the female but a few days, and then seeking
out for another, not to be enjoyed, perhaps, without
a repetition of their former danger.

In this manner, the stag continues to range
from one to the other for about three weeks, the
time the rut continues ; during which he scarcely
eats, sleeps, or rests, but continues to pursue, to
combat, and to enjoy. At the end of this period
of madness, for such in this animal it seems to be,
the creature that was before fat, sleek, and glossy,
becomes lean, feeble, and timid. He then retires
from the herd to seek plenty and repose: he frequents the side of the forest, and chooses the
most nourishing pastures, remaining there till his
strength is renewed. Thus is his whole life passed
in the alternations of plenty and want, of corpu-
lence and inanition, of health and sickness,
without having his constitution much affected by

the violence of the change. As he is above five
years coming to perfection, he lives about forty
years; and it is a general rule, that every animal
lives about seven or eight times the number of
years which it continues to grow. What, therefore, is reported concerning the life of this animal,
has arisen from the credulity of ignorance: some
say, that a stag having been taken in France,
with a collar, on which were written these words,
"Cæsar hoc me donavit;" this was interpreted
of Julius Cæsar; but it is not considered that Cæsar
is a general name for kings; and that one of the
emperors of Germany, who are always styled Cæsars,
might have ordered the inscription.

This animal may differ in the term of his life
according to the goodness of his pasture, or the
undisturbed repose he happens to enjoy. These
are advantages that influence not only his age, but
his size and his vigour. The stags of the plains,
the vallies, and the little hills, which abound in
corn and pasture, are much more corpulent and
much taller than such as are bred on the rocky
waste, or the heathy mountain. The latter are
low, small, and meagre, incapable of going so
swift as the former, although they are found to
hold out much longer. They are also more artful
in evading the hunters; their horns are generally
black and short, while those of the lowland stags
are reddish and flourishing; so that the animal
seems to increase in beauty and stature in proportion to the goodness of the pasture, which he enjoys
in security.

The usual colour of the stag in England was
red; nevertheless, the greater number in other

¶

countries are brown. There are some few that
are white; but these seem to have obtained this
colour in a former state of domestic tameness.
Of all the animals that are natives of this climate,
there are none that have such a beautiful eye as
the stag; it is sparkling, soft, and sensible. His
senses of smelling and hearing are in no less perfection. When he is in the least alarmed, he lifts
the head and erects the ears, standing for a few
minutes as if in a listening posture. Whenever
he ventures upon some unknown ground, or quits
his native covering, he first stops at the skirt of
the plain to examine all around: he next turns
against the wind to examine by the smell if there
be an enemy approaching. If a person should
happen to whistle, or call out at a distance, the
stag is seen to stop short in his slow measured
pace, and gazes upon the stranger with a kind of
awkward admiration: if the cunning animal perceives neither dogs nor fire-arms preparing against
him, he goes forward, quite unconcerned, and
slowly proceeds without offering to fly. Man is
not the enemy he is most afraid of; on the contrary, he seems to be delighted with the sound of
the shepherd's pipe; and the hunter sometimes
makes use of that instrument to allure the poor
animal to his destruction.

The stag eats slowly, and is very delicate in the
choice of his pasture. When he has eaten a sufficiency, he then retires to the covert of some
thicket to chew the cud in security. His rumi-
nation, however, seems performed with much
greater difficulty than with the cow or sheep; for
the grass is not returned from the first stomach

without much straining, and a kind of hiccup, which is easily perceived during the whole time it continues. This may proceed from the greater length of his neck, and the narrowness of the passage, all those of the cow and the sheep kind having it much wider.

This animal's voice is much stronger, louder, and more tremulous, in proportion as he advances in age; in the time of rut it is even terrible. At that season he seems so transported with passion that nothing obstructs his fury; and, when at bay, he keeps the dogs off with great intrepidity. Some years ago, William Duke of Cumberland caused a tiger and a stag to be inclosed in the same area; and the stag made so bold a defence, that the tiger was at last obliged to fly. The stag seldom drinks in the winter, and still less in the spring, while the plants are tender and covered over with dew. It is in the heat of summer, and during the time of rut, that he is seen constantly frequenting the sides of rivers and lakes, as well to slake his thirst as to cool his ardour. He swims with great ease and strength, and best at those times when he is fattest, his fat keeping him buoyant, like oil upon the surface of the water. During the time of rut he even ventures out to sea, and swims from one island to another, although there may be some leagues distance between them.

The cry of the hind, or female, is not so loud as that of the male, and is never excited but by apprehension for herself or her young. It need scarcely be mentioned that she has no horns, or that she is more feeble or unfit for hunting than the male. When once they have conceived, they

separate from the males, and then they both herd
apart. The time of gestation continues between
eight and nine months, and they generally produce
but one at a time. Their usual season for bringing
forth is about the month of May, or the beginning
of June, during which they take great care to hide
their young in the most obscure thickets. Nor is
this precaution without reason, since almost every
creature is then a formidable enemy. The eagle,
the falcon, the osprey, the wolf, the dog, and all
the rapacious family of the cat kind, are in continual employment to find out her retreat. But,
what is more unnatural still, the stag himself is a
professed enemy, and she is obliged to use all her
arts to conceal her young from him, as from the
most dangerous of her pursuers. At this season,
therefore, the courage of the male seems transferred
to the female: she defends her young against her
less formidable opponents by force; and when
pursued by the hunter, she ever offers herself to
mislead him from the principal object of her concern. She flies before the hounds for half the day,
and then returns to her young, whose life she has
thus preserved at the hazard of her own. The calf,
for so the young of this animal is called, never
quits the dam during the whole summer; and in
winter, the hind, and all the males under a year
old, keep together, and assemble in herds, which
are more numerous in proportion as the season is
more severe. In the spring they separate; the
hinds to bring forth, while none but the year olds
remain together; these animals are, however, in
general fond of herding and grazing in company;
it is danger or necessity alone that separates them.

The dangers they have to fear from other animals, are nothing when compared to those from man. The men of every age and nation have made the chase of the stag one of the most favourite pursuits; and those who first hunted from necessity, have continued it for amusement. In our own country, in particular, hunting was ever esteemed as one of the principal diversions of the great.*
At first, indeed, the beasts of chase had the whole island for their range, and knew no other limits than those of the ocean.

The Roman jurisprudence, which was formed on the manners of the first ages, established it as a law, that, as the natural right of things which have no master belongs to the first possessor, wild beasts, birds, and fishes, are the property of whosoever could first take them. But the northern barbarians, who over-ran the Roman empire, bringing with them the strongest relish for this amusement, and, being now possessed of more easy means of subsistence from the lands they had conquered, their chiefs and leaders began to appropriate the right of hunting, and, instead of a natural right to make it a Royal one. When the Saxon kings, therefore, had established themselves into a heptarchy, the chases were reserved by each sovereign for his own particular amusement. Hunting and war, in those uncivilized ages, were the only employment of the great. Their active, but uncultivated minds were susceptible of no pleasures but those of a violent kind, such as gave exercise to their bodies, and prevented the uneasiness of

* British Zoology.

thinking. But as the Saxon kings only appropriated those lands to 'the business of the chase which were unoccupied before, so no individuals received any injury. But it was otherwise when the Norman kings were settled upon the throne. The passion for hunting was then carried to an excess, and every civil right was involved in general ruin. This ardour for hunting was stronger than the consideration of religion, even in a superstitious age. The village communities, nay, even the most sacred edifices, were thrown down, and all turned into one vast waste, to make room for animals, the object of a lawless tyrant's pleasure. Sanguinary laws were enacted to preserve the game ; and, in the reigns of William Rufus and Henry the First, it was less criminal to destroy one of the human species than a beast of chase. Thus it continued while the Norman line filled the throne ; but when the Saxon line was restored, under Henry the Second, the rigour of the forest laws was softened. The barons also for a long time imitated the encroachments, as well as the amusements of the monarch ; but when property became more equally divided, by the introduction of arts and industry, these extensive hunting grounds became more limited ; and as tillage and husbandry increased, the beasts of chase were obliged to give way to others more useful to the community. Those vast tracts of land, before dedicated to hunting, were then contracted ; and, in proportion as the useful arts gained ground, they protected and encouraged the labours of the industrious, and repressed the licentiousness of the sportsman. It is, therefore, among the subjects of a despotic government only

that these laws remain in full force, where large
wastes lie uncultivated for the purposes of hunting,
where the husbandman can find no protection from
the invasions of his lord, or the continual depredations of those animals which he makes the objects
of his pleasure.

In the present cultivated state of this country,
therefore, the stag is unknown in its wild natural
state ; and such of them as remain among us are
kept, under the name of red deer, in parks among
the fallow deer ; but they are become less common
than formerly : its excessive viciousness during
the rutting season, and the badness of its flesh,
inducing most people to part with the species.
The few that still remain wild are to be found on
the moors that border on Cornwall and Devon-
shire ; and in Ireland, on most of the large mountains of that country.

In England, the hunting the stag and the buck
are performed in the same manner ; the animal is
driven from some gentleman's park, and then hunted
through the open country. But those who pursue
the wild animal have a much higher object, as well
as a greater variety in the chase. To let loose
a creature that was already in our possession, in
order to catch it again, is, in my opinion, but a
poor pursuit, as the reward, when obtained, is only
what we before had given away. But to pursue an
animal that owns no proprietor, and which he that
first seizes may be said to possess, has something
in it that seems at least more rational ; this re-
wards the hunter for his toil, and seems to repay
his industry. Besides, the superior strength and
swiftness of the wild animal prolongs the amuse-

ment; it is possessed of more various arts to escape the hunter, and leads him to precipices where the danger ennobles the chase. In pursuing the animal let loose from a park, as it is unused to danger, it is but little versed in the stratagems of escape; the hunter follows as sure of overcoming, and feels none of those alternations of hope and fear which arise from the uncertainty of success. But it is otherwise with the mountain stag: having spent his whole life in a state of continual apprehension; having frequently been followed, and as frequently escaped, he knows every trick to mislead, to confound, or intimidate his pursuers; to stimulate their ardour, and enhance their success.

Those who hunt this animal have their peculiar terms for the different objects of their pursuit. The professors in every art take a pleasure in thus employing a language known only to themselves, and thus accumulate words which to the ignorant have the appearance of knowledge. In this manner, the stag is called the first year, a *calf*, or *hind calf*; the second year, a *knobber*; the third a *brock*; the fourth, a *staggard*; the fifth, a *stag*; the sixth, a *hart*. The female is called a *hind*; the first year she is a *calf*; the second, a *hearse*; the third, a *hind*. This animal is said to *harbour* in the place where he resides. When he cries, he is said to *bell*; the print of his hoof is called the *slot*; his tail is called the *single*; his excrement the *fumet*; his horns are called his *head*: when simple, the first year they are called *broches*; the third year, *spears*; the fourth year, that part which bears the antlers is called the *beam*, and the little impression upon its surface, *glitters*; those which rise from the crust of the *beam*, are called *pearls*. The antlers also have distinct names; the first that branches off is called the *antler*; the second the *sur-antler*; all the rest which grow afterwards, till you come to the top, which is called the *crown*, are called *royal antlers*. The little buds about the tops are called *croches*. The impression on the place where the stag has lain, is called the *layer*. If it be in covert or a thicket, it is called his *harbour*. Where a deer has passed into a thicket, leaving marks whereby his bulk may be guessed, it is called an *entry*. When they cast their heads, they are said to *mew*. When they rub their heads against trees, to bring off the peel of their horns, they are said to *fray*. When a stag hard hunted takes to swimming in the water, he is said to *go sail*; when he turns his head against the hounds, he is said to *bay*; and when the hounds pursue upon the scent, until they have unharboured the stag, they are said to *draw on the slot*.

Such are but a few of the many terms used by hunters in pursuing of the stag, most of which are now laid aside, or in use only among gamekeepers. The chase, however, is continued in many parts of the country where the red deer is preserved, and still makes the amusement of such as have not found out more liberal entertainments. In those few places where the animal is perfectly wild, the amusement, as was said above, is superior. The first great care of the hunter, when he leads out his hounds to the mountain side, where the deer are generally known to harbour, is to make choice

of a proper stag to pursue. His ambition is to
unharbour the largest and the boldest of the whole
herd; and for this purpose he examines the track,
if there be any, which if he finds long and large,
he concludes that it must have belonged to a stag,
and not a hind, the print of whose foot is rounder.
Those marks also which he leaves on trees, by the
rubbing of his horns, show his size, and point him
out as the proper object of pursuit. Now to seek
out a stag in his haunt, it is to be observed, that
he changes his manner of feeding every month.
From the conclusion of rutting time, which is in
November, he feeds on heaths and broomy places.
In December they herd together, and withdraw
into the strength of the forests, to shelter themselves from the severer weather, feeding on holm,
elder trees, and brambles. The three following
months they leave herding, but keep four or five
in a company, and venture out to the corners of
the forest, where they feed on winter pasture;
sometimes making their incursions into the neighbouring corn-fields, to feed upon the tender shoots,
just as they peep above ground. In April and
May they rest in thickets and shady places, and
seldom venture forth; unless roused by approaching danger. In September and October their
annual ardour returns; and then they leave the
thickets, boldly facing every danger, without any
certain place for food or harbour. When by a
knowledge of these circumstances, the hunter has
found out the residence and the quality of his
game, his next care is to uncouple and cast off his
hounds in the pursuit: these no sooner perceive
the timorous animal that flies before them, but

§

they altogether open in full cry, pursuing rather by
the scent than the view, encouraging each other to
continue the chase, and tracing the flying animal
with the most amazing sagacity.   The hunters
also are not less ardent in their speed on horseback,
cheering up the dogs, and directing them where to
pursue.   On the other hand the stag, when unharboured, flies at first with the swiftness of the
wind, leaving his pursuers several miles in the rear;
and at length having gained his former coverts, and
no longer hearing the cries of the dogs and men
that he had just left behind, he stops, gazes round
him, and seems to recover his natural tranquillity.
But this calm is of short duration, for his inveterate pursuers slowly and securely trace him along,
and he once more hears the approaching destruction from behind.   He again, therefore, renews his
efforts to escape, and again leaves his pursuers at
almost the former distance; but this second effort
makes him more feeble than before, and when they
come up a second time he is unable to outstrip them
with equal velocity.   The poor animal now, therefore, is obliged to have recourse to all his little arts
of escape, which sometimes, though but seldom,
avail him.   In proportion as his strength fails him,
the ardour of his pursuers is inflamed; he tracks
more heavily on the ground, and this increasing
the strength of the scent, redoubles the cries of
the hounds and enforces their speed.   It is then
that the stag seeks for refuge among the herd, and
tries every artifice to put off some other head for
his own.   Sometimes he will send forth some little
deer in his stead, in the mean time lying close
himself that the hounds may overshoot him.   He

will break into one thicket after another to find deer, rousing them, gathering them together, and endeavouring to put them upon the tracks he has made. His old companions, however, with a true spirit of ingratitude, now all forsake and shun him with the most watchful industry, leaving the unhappy creature to take his fate by himself. Thus abandoned of his fellows, he again tries other arts by doubling and crossing in some hard beaten highway, where the scent is least perceivable. He now also runs against the wind, not only to cool himself, but the better to hear the voice, and judge of the distance of his implacable pursuers. It is now easily perceivable how sorely he is pressed, by his manner of running, which from the bounding easy pace with which he begun, is converted into a short and stiff manner of going; his mouth also is black and dry, without foam on it; his tongue hangs out; and the tears, as some say, are seen starting from his eyes. His last refuge, when every other method of safety has failed him, is to take the water, and to attempt an escape by crossing whatever lake or river he happens to approach. While swimming, he takes all possible care to keep in the middle of the stream, lest, by touching the bough of a tree, or the herbage on the banks, he may give scent to the hounds. He is also ever found to swim against the stream; whence the huntsmen have made it into a kind of proverb, *That he that would his chase find, must up with the river and down with the wind.* On this occasion too he will often cover himself under water, so as to show nothing but the tip of his nose. Every resource and every art being at length ex-

hausted, the poor creature tries the last remains
of his strength, by boldly opposing those enemies
he cannot escape; he therefore faces the dogs and
men, threatens with his horns, guards himself on
every side, and for some time stands at bay. In
this manner, quite desperate, he furiously aims at
the first dog or man that approaches; and it often
happens that it does not die unrevenged. At that
time, the more prudent, both of the dogs and men,
seem willing to avoid him; but the whole pack
quickly coming up, he is soon surrounded and
brought down, and the huntsman winds a *treble
mort*, as it is called, with his horn.

Such is the manner of pursuing this animal in
England; but every country has a peculiar method
of its own, adapted either to the nature of the
climate, or the face of the soil. The ancient
manner was very different from that practised at
present; they used their dogs only to find out the
game, but not to rouse it. Hence they were not
curious as to the music of their hounds, or the
composition of their pack; the dog that opened
before he had discovered his game, was held in no
estimation. It was their usual manner silently to
find out the animal's retreat, and surround it with
nets and engines, then to drive him up with all
their cries, and thus force him into the toils which
they had previously prepared.

In succeeding times the fashion seemed to alter;
and particularly in Sicily, the manner of hunting
was as follows.* The nobles and gentry being
informed which way a herd of deer passed, gave

* Pier. Hieroglyph. lib. vii. cap. 6.

notice to one another, and appointed a day of hunting. For this purpose, every one was to bring a cross-bow, or a long bow, and a bundle of staves, shod with iron, the heads bored, with a cord passing through them all. Thus provided, they came to where the herd continued grazing, and casting themselves about in a large ring, surrounded the deer on every side. Then each taking his stand, unbound his faggot, set up his stake, and tied the end of the cord to that of his next neighbour, at the distance of about ten feet one from the other. Between each of these stakes was hung a bunch of crimson feathers, and so disposed, that with the least breath of wind they would whirl round, and preserve a sort of fluttering motion. This done, the persons who set up the staves withdrew, and hid themselves in the neighbouring coverts; then the chief huntsman, entering with his hounds within the lines, roused the game with a full cry. The deer, frighted, and flying on all sides, upon approaching the lines, were scared away by the fluttering of the feathers, and wandered about within this artificial paling, still awed by the shining and fluttering plumage that encircled their retreat: the huntsman, however, still pursuing, and calling every person by name, as he passed by their stand, commanded him to shoot the first, third, or sixth, as he pleased; and if any of them missed, or singled out another than that assigned him, it was considered as a most shameful mischance. In this manner, however, the whole herd was at last destroyed; and the day concluded with mirth and feasting.

The stags of China are of a particular kind, for

they are no taller than a common house-dog ; and
hunting them is one of the principal diversions of
the great. Their flesh, while young, is exceed-
ingly good, but when they arrive at maturity,
it begins to grow hard and tough: however, the
tongue, the muzzle, and the ears, are in particular esteem among that luxurious people. Their
manner of taking them is singular enough ; they
carry with them the heads of some of the females
stuffed, and learn exactly to imitate their cry:
upon this the male does not fail to appear, and
looking on all sides, perceives the head, which is
all that the hunter, who is himself concealed, discovers. Upon their nearer approach, the whole
company rise, surround, and often take him alive.

There are very few varieties in the red deer of
this country ; and they are mostly found of the
same size and colour. But it is otherwise in different parts of the world, where they are seen to
differ in form, in size, in horns, and in colour.

The stag of Corsica is a very small animal, being
not above half the size of those common among
us. His body is short and thick, his legs short, and
his hair of a dark brown.

There is, in the forests of Germany, a kind of
stag, named by the ancients the Tragelaphus, and
which the natives call the Bran Deer, or the Brown
Deer. This is of a darker colour than the common
stag, of a lighter shade upon the belly, long hair
upon the neck and throat, by which it appears
bearded, like the goat.

There is also a very beautiful stag, which by
some is said to be a native of Sardinia ; but others
(among whom is M. Buffon) are of opinion that

it comes from Africa or the East Indies. He calls
it the Axis, after Pliny; and considers it as making
the shade between the stag and the fallow-deer.
The horns of the axis are round, like those of the
stag: but the form of its body entirely resembles
that of the buck, and the size also is exactly
the same. The hair is of four colours; namely,
sallow, white, black, and grey. The white is
predominant under the belly, on the inside of
the thighs, and the legs. Along the back there
are two rows of spots in a right line; but those
on other parts of the body are very irregular. A
white line runs along each side of this animal,
while the head and neck are grey. The tail is
black above, and white beneath; and the hair upon
it is six inches long.

Although there are but few individuals of the
deer kind, yet the race seems diffused over all
parts of the earth. The new continent of America,
in which neither the sheep, the goat, nor the
gazelle, have been originally bred, nevertheless
produces stags, and other animals of the deer
kind, in sufficient plenty. The Mexicans have a
breed of white stags in their parks, which they call
Stags Royal.* The stags of Canada differ from
ours in nothing except the size of the horns,
which in them is greater; and the direction of
the antlers, which rather turn back, than project
forward, as in those of Europe. The same difference of size that obtains among our stags is also
to be seen in that country; and, as we are informed
by Ruysch, the Americans have brought them

* Buffon, vol. xii. p. 35.

into the same state of domestic tameness that we
have our sheep, goats, or black cattle. They
send them forth in the day-time to feed in the
forests; and at night they return home with the
herdsman who guards them. The inhabitants have
no other milk but what the hind produces; and
use no other cheese but what is made from thence.
In this manner we find, that an animal which
seems made only for man's amusement, may be
easily brought to supply his necessities. Nature
has many stores of happiness and plenty in reserve,
which only want the call of industry to be produced, and now remain as candidates for human
approbation.*

The Fallow-deer.

No two animals can be more nearly allied than
the stag and the fallow-deer.† Alike in form,
alike in disposition, in the superb furniture of
their heads, in their swiftness and timidity; and

[* Dr. Pallas, in his Travels, has described a curious species
called the tail-less deer. It is an inhabitant of the mountainous
parts of Hircania, Russia, and Siberia, frequenting the most
lofty parts of those regions in the summer, but descending in
winter into the plains.

It is something larger than the roe-buck. The colour is
brown, with the outsides of the limbs and under parts of the
body yellowish. The hinder parts of the thighs are white,
forming a large patch on the back of the animal. The space
round the nose and sides of the lower lip are black, but the
tip of the lip is white. It has no tail, but a mere broadish excrescence.]

† Buffon, vol. xii. p. 36.

yet no two animals keep more distinct, or avoid each other with more fixed animosity. They are never seen to herd in the same place, they never engender together, or form a mixed breed; and even in those countries where the stag is common, the buck seems to be entirely a stranger. In short, they both form distinct families; which, though so seemingly near, are still remote; and although with the same habitudes; yet retain an unalterable aversion.

The fallow-deer, as they are much smaller, so they seem of a nature less robust, and less savage than those of the stag kind. They are found but rarely wild in the forests; they are, in general, bred up in parks, and kept for the purposes of hunting, or of luxury, their flesh being preferred to that of any other animal. It need scarcely be mentioned, that the horns of the buck make its principal distinction, being broad and palmated; whereas those of the stag are in every part round. In the one, they are flatted and spread like the palm of the hand; in the other they grow like a tree, every branch being of the shape of the stem that bears it. The fallow-deer also has the tail longer, and the hair lighter than the stag; in other respects, they pretty nearly resemble one another.

The head of the buck, as of all other animals of this kind, is shed every year, and takes the usual time for repairing. The only difference between it and the stag is, that this change happens later in the buck; and its rutting-time, consequently, falls more into the winter. It is not found so furious at this season as the former; nor

does it so much exhaust itself by the violence of
its ardour. It does not quit its natural pastures
in quest of the female, nor does it attack other
animals with indiscriminate ferocity; however,
the males combat for the female among each
other; and it is not without many contests, that
one buck is seen to become master of the whole
herd.

It often happens, also, that a herd of fallow-
deer is seen to divide into two parties, and engage
each other with great ardour and obstinacy.*
They both seem desirous of gaining some favourite
spot of the park for pasture, and of driving the
vanquished party into the coarser and more
disagreeable parts. Each of these factions has
its particular chief: namely, the two oldest and
strongest of the herd. These lead on to the
engagement; and the rest follow under their
direction. These combats are singular enough,
from the disposition and conduct which seems to
regulate their mutual efforts. They attack with
order, and support the assault with courage; they
come to each other's assistance, they retire, they
rally, and never give up the victory upon a single
defeat. The combat is renewed for several days
together; until at length the most feeble side is
obliged to give way, and is content to escape to the
most disagreeable part of the park, where only they
can find safety and protection.

The fallow-deer is easily tamed, and feeds upon
many things which the stag refuses. By this
means it preserves its venison better; and even

* Buffon, vol. xli, p. 36.

after rutting it does not appear entirely exhausted. It continues almost in the same state through the whole year, although there are particular seasons when its flesh is chiefly in esteem. This animal also browzes closer than the stag; for which reason it is more prejudicial among young trees, which it often strips too close for recovery. The young deer eat much faster and more greedily than the old; they seek the female at their second year, and, like the stag, are fond of variety. The doe goes with young about eight months, like the hind; and commonly brings forth one at a time; but they differ in this, that the buck comes to perfection at three, and lives till sixteen; whereas the stag does not come to perfection till seven, and lives till forty.

As this animal is a beast of chase, like the stag, so the hunters have invented a number of names relative to him. The buck is the first year called a *fawn*; the second, a *pricket*; the third, a *sorel*; the fourth, a *sore*; the fifth, a *buck of the first head*; and the sixth, a *great buck*: the female is called a *doe*; the first year a *fawn*; and the second a *tegg*. The manner of hunting the buck is pretty much the same as that of stag-hunting, except that less skill is required in the latter. The buck is more easily roused; it is sufficient to judge by the view, and mark what grove or covert it enters, as it is not known to wander far from thence; nor, like the stag, to change his *layer*, or place of repose. When hard hunted, it takes to some strong hold or covert with which it is acquainted, in the more gloomy parts of the

wood, or the steeps of the mountain; not like
the stag, flying far before the hounds, nor crossing
nor doubling, nor using any of the subtleties
which the stag is accustomed to. It will take
the water when sorely pressed, but seldom a great
river; nor can it swim so long, nor so swiftly,
as the former. In general, the strength, the
cunning, and the courage of this animal, are inferior to those of the stag; and, consequently, it
affords neither so long, so various, nor so obstinate
a chase: besides, being lighter, and not tracking
so deeply, it leaves a less powerful and lasting
scent, and the dogs in the pursuit are more frequently at a fault.

As the buck is a more delicate animal than the
stag, so also is it subject to greater varieties.* We
have in England two varieties of the fallow-deer,
which are said to be of foreign origin: the beautiful spotted kind, which is supposed to have been
brought from Bengal; and the very deep brown
sort, that are now so common in several parts of
this kingdom. These were introduced by king
James the First, from Norway; for, having observed their hardiness, and that they could endure
the winter, even in that severe climate, without
fodder, he brought over some of them into Scotland, and disposed of them among his chases.
Since that time they have multiplied in many
parts of the British empire; and England is now
become more famous for its venison, than any
other country in the world. Whatever pains the

---

* British Zoology.

French have taken to rival us in this particular, the flesh of their fallow-deer, of which they keep but a few, has neither the fatness nor the flavour of that fed upon English pasture.

However, there is scarcely a country in Europe, except far to the northward, in which this animal is a stranger. The Spanish fallow-deer are as large as stags, but of a darker colour, and a more slender neck: their tails are longer than those of ours; they are black above, and white below. The Virginian deer are larger and stronger than ours; with great necks, and their colour inclinable to grey. Other kinds have the hoofs of their hind legs marked outwardly with a white spot; and their ears and tails much longer than the common. One of these has been seen full of white spots, with a black list down the middle of his back. In Guiana, a country of South America, according to Labat, there are deer without horns, which are much less than those of Europe, but resembling them in every other particular. They are very lively, light of course, and excessively fearful; their hair is of a reddish sallow, their heads are small and lean, their ears little, their necks long and arched, the tail short, and the sight piercing. When pursued, they fly into places where no other animal can follow them. The Negroes, who pursue them, stand to watch for them in narrow paths, which lead to the brook or the meadow where they feed; there waiting in the utmost silence, (for the slightest sound will drive them away,) the Negro, when he perceives the animal within reach, shoots, and is happy if he can bring down his game. Their flesh, though seldom fat, is considered as a great delicacy, and the hunter is well rewarded for his trouble.*

The Roe-buck.

The Roe-buck is the smallest of the deer kind known in our climate, and is now almost extinct among us, except in some parts of the highlands of Scotland. It is generally about three feet long, and about two feet high. The horns are from eight to nine inches long, upright, round, and divided into only three branches. The body is covered with very long hair, well adapted to the rigour of its mountainous abode. The lower part of each hair is ash-colour; near the ends is a narrow bar of black, and the points are yellow. The hairs on the face are black, tipped with ash-colour. The ears are long, their insides of a pale yellow,

[* The accurate observer of nature, Mr. White, in his Natural History of Selborne, communicates an extraordinary provision with which these animals are endowed. When they drink, they plunge their noses deep under water, and continue them in that situation a long time: but to obviate any inconvenience which might arise from this kind of immersion, they are furnished with two spiracles or vents; one at the inner corner of each eye, communicating with the nostrils, and which they can open at pleasure. These seem to be highly serviceable to them in the chase, by affording them the means of free respiration; for, without doubt, these additional nostrils are thrown open when they are hard run. Mr. Pennant has likewise observed something analogous to this in the antelope. "This animal," says he, "has also a long slit beneath each eye, which can be opened and shut at pleasure: on holding an orange to one, the creature made the same use of those orifices as of his nostrils, applying them to the fruit, and seeming to smell it through them.]

and covered with long hair. The spaces bordering on the eyes and mouth are black. The chest, belly, and legs, and the inside of the thighs, are of a yellowish white; the rump is of a pure white, and the tail very short. The make of this little animal is very elegant; and its swiftness equals its beauty. It differs from the fallow-deer, in having round horns, and not flatted like theirs. It differs from the stag, in its smaller size, and the proportionable paucity of its antlers: and it differs from all of the goat kind, as it annually sheds its head, and obtains a new one, which none of that kind are ever seen to do.

As the stag frequents the thickest forests, and the sides of the highest mountains, the roe-buck, with humbler ambition, courts the shady thicket, and the rising slope. Although less in size, and far inferior in strength to the stag, it is yet more beautiful, more active, and even more courageous: its hair is always smooth, clean, and glossy; and it frequents only the driest places, and of the purest air. Though but a very little animal, as we have already observed, yet when its young is attacked, it faces even the stag himself, and often comes off victorious.* All its motions are elegant and easy; it bounds without effort, and continues the course with but little fatigue. It is also possessed of more cunning in avoiding the hunter, is more difficult to pursue, and; although its scent is much stronger than that of the stag, it is more frequently found to make good a retreat. It is not with the roe-buck, as with the stag, who never offers to use

* Buffon, vol. xii. p. 75.

art until his strength is beginning to decline; this
more cunning animal, when it finds that its first
efforts to escape are without success, returns upon
its former track, again goes forward, and again
returns, until by its various windings it has entirely
confounded the scent, and joined the last emana-
tions to those of its former course. It then, by a
bound, goes to one side, lies flat upon its belly,
and permits the pack to pass by very near, without
offering to stir.

But the roe-buck differs not only from the stag
in superior cunning, but also in its natural appetites,
its inclinations, and its whole habits of living.
Instead of herding together, these animals live in
separate families; the sire, the dam, and the young
ones associate together, and never admit a stranger
into their little community. All others of the deer
kind are inconstant in their affection; but the
roe-buck never leaves its mate; and as they have
been generally bred up together, from their first
fawning, they conceive so strong an attachment,
the male for the female, that they never after separate. Their rutting season continues but fifteen
days; from the latter end of October to about the
middle of November. They are not at that time,
like the stag, overloaded with fat: they have not
that strong odour, which is perceived in all others
of the deer kind; they have none of those furious
excesses; nothing, in short, that alters their state:
they only drive away their fawns upon these occasions; the buck forcing them to retire, in order to
make room for a succeeding progeny: however,
when the copulating season is over, the fawns
return to their does, and remain with them some

time longer ; after which they quit them entirely,
in order to begin an independent· family of their
own. The female goes with young but five months
and a half ; which alone serves to distinguish this
animal from all others of the deer kind, that continue pregnant more than eight. In this respect,
she rather approaches more nearly to the goat
kind ; from which, however, this race is separated
by the male's annual casting its horns.

When the female is ready to bring forth, she
seeks a retreat in the thickest part of the woods,
being not less apprehensive of. the buck, from
whom she then separates, than of the wolf, the
wild cat, and almost every ravenous animal of the
forest ; she generally produces two at a time, and
three but very rarely. In about ten or twelve days
these are able to follow their dam, except in cases
of warm pursuit, when their strength is not equal
to the fatigue. Upon such occasions, the tenderness of the dam is very extraordinary ; leaving
them in the deepest thickets, she offers herself to
the danger, flies before the hounds, and does all in
her power to lead them from the retreat where she
has lodged her little ones. Such animals as are
nearly upon her own. level she boldly encounters ;
attacks the stag, the wild cat, and even the wolf;
and while she ·has life, continues her efforts to protect her young. Yet all her endeavours are often
vain ; about the month of May, which is her fawning time, there is a greater destruction among those
animals than at any other season of the year.
Numbers of the fawns are taken alive; by the peasants ; numbers are found out, and worried. by the
dogs ; and still more by the wolf, which has always

been their most inveterate enemy. By these continual depredations upon this beautiful creature, the roe-buck is every day becoming scarcer, and the whole race in many countries is wholly worn out. They were once common in England; the huntsmen, who characterised only such beasts as they knew, have given names to the different kinds and ages, as to the stag: thus they called it the first year, a *hind;* the second, a *gyrle;* and the third, a *hemuse;* but these names at present are utterly useless, since the animal no longer exists among us. Even in France, where it was once extremely common, it is now confined to a few provinces; and it is probable that in an age or two the whole breed will be utterly extirpated. M. Buffon, indeed, observes, that in those districts where it is mostly found, it seems to maintain its usual plenty, and that the balance between its destruction and increase is held pretty even; however, the number in general is known to decrease; for wherever cultivation takes place, the beasts of nature are known to retire. Many animals that once flourished in the world may now be extinct; and the descriptions of Aristotle and Pliny, though taken from life, may be considered as fabulous, as their archetypes are no longer existing.

The fawns continue to follow the deer eight or nine months in all; and upon separating, their horns begin to appear, simple and without antlers the first year, as in those of the stag kind.* These they shed at the latter end of autumn, and renew during the winter; differing in this from the stag,

* Buffon, vol. xii. p. 88.

who sheds them in spring, and renews them in
summer. When the roe-buck's head is completely
furnished, it rubs the horns against trees in the
manner of the stag, and thus strips them of the
rough skin and the blood-vessels, which no longer
contribute to their nourishment and growth.
When these fall, and new ones begin to appear,
the roe-buck does not retire as the stag to the
covert of the wood, but continues its usual haunts,
only keeping down its head to avoid striking its
horns against the branches of trees, the pain of
which it seems to feel with exquisite sensibility.
The stag, who sheds his horns in summer, is
obliged to seek a retreat from the flies, that at that
time greatly incommode him; but the roe-buck,
who sheds them in winter, is under no such
necessity; and, consequently, does not separate
from its little family, but keeps with the female all
the year round.*

As the growth of the roe-buck, and its arrival
at maturity, is much speedier than that of the stag,
so its life is proportionably shorter. It seldom is
found to extend above twelve or fifteen years; and if
kept tame, it does not live above six or seven. It is
an animal of a very delicate constitution, requiring
variety of food, air, and exercise. It must be
paired with a female, and kept in a park of at least
a hundred acres. They may easily be subdued, but
never thoroughly tamed. No arts can teach them
to be familiar with the feeder, much less attached
to him. They still preserve a part of their natural
wildness, and are subject to terrors without a

* Buffon, vol. vii. p. 98.

cause. They sometimes, in attempting to escape, strike themselves with such force against the walls of their inclosure, that they break their limbs, and become utterly disabled. Whatever care is taken to tame them, they are never entirely to be relied on, as they have capricious fits of fierceness, and sometimes strike at those they dislike, with a degree of force that is very dangerous.

The cry of the roe-buck is neither so loud nor so frequent as that of the stag. The young ones have a particular manner of calling to the dam, which the hunters easily imitate, and often thus allure the female to her destruction. Upon some occasions also they become in a manner intoxicated with their food, which, during the spring, is said to ferment in their stomachs, and they are then very easily taken. In summer they keep close under covert of the forest, and seldom venture out, except in violent heats, to drink at some river or fountain. In general, however, they are contented to slake their thirst with the dew that falls on the grass and the leaves of trees, and seldom risk their safety to satisfy their appetite. They delight chiefly in hilly grounds, preferring the tender branches and buds of trees to corn, or other vegetables; and it is universally allowed that the flesh of those between one and two years old is the greatest delicacy that is known. Perhaps, also, the scarceness of it enhances its flavour.

In America this animal is much more common than in Europe. With us there are but two known varieties; the red, which is the larger sort; and the brown, with a spot behind, which is less. But in the new continent the breed is extremely nume-

De Suve del.   Warner.

The Female Moofe or Elk.

rous, and the varieties in equal proportion. In Louisiana, where they are extremely common, they are much larger than in Europe; and the inhabitants live in a great measure upon its flesh, which tastes like mutton when well fatted. They are found also in Brasil, where they have the name of Cuguacu Apara, only differing from ours in some slight deviations in the horns. This animal is also said to be common in China; although such as have described it, seem to confound it with the musk-goat, which is of a quite different nature.

The Elk.*

We have hitherto been describing minute animals in comparison of the Elk; the size of which, from concurrent testimony, appears to be equal to that of the elephant itself. It is an animal rather of the buck than the stag kind, as its horns are flatted towards the top; but it is far beyond both in stature, some of them being known to be above ten feet high. It is a native both of the old and new continent, being known in Europe under the name of the Elk, and in America by that of the Moose-deer. It is sometimes taken in the German and Russian forests, although seldom appearing;

[* The Elk varies much in size, according to the climate where it ranges. Its common height and bulk, when full grown, is about that of a middle-sized horse. It inhabits only the colder countries, and it is generally found larger in Asia and America than in Europe: in Siberia in particular, it is found of a magnitude truly gigantic. Its common gait is that of a shambling quick trot, during which the hoofs clatter much like those of the Rein-deer.]

but it is extremely common in North America, where the natives pursue, and attack it in the snow. The accounts of this animal are extremely various ; some describing it as being no higher than a horse, and others above twelve feet high.

As the stature of this creature makes its chief peculiarity, so it were to be wished that we could come to some precision upon that head. · If we were to judge of its size by the horns, which are sometimes fortuitously dug up in many parts of Ireland, we should not be much amiss in ascribing them to an animal at least ten feet high. One of these I have seen, which was ten feet nine inches from one tip to the other. From such dimensions, it is easy to perceive that it required an animal far beyond the size of a horse to support them. To bear a head with such extensive and heavy antlers, required no small degree of strength ; and without all doubt the bulk of the body must have been proportionable to the size of the horns. I remember, some years ago, to have seen a small moose-deer, which was brought from America, by a gentleman of Ireland ; it was about the size of a horse, and the horns were very little larger than those of a common stag : this, therefore, serves to prove that the horns bear an exact proportion to the animal's size. The small elk has but small horns ; whereas those enormous ones, which we have described above, must have belonged to a proportionable creature. In all the more noble animals, Nature observes a perfect symmetry ; and it is not to be supposed that she fails in this single instance. We have no reason, therefore, to doubt the accounts of Josselyn and Dudley, who affirm, that they have been found fourteen spans; which, at nine inches to a span, makes the animal almost eleven feet high. Others have extended their accounts to twelve and fourteen feet, which makes this creature one of the most formidable of the forest.

There is but very little difference between the European elk, and the American moose-deer, as they are but varieties of the same animal. It may be rather larger in America than with us; as in the forests of that unpeopled country it receives less disturbance than in our own. In all places, however, it is timorous and gentle; content with its pasture, and never willing to disturb any other animal, when supplied itself.

The European elk grows to above seven or eight feet high. In the year 1742, there was a female of this animal shown at Paris, which was caught in a forest of Red Russia, belonging to the Cham of Tartary :* it was then but young, and its height was even at that time six feet seven inches ; but the describer observes, that it has since become much taller and thicker, so that we may suppose this female at least seven feet high. There have been no late opportunities of seeing the male; but by the rule of proportion, we may estimate his size at eight or nine feet at the least, which is about twice as high as an ordinary horse. The height, however, of the female, which was measured, was but six feet seven inches, Paris measure; or almost seven English feet high. It was ten feet from the tip of the nose to the insertion of the tail;

* Dictionnaire Raisonné des Animaux. Au nom, Elan.

and eight feet round the body. The hair was very long and coarse, like that of a wild boar. The ears resembled those of a mule, and were a foot and a half long. The upper jaw was longer, by six inches, than the lower; and, like other ruminating animals, it had no teeth (cutting teeth I suppose the describer means). It had a large beard under the throat, like a goat; and in the middle of the forehead, between the horns, there was a bone as large as an egg. The nostrils were four inches long on each side of the mouth. It made use of its fore-feet, as a defence against its enemies. Those who showed it, asserted, that it ran with astonishing swiftness; that it swam also with equal expedition, and was very fond of the water. They gave it thirty pounds of bread every day, beside hay, and it drank eight buckets of water. It was tame and familiar, and submissive enough to its keeper.

This description differs in many circumstances from that which we have of the moose, or American elk, which the French call the Original. Of these there are two kinds, the common light grey moose, which is not very large; and the black moose, which grows to an enormous height. Mr. Dudley observes, that a doe or a hind of the black moose kind, of the fourth year, wanted but an inch of seven feet high. All, however, of both kinds, have flat palmed horns, not unlike the fallow-deer, only that the palm is much larger, having a short trunk at the head, and then immediately spreading above a foot broad, with a kind of small antlers, like teeth, on one of the edges. In this particular, all of the elk kind agree; as well the European elk, as the grey and the black moose-deer.

The grey moose-deer is about the size of a horse: and although it has large buttocks, its tail is not above an inch long. As in all of this kind the upper lip is much longer than the under, it is said that they continue to go backward as they feed. Their nostrils are so large that a man may thrust his hand in a considerable way; and their horns are as long as those of a stag, but, as was observed, much broader.

The black moose is the enormous animal mentioned above, from eight to twelve feet high. Josselyn, who is the first English writer that mentions it, says, that it is a goodly creature, twelve feet high, with exceeding fair horns, that have broad palms, two fathoms from the top of one horn to another. He assures us that it is a creature, or rather a monster of superfluity, and many times bigger than an English ox. This account is confirmed by Dudley; but he does not give so great an expansion to the horns, measuring them only thirty-one inches between one tip and the other; however, that such an extraordinary animal as Josselyn describes, has actually existed, we can make no manner of doubt of, since there are horns common enough to be seen among us, twelve feet from one tip to the other.

These animals delight in cold countries, feeding upon grass in summer, and the bark of trees in winter. When the whole country is deeply covered with snow, the moose-deer herd together under the tall pine-trees, strip off the bark, and remain in that part of the forest while it yields

them subsistence. It is at that time that the
natives prepare to hunt them; and particularly
when the sun begins to melt the snow by day, which
is frozen again at night; for then the icy crust
which covers the surface of the snow is too
weak to support so great a bulk, and only retards
the animal's motion. When the Indians, therefore, perceive a herd of these at a distance, they
immediately prepare for their pursuit, which is
not, as with us, the sport of an hour, but is
attended with toil, difficulty and danger.* The
timorous animal no sooner observes its enemies
approach, than it immediately endeavours to escape,
but sinks at every step it takes. Still, however,
it pursues its way through a thousand obstacles;
the snow, which is usually four feet deep, yields
to its weight and embarrasses its speed; the sharp
ice wounds its feet; and its lofty horns are entangled in the branches of the forest, as it passes
along. The trees, however, are broken down with
ease; and wherever the moose-deer runs, it is
perceived by the snapping off the branches of trees,
as thick as a man's thigh, with its horns. The
chase lasts in this manner for the whole day; and
sometimes it has been known to continue for two,
nay three days together; for the pursuers are often
not less excited by famine, than the pursued by
fear. Their perseverance, however, generally
succeeds; and the Indian who first comes near
enough, darts his lance, with unerring aim, which
sticks in the poor animal, and at first increases its
efforts to escape. In this manner the moose trots

* Phil. Trans. vol. ii. p. 486.

heavily on, (for that is its usual pace,) till its pursuers once more come up, and repeat their blow;
upon this, it again summons up sufficient vigour
to get a-head; but, at last, quite tired, and spent
with loss of blood, it sinks, as the describer expresses
it, like a ruined building, and makes the earth
shake beneath its fall.

This animal, when killed, is a very valuable
acquisition to the hunters; the flesh very well
tasted, and is said to be very nourishing. The
hide is strong, and so thick, that it has been often
known to turn a musket-ball; however, it is soft
and pliable, and, when tanned, the leather is extremely light, yet very lasting. The fur is a
light grey in some, and blackish in others; and,
when viewed through a microscope, appears spongy
like a bulrush, and is smaller at the roots and
points than in the middle; for this reason, it lies
very flat and smooth, and though beaten or abused
never so much, it always returns to its former
state. The horns also are not less useful, being
applied to all the purposes for which hartshorn is
beneficial: these are different in different animals;
in some they resemble entirely those of the European elk, which spread into a broad palm, with
small antlers on one of the edges; in others they
have a branched brow-antler between the bur and
the palm, which the German elk has not; and in
this they entirely agree with those whose horns
are so frequently dug up in Ireland. This animal
is said to be troubled with the epilepsy, as it is
often found to fall down when pursued, and thus
becomes an easier prey; for this reason, an imaginary virtue has been ascribed to the hinder hoof,

which some have supposed to be a specific against
all epileptic disorders. This, however, may be
considered as a vulgar error; as well as that of its
curing itself of this disorder by applying the
hinder hoof behind the ear. After all, this animal
is but very indifferently and confusedly described
by travellers; each mixing his account with something false or trivial; often mistaking some other
quadruped for the elk, and confounding its history. Thus some have mistaken it for the rein-
deer, which in every thing but size it greatly
resembles; some have supposed it to be the same
with the Tapurette,* from which it entirely
differs; some have described it as the common red
American stag, which scarcely differs from our
own; and, lastly, some have confounded it with
the Bubalus, which is more properly a gazelle of
Africa.†

The Rein-deer.‡

Of all animals of the deer kind, the Rein-deer
is the most extraordinary and the most useful. It
is a native of the icy regions of the north; and
though many attempts have been made to accustom it to a more southern climate, it shortly feels
the influence of the change, and in a few months
declines and dies. Nature seems to have fitted it

* Condamine.   † Dapper, Description de l'Afrique, p. 17.
[‡ In the elk the horns are stemless, or branched from the
base; in the rein-deer the horns are round, bent back, and palmated at the extremities.]

12

De Sève del.   Warner sc.

The Rein Deer.

entirely to answer the necessities of that hardy race of mankind that live near the pole. As these would find it impossible to subsist among their barren snowy mountains without its aid, so this animal can live only there, where its assistance is most absolutely necessary. From it alone the natives of Lapland and Greenland supply most of their wants; it answers the purposes of a horse, to convey them and their scanty furniture from one mountain to another; it answers the purposes of a cow, in giving milk; and it answers the purposes of the sheep, in furnishing them with a warm, though a homely kind of clothing. From this quadruped alone, therefore, they receive as many advantages as we derive from three of our most useful creatures; so that Providence does not leave these poor outcasts entirely destitute, but gives them a faithful domestic, more patient and serviceable than any other in nature.

The rein-deer resembles the American elk in the fashion of its horns. It is not easy in words to describe these minute differences; nor will the reader, perhaps, have a distinct idea of the similitude, when told that both have brow-antlers, very large, and hanging over their eyes, palmated towards the top, and bending forward, like a bow. But here the similitude between these two animals ends; for, as the elk is much larger than the stag, so the rein-deer is much smaller. It is lower and stronger built than the stag; its legs are shorter and thicker, and its hoofs much broader than in that animal; its hair is much thicker and warmer, its horns much larger in proportion, and branching forward over its eyes; its ears are much

larger; 'its pace is rather a trot than a bounding;
and this it can continue for a whole day; its hoofs
are cloven and moveable, so that it spreads them
abroad as it goes, to prevent its sinking in the
snow. When it proceeds on a journey, it lays
its great horns on its back, while there are two
branches which always hang over its forehead,
and almost cover its face. One thing seems peculiar to this animal and the elk, which is, that as
they move along, their hoofs are heard to crack
with a pretty loud noise. This arises from their
manner of treading; for as they rest upon their
cloven hoof, it spreads on the ground, and the
two divisions separate from each other; but when
they lift it, the divisions close again, and strike
against each other with a crack. The female also
of the rein-deer has horns as well as the male, by
which the species is distinguished from all other
animals of the deer kind whatsoever.

When the rein-deer first shed their coat of hair,
they are brown; but in proportion as summer
approaches, their hair begins to grow whitish,
until, at last, they are nearly grey.* They are,
however, always black about the eyes. The neck
has long hair, hanging down, and coarser than
upon any other part of the body. The feet, just
at the insertion of the hoof, are surrounded with
a ring of white. The hair in general stands so
thick over the whole body, that if one should
attempt to separate it, the skin will no where

* For the greatest part of this description of the rein-deer,
I am obliged to Mr. Hoffberg; upon whose authority, being a
native of Sweden, and an experienced naturalist, we may confi-
dently rely.

appear uncovered: whenever it falls also, it is not seen to drop from the root, as in other quadrupeds, but seems broken short near the bottom; so that the lower part of the hair is seen growing, while the upper falls away.

The horns of the female are made like those of the male, except that they are smaller and less branching. As in the rest of the deer kind, they sprout from the points; and also in the beginning are furnished with a hairy crust, which supports the blood-vessels, of most exquisite sensibility. The rein-deer shed their horns after rutting-time, at the latter end of November; and they are not completely furnished again till towards autumn. The female always retains hers till she brings forth, and then sheds them, about the beginning of November. If she be barren, however, which is not unfrequently the case, she does not shed them till winter. The castration of the rein-deer does not prevent the shedding of their horns: those which are the strongest, cast them early in winter; those which are more weakly, not so soon. Thus, from all these circumstances, we see how greatly this animal differs from the common stag. The female of the rein-deer has horns, which the hind is never seen to have; the rein-deer, when castrated, renews its horns, which we are assured the stag never does: it differs not less in its habits and manner of living, being tame, submissive, and patient; while the stag is wild, capricious, and unmanageable.

The rein-deer, as was said, is naturally an inhabitant of the countries bordering on the arctic circle. It is not unknown to the natives of Siberia.

The North Americans also hunt it, under the name of the Caribou. But in Lapland, this animal is converted to the utmost advantage; and some herdsmen of that country are known to possess above a thousand in a single herd.

. Lapland is divided into two districts, the mountainous and the woody. The mountainous part of the country is at best barren and bleak, excessively cold, and uninhabitable during the winter; still, however, it is the most desirable part of this frightful region, and is most thickly peopled during the summer. The natives generally reside on the declivity of the mountains, three or four cottages together, and lead a cheerful and social life. Upon the approach of winter they are obliged to migrate into the plains below, each bringing down his whole herd, which often amounts to more than a thousand, and leading them where the pasture is in greatest plenty. The woody part of the country is much more desolate and hideous. The whole face of nature there presents a frightful scene of trees without fruit, and plains without verdure. As far as the eye can reach, nothing is to be seen, even in the midst of summer, but barren fields, covered only with a moss, almost as white as snow: no grass, no flowery landscapes, only here and there a pine-tree, which may have escaped the frequent conflagrations by which the natives burn down their forests. But what is very extraordinary, as the whole surface of the country is clothed in white, so, on the contrary, the forests seem to the last degree dark and gloomy. While one kind of moss makes the fields look as if they were covered with snow,

another kind blackens over all the trees, and even
hides their verdure. This moss, however, which
deforms the country, serves for its only support, as
upon it alone the rein-deer can subsist. The inhabitants, who, during the summer, lived among
the mountains, drive down their herds in winter,
and people the plains and woods below. Such of
the Laplanders as inhabit the woods and the plains
all the year round, live remote from each other,
and having been used to solitude, are melancholy,
ignorant, and helpless. They are much poorer
also than the mountaineers, for, while one of those
is found to possess a thousand rein-deer at a time,
none of these are ever known to rear the tenth
part of that number. The rein-deer makes the
riches of this people; and the cold mountainy
parts of the country agree best with its constitution. It is for this reason, therefore, that the
mountains of Lapland are preferred to the woods;
and that many claim an exclusive right to the tops
of hills, covered in almost eternal snow.

As soon as the summer begins to appear, the
Laplander who had fed his rein-deer upon the lower
grounds during the winter, then drives them up to
the mountains, and leaves the woody country, and
the low pasture, which at that season are truly
deplorable. The gnats, bred by the sun's heat in the
marshy bottoms, and the weedy lakes, with which
the country abounds more than any other parts of
the world, are all upon the wing, and fill the whole
air, like clouds of dust in a dry windy day. The
inhabitants, at that time, are obliged to daub their
faces with pitch, mixed with milk, to shield their
skins from their depredations. All places are then

so greatly infested, that the poor natives can scarcely
open their mouths without fear of suffocation;
the insects enter, from their numbers and minute-
ness, into the nostrils and the eyes, and do not
leave the sufferer a moment at ease.   But they are
chiefly enemies to the rein-deer: the horns of that
animal being then in their tender state, and possessed of extreme sensibility, a famished cloud of
insects instantly settle upon them, and drive the
poor animal almost to distraction.   In this extremity, there are but two remedies, to which the
quadruped, as well as its master, are obliged to
have recourse.   The one is, for both to take shelter
near the cottage, where a large fire of tree moss
is prepared, which filling the whole place with
smoke, keeps off the gnat, and thus, by one inconvenience, expels a greater;   the other is, to
ascend to the highest summit of the mountains,
where the air is too thin, and the weather too
cold, for the gnats to come.   There the rein-deer
are seen to continue the whole day, although
without food, rather than to venture down into the
lower parts, where they can have no defence against
their unceasing persecutors.

Besides the gnat, there is also a gadfly, that,
during the summer season, is no less formidable
to them.   This insect is bred under their skins,
where the egg has been deposited the preceding
summer; and it is no sooner produced as a fly,
than it again endeavours to deposit its eggs in
some place similar to that from whence it came.
Whenever, therefore, it appears flying over a herd
of rein-deer, it puts the whole body, how numerous soever, into motion; they know their enemy,

and do all they can, by tossing their horns, and
running among each other, to terrify or avoid it.
All their endeavours, however, are too generally
without effect; the gadfly is seen to deposite its
eggs, which burrowing under the skin, wound it
in several places, and often bring on an incurable
disorder.

In the morning, therefore, as soon as the Lapland herdsman drives his deer to pasture, his greatest
care is to keep them from scaling the summits of
the mountains where there is no food, but where
they go merely to be at ease from the gnats and
gadflies that are ever annoying them. At this time
there is a strong contest between the dogs and the
deer; the one endeavouring to climb up against
the side of the hill, and to gain those summits that
are covered in eternal snows; the other, forcing
them down, by barking and threatening, and, in a
manner, compelling them into the places where
their food is in the greatest plenty. There the
men and dogs confine them; guarding them with
the utmost precaution the whole day, and driving
them home at the proper seasons for milking.

The female brings forth in the middle of May,
and gives milk till about the middle of October.
Every morning and evening, during the summer,
the herdsman returns to the cottage with his deer
to be milked, where the women previously have
kindled up a smoky fire, which effectually drives
off the gnats, and keeps the rein-deer quiet while
milking. The female furnishes about a pint, which,
though thinner than that of the cow, is, nevertheless, sweeter and more nourishing. This done,
the herdsman drives them back to pasture; as he

neither folds nor houses them, neither provides 'for
their subsistence during the winter, nor improves
their pasture by cultivation.

Upon the return of the winter, when the gnats
and flies are no longer to be feared, the Laplander
descends into the lower grounds : and, as there
are but few to dispute the possession of that desolate country, he has an extensive range to feed
them in. Their chief, and almost their only food
at that time, is the white moss already mentioned ;
which, from its being fed upon by this animal,
obtains the name of the *Lichen rangiferinus.*
This is of two kinds : the woody lichen, which
covers almost all the desert parts of the country
like snow ; the other is black, and covers the
branches of the trees in very great quantities.
However unpleasing these may be to the spectator,
the native esteems them as one of his choicest
benefits, and the most indulgent gift of Nature.
While his fields are clothed with moss, he envies
neither the fertility nor the verdure of the more
southern landscape ; dressed up warmly in his deer-
skin clothes, with shoes and gloves of the same
materials, he drives his herd along the desert ;
fearless and at ease, ignorant of any higher luxury
than what their milk and smoke-dried flesh afford
him.   Hardened to the climate, he sleeps in the
midst of ice ; or awaking, dozes away his time
with tobacco ; while his faithful dogs supply his
place, and keep the herd from wandering. The
deer, in the mean time, with instincts adapted to
the soil, pursue their food, though covered in
the deepest snow. They turn it up with their
noses, like swine ; and even though its surface be

frozen and stiff, yet the hide is so hardened in that part, that they easily overcome the difficulty. It sometimes, however, happens, though but rarely, that the winter commences with rain, and a frost ensuing, covers the whole country with a glazed crust of ice. Then, indeed, both the rein-deer and the Laplander are undone; they have no provisions laid up in case of accident, and the only resource is to cut down the large pine-trees, that are covered with moss, which furnishes but a scanty supply; so that the greatest part of the herd is then seen to perish, without a possibility of assistance. It sometimes also happens, that even this supply is wanting; for the Laplander often burns down his woods, in order to improve and fertilize the soil which produces the moss, upon which he feeds his cattle.

In this manner the pastoral life is still continued near the pole; neither the coldness of the winter, or the length of the nights, neither the wildness of the forest, nor the vagrant disposition of the herd, interrupt the even tenour of the Laplander's life. By night and day he is seen attending his favourite cattle, and remains unaffected, in a season which would be speedy death to those bred up in a milder climate. He gives himself no uneasiness to house his herds, or to provide a winter subsistence for them; he is at the trouble neither of manuring his grounds nor bringing in his harvests; he is not the hireling of another's luxury; all his labours are to obviate the necessities of his own situation; and these he undergoes with cheerfulness, as he is sure to enjoy the fruits of his own industry. If, therefore, we compare the Laplander with the peasant

of more southern climates, we shall have little reason to pity his situation.; the climate in which he
lives is rather terrible to us than to him; and, as
for the rest, he is blessed with liberty, plenty, and
ease. The rein-deer alone supplies him with all
the wants of life, and some of the conveniences,
serving to show how many advantages Nature is
capable of supplying, when necessity gives the
call. Thus, the poor, little, helpless native, who
was originally, perhaps, driven by fear or famine
into those inhospitable climates, would seem, at
first view, to be the most wretched of mankind:
but it is far otherwise; he looks round among the
few wild animals that this barren country can maintain, and singles out one from among them, and
that of a kind which the rest of mankind have not
thought worth taking from a state of nature; this
he cultivates, propagates, and multiplies, and from
this alone derives every comfort that can soften
the severity of his situation.

The rein-deer of this country are of two kinds,
the wild and the tame. The wild are larger and
stronger, but more mischievous than the others.
Their breed, however, is preferred to that of the
tame: and the female of the latter is often sent
into the woods, from whence she returns home
impregnated by one of the wild kind. These are
fitter for drawing the sledge, to which the Laplander accustoms them betimes, and yokes them
to it by a strap, which goes round the neck, and
comes down between their legs. The sledge is
extremely light, and shod at the bottom with the
skin of a young deer, the hair turned to slide on
the frozen snow. The person who sits on this

guides the animal with a cord, fastened round
the horns, and encourages it to proceed with his
voice, and drives it with a goad. Some of the
wild breed, though by far the strongest, are yet
found refractory, and often turn upon their
drivers; who have then no other resource but to
cover themselves with their sledge, and let the ·
animal vent its fury upon that. But it is otherwise
with those that are tame; no creature can be more
active, patient, and willing; when hard pushed,
they will trot nine or ten Swedish miles, or
between fifty and sixty English miles, at one stretch.
But, in such a case, the poor obedient creature
fatigues itself to death; and, if not prevented by
the Laplander, who kills it immediately, it will
die a day or two after. In general, they can
go about thirty miles without halting, and this
without any great or dangerous efforts. This,
which is the only manner of travelling in that
country, can be performed only in winter, when
the snow is glazed over with ice; and although
it be a very speedy method of conveyance, yet it
is inconvenient, dangerous, and troublesome.

In order to make these animals more obedient,
and more generally serviceable, they castrate them;
which operation the Laplanders perform with their
teeth: these become sooner fat when taken from
labour; and they are found to be stronger in
drawing the sledge. There is usually one male left
entire for every six females; these are in rut from
the feast of St. Matthew to about Michaelmas.
At this time, their horns are thoroughly burnished,
and their battles among each other are fierce
and obstinate. The females do not begin to breed

till they are two years old : and then they continue
regularly breeding every year till they are super-
annuated.   They go with young above eight
months, and generally bring forth two at a time
The fondness of the dam for her young is very
remarkable ; it often happens that when they are
separated from her, she will return from pasture,
keep calling round the cottage for them, and will
not desist until, dead or alive, they are brought
and laid at her feet.   They are at first of a light
brown ; but they become darker with age ; and
at last the old ones are of a brown almost approaching to blackness.   The young follow the
dam for two or three years ; but they do not
acquire their full growth until four.   They are then
broke in, and managed for drawing the sledge ;
and they continue serviceable for four or five years
longer.   They never live above fifteen or sixteen
years ; and when they arrive at the proper age,
the Laplander generally kills them for the sake of
their skins and their flesh.   This he performs by
striking them on the back of the neck, with his
knife, into the spinal marrow ; upon which they
instantly fall, and he then cuts the arteries that lead
to the heart, and lets the blood discharge itself
into the cavity of the breast.

There is scarcely any part of this animal that is
not converted to its peculiar uses.   As soon as it
begins to grow old, and some time before the rut,
it is killed, and the flesh dried in the air.   It is
also sometimes hardened with smoke, and laid up
for travelling provision, when the natives migrate
from one part of the country to another.   During
the winter, the rein-deer are slaughtered as sheep

†

with us; and every four persons in the family are
allowed one rein-deer for their week's subsistence.
In spring, they spare the herd as much as they
can, and live upon fresh fish. In summer, the
milk and curd of the rein-deer makes their chief
provision; and, in autumn, they live wholly upon
fowls, which they kill with a cross-bow, or catch
in springes. Nor is this so scanty an allowance:
since, at that time, the sea-fowls come in such
abundance, that their ponds and springs are covered over. These are not so shy as with us, but
yield themselves an easy prey. They are chiefly
allured to those places by the swarms of gnats
which infest the country during summer, and
now repay the former inconveniences, by inviting such numbers of birds as supply the natives
with food a fourth part of the year in great abundance.

The milk, when newly taken, is warmed in a
cauldron, and thickened with rennet, and then
the curd is pressed into cheeses, which are little
and well tasted. These are never found to breed
mites as the cheese of other countries, probably
because the mite-fly is not to be found in Lapland.
The whey which remains is warmed up again, and
becomes of a consistence as if thickened with the
white of eggs. Upon this the Laplanders feed
during the summer; it is pleasant and well tasted,
but not very nourishing. As to butter they very
seldom make any, because the milk affords but a
very small quantity, and this, both in taste and consistence, is more nearly resembling to suet. They
never keep their milk till it turns sour; and do
not dress it into the variety of dishes which the

more southern countries are known to do. The
only delicacy they make from it is with wood-sorrel,
which being boiled up with it, and coagulating, the
whole is put into casks or deer-skins, and kept
under ground to be eaten in winter.

The skin is even a more valuable part of this
animal than either of the former. From that part
of it which covered the head and feet, they make
their strong snow shoes, with the hair on the
outside. Of the other parts they compose their
garments, which are extremely warm, and which
cover them all over. The hair of these also is on
the outside; and they sometimes line them within
with the fur of the glutton, or some other warm-
furred animal of that climate. These skins also
serve them for beds. They spread them on each
side of the fire, upon some leaves of the dwarf
birch-tree, and in this manner lie both soft and
warm. Many garments, made of the skin of the
rein-deer, are sold every year to the inhabitants of
the more southern parts of Europe; and they are
found so serviceable in keeping out the cold, that
even people of the first rank are known to wear
them.

In short, no part of this animal is thrown away
as useless. The blood is preserved in small casks,
to make sauce with the marrow in spring. The
horns are sold to be converted into glue. The
sinews are dried, and divided so as to make the
strongest kind of sewing thread, not unlike catgut.
The tongues, which are considered as a great
delicacy, are dried, and sold into the more southern
provinces. The intestines themselves are washed
like our tripe, and in high esteem among the

natives. Thus the Laplander finds all his necessities amply supplied from this single animal; and he who has a large herd of these animals, has no idea of higher luxury.

But, although the rein-deer be a very hardy and vigorous animal, it is not without its diseases. I have already mentioned the pain it feels from the gnat, and the apprehensions it is under from the gad-fly. Its hide its often found pierced in a hundred places, like a sieve, from this insect; and not a few die in their third year, from this very cause. Their teats also are subject to cracking, so that blood comes instead of milk. They sometimes take a loathing for their food; and, instead of eating, stand still, and chew the cud. They are also troubled with a vertigo, like the elk, and turn round often till they die. The Laplander judges of their state by the manner of their turning. If they turn to the right, he judges their disorder but slight; if they turn to the left, he deems it incurable. The rein-deer are also subject to ulcers near the hoof, which unqualifies them for travelling, or keeping with the herd. But the most fatal disorder of all is that which the natives call the suddataka, which attacks this animal at all seasons of the year. The instant it is seized with this disease, it begins to breathe with greater difficulty, its eyes begin to stare, and its nostrils to expand. It acquires also an unusual degree of ferocity, and attacks all it meets indiscriminately. Still, however, it continues to feed as if in health, but is not seen to chew the cud, and it lies down more frequently than before. In this manner it continues, every day consuming, and growing

A A 2

more lean, till at last it dies from mere inanition;
and not one of those that are attacked with this
disorder are ever found to recover. Notwithstanding, it is but very lately known in that part
of the world: although, during the last ten or
fifteen years, it has spoiled whole provinces of this
necessary creature.   It is contagious; and the
moment the Laplander perceives any of his herd
infected, he hastens to kill them immediately, before
it spreads any farther.   When examined internally,
there is a frothy substance found in the brain, and
round the lungs; the intestines are lax and flabby,
and the spleen is diminished to almost nothing.
The Laplander's only cure in all these disorders
is to anoint the animal's back with tar; if this does
not succeed, he considers the disease as beyond
the power of art; and, with his natural phlegm,
submits to the severities of fortune.

Besides the internal maladies of this animal,
there are some external enemies which it has to
fear.   The bears now and then make depredations
upon the herd; but of all their persecutors, the
creature called the glutton is the most dangerous
and the most successful.   The war between these
is carried on not less in Lapland than in North
America, where the rein-deer is called the Caribou,
and the glutton the Carcajou.   This animal, which
is not above the size of a badger, waits whole
weeks together for its prey, hid in the branches of
some spreading tree; and when the wild rein-deer
passes underneath, it instantly drops down upon
it, fixing its teeth and claws into the neck, just
behind the horns.   It is in vain that the wounded
animal then flies for protection, that it rustles

among the branches of the forest, the glutton
still holds its former position; and although it
often loses a part of its skin and flesh, which are
rubbed off against the trees, yet it still keeps fast,
until its prey drops with fatigue and loss of blood.
The deer has but one only method of escape,
which is by jumping into the water; that element
its enemy cannot endure; for, as we are told, it
quits its hold immediately, and then thinks only of
providing for its own proper security.*

CHAP. XIX.

Of Quadrupeds of the Hog Kind.†

ANIMALS of the hog kind seem to unite in
themselves all those distinctions by which others

[* Mr. Pennant has described a remarkably small kind of
deer, which was brought from Bengal, and was in the possession
of the late Lord Clive. Its general colour was brown; the
belly and rump lighter; the horns were slender, about thirteen
inches long, with a single branch at the base of each, and forked
at the tips. The body, from the tip of the nose to the tail,
was three feet six inches long; the tail measured eight inches;
the height from the shoulder to the hoof, was two feet two
inches; behind, it was about two inches higher; the legs were
so fine and slender, that, like those of the pigmy antelope and
musk, they were often capped with gold, and made use of as
tobacco-stoppers.]

[† The animals of this tribe have four front teeth in the upper
jaw, which converge at their points; and generally six in the
lower jaw, which project. The canine teeth, or tusks, are two
in each jaw; those in the upper jaw short, those in the lower
jaw extending beyond the mouth. The snout is prominent,
moveable, and has the appearance of having been abruptly cut
off; the hoofs are cloven.]

¶

are separated. They resemble those of the horse
kind in the number of their teeth, which in all
amount to forty-four, in the length of their head,
and in having but a single stomach. They resemble the cow kind in their cloven hoofs and the
position of their intestines; and they resemble those
of the claw-footed kind in their appetite for flesh,
in their not chewing the cud, and in their numerous
progeny. Thus this species serves to fill up that
chasm which is found between the carnivorous
kinds and those that live upon grass; being
possessed of the ravenous appetite of the one,
and the inoffensive nature of the other. We
may consider them, therefore, as of a middle
nature, which we can refer neither to the rapacious
nor the peaceful kinds, and yet partaking somewhat of the nature of both. Like the rapacious
kinds, they are found to have short intestines;
their hoofs, also, though cloven to the sight, will,
upon anatomical inspection, appear to be supplied
with bones like beasts of prey; and the number
of their teats also increase the similitude; on the
other hand, in a natural state they live upon vegetables, and seldom seek after animal food, except
when urged by necessity. They offend no other
animal of the forest, at the same time that they are
furnished with arms to terrify the bravest.

The Wild Boar, which is the original of all the
varieties we find in this creature, is by no means
so stupid nor so filthy an animal as that we have
reduced to tameness; he is much smaller than the
tame hog, and does not vary in his colour as those
of the domestic kind do, but is always found of
an iron grey, inclining to black: his snout is much

longer than that of the tame hog, and the ears are
shorter, rounder, and black; of which colour are
also the feet and the tail. He roots the ground
in a different manner from the common hog; for
as this turns up the earth in little spots here and
there, so the wild boar ploughs it up like a
furrow, and does irreparable damage in the cultivated lands of the farmer. The tusks also of this
animal are larger than in the tame breed, some of
them being seen almost a foot long.* These, as
is well known, grow from both the under and
upper jaw, bend upwards circularly, and are
exceeding sharp at the points. They differ from
the tusks of the elephant in this, that they never
fall; and it is remarkable of all the hog kind, that
they never shed their teeth, as other animals are
seen to do. The tusks of the lower jaw are always
the most to be dreaded, and are found to give very
terrible wounds.

The wild boar can properly be called neither a
solitary nor a gregarious animal. The three first
years the whole litter follows the sow, and the
family lives in a herd together. They are then
called beasts of company, and unite their common
forces against the invasions of the wolf, or the
more formidable beasts of prey. Upon this their
principal safety while young depends; for when
attacked they give each other mutual assistance,
calling to each other with a very loud and fierce
note; the strongest face the danger; they form a
ring, and the weakest fall into the centre. In
this position few ravenous beasts dare venture to

* Buffon, vol. ix, p. 147.

attack them, but pursue the chase where there is less resistance and danger. However, when the wild boar is come to a state of maturity, and when conscious of his own superior strength, he then walks the forest alone and fearless. At that time he dreads no single creature, nor does he turn out of his way even for man himself. He does not seek danger, and he does not much seem to avoid it.

This animal is therefore seldom attacked, but at a disadvantage, either by numbers, or when found sleeping by moon-light. The hunting the wild boar is one of the principal amusements of the nobility in those countries where it is to be found. The dogs provided for this sport are of the slow heavy kind. Those used for hunting the stag, or the roe-buck, would be very improper, as they would too soon come up with their prey; and, instead of a chase, would only furnish out an engagement. A small mastiff is therefore chosen; nor are the hunters much mindfull of the goodness of their nose, as the wild boar leaves so strong a scent, that it is impossible for them to mistake its course. They never hunt any but the largest and the oldest, which are known by their tracks. When the boar is rear'd, as is the expression for driving him from his covert, he goes slowly and uniformly forward, not much afraid, nor very far before his pursuers. At the end of every half mile, or thereabouts, he turns round, stops till the hounds come up, and offers to attack them. These, on the other hand, knowing their danger, keep off, and bay him at a distance. After they have for a while gazed upon each other, with mutual animo-

vity, the boar again slowly goes on his course, and
the dogs renew their pursuit. In this manner the
charge is sustained, and the chase continues till
the boar is quite tired, and refuses to go any farther. The dogs then attempt to close in upon
him from behind; those which are young, fierce,
and unaccustomed to the chase, are generally the
foremost, and often lose their lives by their ardour.
Those which are older and better trained are content to wait until the hunters come up, who strike
at him with their spears, and, after several blows,
dispatch or disable him. The instant the animal
is killed, they cut off the testicles, which would
otherwise give a taint to the flesh; and the huntsmen celebrate the victory with their horns.

The hog, in a natural state, is found to feed
chiefly upon roots and vegetables; it seldom
attacks any other animal, being content with such
provisions as it procures without danger. Whatever animal happens to die in the forest, or is so
wounded that it can make no resistance, becomes
a prey to the hog, who seldom refuses animal food,
how putrid soever, although it is never at the
pains of taking or procuring it alive. For this
reason it seems a glutton rather by accident than
choice, content with vegetable food, and only
devouring flesh when pressed by necessity, and
when it happens to offer. Indeed, if we behold
the hog in its domestic state, it is the most sordid
and brutal animal in nature.* The awkwardness
of its form seems to influence its appetites; and all
its sensations are as gross as its shapes are unsightly.

* Buffon, vol. ix. p. 14.

was possessed only of an insatiable desire of
ㅤg; and seems to make choice only of what
ㅤer animals find the most offensive. But we
ㅤght to consider that the hog with us is in an
unnatural state, and that it is in a manner compelled
to feed in this filthy manner, from wanting that
proper nourishment which it finds in the forest.
When in a state of wildness, it is of all other quadrupeds the most delicate in the choice of what
vegetables it shall feed on, and rejects a greater
number than any of the rest. The cow, for instance,
as we are assured by Linnæus, eats two hundred
and seventy-six plants, and rejects two hundred
and eighteen; the goat eats four hundred and
forty-nine, and rejects a hundred and twenty-six;
the sheep eats three hundred and eighty seven,
and rejects a hundred and forty-one; the horse
eats two hundred and sixty-two, and rejects two
hundred and twelve; but the hog, more nice in
its provision than any of the former, eats but
seventy-two plants, and rejects a hundred and
seventy-one. The indelicacy of this animal is,
therefore, rather in our apprehensions than in
its nature; since we find it makes a very distinguishing choice in the quality of its food;
and if it does not reject animal putrefaction, it
may be because it is abridged in that food which
is most wholesome and agreeable to it in a state
of nature. This is certain, that its palate is not
insensible to the difference of eatables; for, where
it finds variety, it will reject the worst, with as
distinguishing a taste as any other quadruped
whatsoever.* In the orchards of peach-trees in

* British Zoology, vol. i. p. 42.

North America, where the hog has plenty of delicious food, it is observed, that it will reject the fruit that has lain but a few hours on the ground, and continue on the watch whole hours together for a fresh windfall.

However, the hog is naturally formed in a more imperfect manner than the other animals that we have rendered domestic around us, less active in its motions, less furnished with instinct in knowing what to pursue or avoid. Without attachment, and incapable of instruction, it continues, while it lives, an useless, or rather a rapacious dependant. The coarseness of its hair, and the thickness of its hide, together with the thick coat of fat that lies immediately under the skin, render it insensible to blows or rough usage. Mice have been known to burrow in the back of these animals while fattening in the sty,* without their seeming to perceive it. Their other senses seem to be in tolerable perfection; they scent the hounds at a distance; and, as we have seen, they are not insensible in the choice of their provisions.

The hog is, by nature, stupid, inactive, and drowsy; if undisturbed it would sleep half its time; but it is frequently awaked by the calls of appetite, which when it has satisfied, it goes to rest again. Its whole life is thus a round of sleep and gluttony; and, if supplied with sufficient food, it soon grows unfit even for its own existence; its flesh becomes a greater load than its legs are able to support, and it continues to feed lying down, or kneeling, a helpless instance of indulged

* Buffon.

sensuality. The only times it seems to have passions of a more active nature, are, when it is incited by venery, or when the wind blows with any vehemence. Upon this occasion, it is so agitated as to run violently towards its sty, screaming horribly at the same time, which seems to argue that it is naturally fond of a warm climate. It appears also to foresee the approach of bad weather, bringing straw to its sty in its mouth, preparing a bed, and hiding itself from the impending storm. Nor is it less agitated when it hears any of its kind in distress: when a hog is caught in a gate, as is often the case, or when it suffers any of the usual domestic operations of ringing or spaying, all the rest are then seen to gather round it, to lend their fruitless assistance, and to sympathize with its sufferings. They have often also been known to gather round a dog that had teazed them, and kill him upon the spot.

Most of the diseases of this animal arise from intemperance; measles, imposthumes, and scrophulous swellings, are reckoned among the number. It is thought by some that they wallow in the mire to destroy a sort of louse or insect that is often found to infest them; however, they are generally known to live, when so permitted, to eighteen or twenty years; and the females produce till the age of fifteen. As they produce from ten to twenty young at a litter, and that twice a year, we may easily compute how numerous they would shortly become, if not diminished by human industry. In the wild state they are less prolific; and the sow of the woods brings forth but once a year, probably because exhausted by rearing up her former numerous progeny.

It would be superfluous to dwell longer upon the nature and qualities of an animal too well known to need a description: there are few, even in cities, who are unacquainted with its uses, its appetites, and way of living. The arts of fattening, rearing, guarding, and managing hogs, fall more properly under the cognizance of the farmer than the naturalist; they make a branch of domestic economy, which, properly treated, may be extended to a great length: but the history of nature ought always to end where that of art begins. It will be sufficient, therefore, to observe that the wild boar was formerly a native of our country, as appears from the laws of Hoel Dda,* the famous Welsh legislator, who permitted his grand huntsman to chase that animal from the middle of November to the beginning of December. William the Conqueror also punished such as were convicted of killing the wild boar in his forests, with the loss of their eyes. At present the whole wild breed is extinct; but no country makes greater use of the tame kinds, as their flesh, which bears salt better than that of any other animal, makes a principal part of the provisions of the British navy.

As this animal is a native of almost every country, there are some varieties found in the species. That which we call the East-India breed, is lower, less furnished with hair, is usually black, and has the belly almost touching the ground; it is now.

* British Zoology, vol. i. p. 44.

common in England, fattens more easily than the ordinary kinds, and makes better bacon.

There is a remarkable variety of this animal about Upsal,* which is single-hoofed, like the horse; but in no other respect differing from the common kinds. The authority of Aristotle, who first made mention of this kind, has been often called in question; some have asserted, that such a quadruped never existed, because it happened not to fall within the sphere of their own confined observation; however, at present, the animal is too well known to admit of any doubt concerning it. The hog common in Guinea differs also in some things from our own; though shaped exactly as ours, it is of a reddish colour, with long ears, which end in a sharp point, and a tail which hangs down to the pastern; the whole body is covered with short red shining hair, without any bristles, but pretty long near the tail. Their flesh is said to be excellent, and they are very tame.

All these, from their near resemblance to the hog, may be considered as of the same species; the East-Indian hog, we well know, breeds with the common kind; whether the same obtains between it and those of Upsal and Guinea, we cannot directly affirm; but where the external similitude is so strong, we may be induced to believe that the appetites and habits are the same. It is true, we are told, that the Guinea breed will not mix with ours, but keep separate, and herd only together: however, this is no proof of their diversity, since every animal will prefer its own likeness in

* Amœnit. Acad. vol. 5. p. 465.

13

Do Seve del.   Harive sc.

The Peccary.

its mate; and they will only then mix with another sort, when deprived of the society of their own. These, therefore, we may consider as all of the hog kind; but there are other quadrupeds, that, in general, resemble this species, which, nevertheless, are very distinct from them. Travellers, indeed, from their general form, or from their habits and way of living, have been content to call these creatures hogs also; but upon a closer inspection, their differences are found to be such as entirely to separate the kinds, and make each a distinct animal by itself. *

The Peccary or Tajacu.

That animal which of all others most resembles a hog, and yet is of a formation very distinct from

[* A singular variety of the hog has lately been brought from Ethiopia, and was exhibited alive at the Hague. In its general form it resembled the common hog, but was peculiarly distinguished by a pair of large, flat, fleshy, semicircular lobes, placed immediately under the eyes. Its colour was a dusky blackish brown; the body strong, and the tail slender and a little flattened. It is said to be a fierce and dangerous animal, and to reside in subterraneous recesses, which it digs with its nose and hoofs.

Dr. Sparrman, while he was in Africa, witnessed a curious method by which this animal protected its young, when pursued. He followed several pigs with the old sows, with the intention of shooting one of them: but though he failed in this object, their chase afforded him singular pleasure. The heads of the females, which had before seemed of a tolerable size, appeared, on a sudden, to have grown larger and more shapeless than they were. This he found out to have been occasioned by the fact, that each of the old ones, during its flight, had taken up and carried forwards a young pig in its mouth; and this explained to him

it, is called the Peccary, or Tajacu. It is a native
of America, and found there in such numbers,
that they are seen in herds of several hundreds
together, grazing among the woods, and inoffensive, except when offended.

The Peccary at first view resembles a small hog;
the form of its body, the shape of its head, the
length of its snout, and the form of its legs, are
entirely alike: however, when we come to examine it nearer, the differences begin to appear.
The body is not so bulky; its legs not so long;
its bristles much thicker and stronger than those
of the hog, resembling rather the quills of a porcupine, than hair; instead of a tail, it has only a
little fleshy protuberance,, which does not even
cover its posteriors; but that which is still more
extraordinary, and in which it differs from all
other quadrupeds whatsoever, is, that it has got
upon its back a lump resembling the navel in other
animals, which is found to suppurate a liquor of a
very strong smell. The Peccary is the only creature that has those kind of glands which discharge
the musky substance, on that part of its body.
Some have them under the belly, and others under
the tail; but this creature, by a conformation
peculiar to itself, has them on its back. This lump,
or navel, is situated on that part of the back which
is over the hinder legs; it is, in general, so
covered with long bristles, that it cannot be seen,
except they be drawn aside. A small space then

another subject of his surprise, which was, that all the pigs
which he had just before been chasing with the old ones, had
vanished on a sudden. He was twice afterwards witness to the
same circumstance.].

appears, that is almost bare, and only beset with a few short fine hairs; but the middle is raised like a lump; and in this there is an orifice, into which one may thrust a common goose-quill. This hole or bag is not above an inch in depth; and round it, under the skin, are situated a number of small glands, which distil a whitish liquor, in colour and substance resembling that obtained from the civet animal. Perhaps it was this analogy, that led Dr. Tyson to say, that it smelt agreeably also, like that perfume. But this M. Buffon absolutely denies; affirming, that the smell is at every time, and in every proportion, strong and offensive; and to this I can add my own testimony, if that able naturalist should want a voucher.

But, to be more particular in the description of the other parts of this quadruped; the colour of the body is grizzly, and beset with bristles, thicker and stronger than those of a common hog; though not near so thick as those of a porcupine, they resemble them in this respect, that they are variegated with black and white rings. The belly is almost bare; and the short bristles on the sides gradually increase in length as they approach the ridge of the back, where some are five inches long. On the head also, between the ears, there is a large tuft of bristles, that are chiefly black. The ears are about two inches and a half long, and stand upright; and the eyes resemble those of a common hog, only they are smaller. From the lower corner of the eye to the snout is usually six inches; and the snout itself is like that of a hog, though it is but small. One side of the lower lip is generally smooth, by the rubbing of the tusk of the upper jaw. The feet and hoofs are perfectly like those of a common hog; but, as was already observed, it has no tail. There are some anatomical differences in its internal structure, from that of the common hog. Dr. Tyson was led to suppose that it had three stomachs, whereas the hog has but one; however, in this he was deceived, as M. Daubenton has plainly shown that the stomach is only divided by two closings, which gives it the appearance as if divided into three; and there is no conformation that prevents the food in any part of it from going or returning to any other.

. The peccary may be tamed like the hog, and has pretty nearly the same habits and natural inclinations. It feeds upon the same aliments; its flesh, though drier and leaner than that of the hog, is pretty good eating; it is improved by castration; and, when killed, not only the parts of generation must be taken instantly away, but also the navel on the back, with all the glands that contribute to its supply. If this operation be deferred for only half an hour, the flesh becomes utterly unfit to be eaten.

The peccary is extremely numerous in all the parts of Southern America. They go in herds of two or three hundred together; and unite, like hogs, in each other's defence. They are particularly fierce when their young are attempted to be taken from them. They surround the plunderer, attack him without fear, and frequently make his life pay the forfeit of his rashness. When any of the natives are pursued by a herd in this manner, they frequently climb a tree to avoid them; while the peccaries gather round the root, threaten with their tusks, and their rough bristles standing erect, as in the hog kind, they assume a very terrible appearance. In this manner they remain at the foot of the tree for hours together; while the hunter is obliged to wait patiently, and not without apprehensions, until they think fit to retire.

The peccary is rather fond of the mountainous parts of the country, than the lowlands; it seems to delight neither in the marshes nor the mud, like our hogs; it keeps among the woods; where it subsists upon wild fruits, roots, and vegetables; it is also an unceasing enemy to the lizard, the toad, and all the serpent kinds, with which these uncultivated forests abound. As soon as it perceives a serpent, or a viper, it at once seizes it with its fore hoofs and teeth, skins it in an instant, and devours the flesh. This is often seen, and may, therefore, be readily credited; but as to its applying to a proper vegetable immediately after, as an antidote to the poison of the animal it had devoured, this part of the relation we may very well suspect. The flesh neither of the toad or viper, as every one now knows, are poisonous; and, therefore, there is no need of a remedy against their venom. Ray gives no credit to either part of the account; however, we can have no reason to disbelieve that it feeds upon toads and serpents; it is only the making use of a vegetable antidote that appears improbable, and which perhaps had its rise in the ignorance and credulity of the natives.

The peccary, like the hog, is very prolific; the young ones follow the dam, and do not separate till they have come to perfection. If taken at first, they are very easily tamed, and soon lose all their natural ferocity; however, they never show any remarkable signs of docility, but continue stupid and rude, without attachment, or even seeming to know the hand that feeds them. They only continue to do no mischief; and they may be permitted to run tame, without apprehending any dangerous consequences. They seldom stray far from home; they return of themselves to the sty; and do not quarrel among each other, except when they happen to be fed in common. At such times, they have an angry kind of growl, much stronger and harsher than that of a hog; but they are seldom heard to scream as the former, only now and then, when frighted, or irritated, they have an abrupt angry manner of blowing, like the boar.

The peccary, though like the hog in so many various respects, is, nevertheless, a very distinct race, and will not mix, nor produce an intermediate breed. The European hog has been transplanted into America, and suffered to run wild among the woods; it is often seen to herd among a drove of peccaries, but never to breed from them. They may, therefore, be considered as two distinct creatures; the hog is the larger, and the more useful animal; the peccary, more feeble and local; the hog subsists in most parts of the world, and in almost every climate; the peccary is a native of the warmer regions, and cannot subsist in ours, without shelter and assistance. It is more than probable, however, that we could readily propagate the breed of this quadruped; and that, in two or three generations, it might be familiarized to our

De Seve del.   Warner sc.

The Cabiai.

climate; but, as it is inferior to the hog in every respect, so it would be needless to admit a new domestic, whose services are better supplied in the old. ....

....

....

The Capibara, or Cabiai.*

There are some quadrupeds so entirely different from any that we are acquainted with, that it is hard to find a well-known animal to which to resemble them. In this case, we must be content to place them near such as they most approach in form and habits, so that the reader may at once have some idea of the creature's shape or disposition, although, perhaps, an inadequate and a very confused one.

Upon that confused idea, however, it will be our business to work; to bring it, by degrees, to greater precision; to mark out the differences or form, and thus give the clearest notions that words can easily convey. The known animal is a kind of rude sketch of the figure we want to exhibit; from which, by degrees, we fashion out the shape of the creature we desire should be known; as a

[* This animal is by modern zoologists enumerated among the Cavys. It is extremely shy and timid, always going in pairs, and escaping but indifferently on account of the length of its feet. It will sometimes sit up while feeding, like a squirrel, holding its food between its paws. The fore feet are divided into four toes, connected to each other by a small web at the base, and tipped with thick claws, or rather small hoofs, at the extremities: the hind feet are formed in the same manner, but are divided into three toes only.]

statuary seldom begins his work till the rude out-line of the figure is given by some other hand—in this manner, I have placed the Capibara among the hog kind, merely because it is more like a hog than any other animal commonly known ; and yet, more closely examined, it will be found to differ in some of the most obvious particulars.

The Capibara resembles a hog of about two years old, in the shape of its body, and the coarse-ness and colour of its hair. Like the hog, it has a thick, short neck, and a rounded bristly back ; like the hog, it is fond of the water and marshy places, brings forth many at a time, and, like it, feeds upon animal and vegetable food. But, when examined more nearly, the differences are many and obvious. The head is longer, the eyes are larger, and the snout, instead of being rounded, as in the hog, is split, like that of a rabbit or hare, and furnished with thick strong whiskers ; the mouth is not so wide, the number and the form of the teeth are different, for it is without tusks : like the peccary, it wants a tail ; and, unlike to all others of this kind, instead of a cloven hoof, it is in a manner web-footed, and thus entirely fitted for swimming and living in the water. The hoofs before are divided into four parts ; and those behind into three ; between the divisions, there is a prolongation of the skin, so that the foot, when spread in swimming, can beat a greater surface of water.

As its feet are thus made for water, so it is seen to delight entirely in that element ; and some naturalists have called it the Water-hog for that reason. It is a native of South America, and is

15

The Babirouefsa.

chiefly seen frequenting the borders of lakes and
rivers, like the otter. It seizes the fish upon which
it preys, with its hoofs and teeth, and carries them
to the edge of the lake, to devour them at its ease.
It lives also upon fruits, corn, and sugar-canes.
As its legs are long and broad, it is often seen
sitting up, like a dog that is taught to beg. Its cry
more nearly resembles the braying of an ass, than
the grunting of a hog. It seldom goes out,
except at night, and that always in company. It
never ventures far from the sides of the river or
the lake in which it preys; for as it runs ill,
because of the length of its feet, and the shortness
of its legs, so its only place of safety is the water,
into which it immediately plunges when pursued,
and keeps so long at the bottom, that the hunter
can have no hopes of taking it there. The Capibara, even in a state of wildness, is of a gentle
nature, and, when taken young, is easily tamed.
It comes and goes at command, and even shows an
attachment to its keeper. Its flesh is said to be
fat and tender, but, from the nature of its food, it
has a fishy taste, like that of all those which are
bred in the water. Its head, however, is said to
be excellent; and, in this, it resembles the beaver,
whose fore parts taste like flesh, and the hinder
like the fish it feeds on.

The Babyrouessa, or Indian Hog.

The Babyrouessa is still more remote from the
hog kind than the Capibara; and yet most travellers who have described this animal, do not

scruple to call it the Hog of Borneo, which is an
island in the East Indies, where it is principally
to be found. Probably the animal's figure upon
the whole most resembles that of the hog kind, and
may have induced them to rank it among the
number; however, when they come to its description, they represent it as having neither the hair,
the bristles, the head, the stature, nor the tail of
a hog. Its legs, we are told, are longer, its snout
shorter, its body more slender, and somewhat resembling that of a stag; its hair is finer, of a gray
colour, rather resembling wool than bristles, and its
tail also tufted with the same. From these varieties, therefore, it can scarcely be called a hog; and
yet, in this class we must be content to rank it
until its form and nature come to be better known.
What we at present principally distinguish it by,
are four enormous tusks, that grow out of the
jaws; the two largest from the upper, and the
two smallest from the under. The jaw-bones of
this extraordinary animal are found to be very
thick and strong; from whence these monstrous
tusks are seen to proceed, that distinguish it from
all other quadrupeds whatsoever. The two that
go from the lower jaw are not above a foot long,
but those of the upper are above half a yard; as
in the boar, they bend circularly, and the two
lower stand in the jaw as they are seen to do in
that animal: but the two upper rise from the
upper jaw, rather like horns than teeth; and,
bending upwards and backwards, sometimes have
their points directed to the animal's eyes, and are
often fatal by growing into them. Were it not that
the Babyrouessa had two stick large teeth in the mouth,

we might easily suppose the two upper to be horns; and, in fact, their sockets are directed upwards; for which reason Doctor Grew was of that opinion. But, as the teeth of both jaws are of the same consistence, and as they both grow out of sockets in the same manner, the analogy between both is too strong not to suppose them of the same nature. The upper teeth, when they leave the socket, immediately pierce the upper lips of the animal, and grow as if they immediately went from its cheek. The tusks in both jaws are of a very fine ivory, smoother and whiter than that of the elephant, but not so hard or serviceable.

These enormous tusks give this animal a very formidable appearance; and yet it is thought to be much less dangerous than the wild boar.* Like animals of the hog kind, they go together in a body, and are often seen in company with the wild boar, with which, however, they are never known to engender. They have a very strong scent, which discovers them to the hounds; and, when pursued, they growl dreadfully, often turning back upon the dogs, and wounding them with the tusks of the lower jaw, for those of the upper are rather an obstruction than a defence. They run much swifter than the boar, and have a more exquisite scent, winding the men and the dogs at a great distance. When hunted closely, they generally plunge themselves into the sea, where they swim with great swiftness and facility, diving, and rising again at pleasure; and in this

* Buffon, vol. xxv. p. 179.

manner they most frequently escape their pursuers.
Although fierce and terrible when offended, yet
they are peaceable and harmless when unmolested.
They are easily tamed, and their flesh is good
to be eaten; but it is said to putrefy in a very
short time. They have a way of reposing themselves different from most other animals of the
larger kind; which is by hitching one of their
upper tusks on the branch of a tree, and then suffering their whole body to swing down at ease.
Thus suspended from a tooth, they continue the
whole night quite secure, and out of the reach of
such animals as hunt them for prey.

The Babyrouessa, though by its teeth and tusks
it seems fitted for a state of hostility, and probably
is carnivorous, yet, nevertheless, seems chiefly to
live upon vegetables and the leaves of trees. It
seldom seeks to break into gardens, like the bear,
in order to pillage the more succulent productions
of human industry, but lives remote from mankind,
content with coarser fare and security. It has been
said that it was only to be found in the island of
Borneo; but this is a mistake, as it is well known
in many other parts, both of Asia and Africa, as at
the Celebes, at Estrila, Senegal, and Madagascar.*

Such are the animals of the hog kind, which
are not distinctly known; and even all these, as
we see, have been but imperfectly examined, or
described. There are some others of which we
have still more imperfect notices; such as the
Warree, a hog of the isthmus of Darien, described
by Wafer, with large tusks, small ears, and bristles

* Anderson's Natural History of Greenland.

like a coarse fur all over the body. This, however, may be the European hog, which has run
wild in that part of the new world, as no other
traveller has taken notice of the same. The Ca-
nary boar seems different from other animals of
this kind, by the largeness of its tusks ; and, as is
judged from the skeleton, by the aperture of its
nostrils, and the number of its grinders. I cannot
conclude this account of those animals that are
thus furnished with enormous tusks, without observing that there is a strong consent between
these and the parts of generation. When castrated,
it is well known that the tusks grow much smaller,
and are scarcely seen to appear without the lips ;
but what is still more remarkable, is that in a
boar, if the tusks by any accident or design be
broke away, the animal abates of its fierceness
and venery, and it produces nearly the same effect
upon its constitution as if castration had actually
taken place.*

CHAP. XX.

Animals of the Cat Kind.†

WE have hitherto been describing a class of
peaceful and harmless animals, that serve as the

---

* Lisle's Husbandry, vol. ii. p. 329.

[† The quadrupeds of this family are distinguished by having
six front teeth, the intermediate ones of which are equal; the
grinders are three on each side in each jaw ; the tongue is furnished with rough prickles pointing backwards; and the claws
are sheathed and retractile, except in the lion, which has them
retractile but not sheathed.]

instruments of man's happiness, or at least that do
not openly oppose him. We come now to a bloody
and unrelenting tribe, that disdain to own his
power, and carry on unceasing hostilities against
him. All the class of the cat kind are chiefly distinguished by their sharp and formidable claws,
which they can hide and extend at pleasure. They
lead a solitary ravenous life, neither uniting for
their mutual defence, like vegetable feeders, nor
for their mutual support, like those of the dog
kind. The whole of this cruel and ferocious tribe
seek their food alone; and, except at certain seasons, are even enemies to each other. The dog,
the wolf, and the bear, are sometimes known to
live upon vegetable or farinaceous food; but all of
the cat kind, such as the lion, the tiger, the leopard, and the ounce, devour nothing but flesh, and
starve upon any other provision.

They are, in general, fierce, rapacious, subtle,
and cruel, unfit for society among each other, and
incapable of adding to human happiness. However, it is probable that even the fiercest could
be rendered domestic, if man thought the conquest
worth the trouble. Lions have been yoked to the
chariots of conquerors, and tigers have been taught
to tend those herds which they are known at present to destroy; but these services are not sufficient to recompense for the trouble of their keeping; so that, ceasing to be useful, they continue
to be noxious, and become rebellious subjects because not taken under equal protection with the
rest of the brute creation.

Other tribes of animals are classed with difficulty; have often but few points of resemblance;

and, though alike in form, have different dispositions, and different appetites. But all those of the
cat kind, although differing in size, or in colour,
are yet nearly allied to each other; being equally
fierce, rapacious, and artful; and he that has seen
one, has seen all. In other creatures there are many
changes wrought by human assiduity; the dog, the
hog, or the sheep, are altered in their natures and
forms, just as the necessities or the caprice of mankind have found fitting; but all of this kind are
inflexible in their forms, and wear the print of their
natural wildness strong upon them. The dogs or
cows vary in different countries, but lions or tigers
are still found the same; the very colour is nearly
alike in all; and the slightest alterations are sufficient to make a difference in the kinds, and to
give the animal a different denomination.

The cat kind are not less remarkable for the
sharpness and strength of their claws, which thrust
forth from their sheath when they seize their prey,
than for the shortness of their snout, the roundness
of their head, and the large whiskers which grow on
the upper lip. Their teeth also, which amount
to the number of thirty, are very formidable; but
are rather calculated for tearing their prey than
for chewing it; for this reason they feed but
slowly; and while they eat, generally continue
growling, to deter others from taking a share. In
the dog kind, the chief power lies in the under
jaw, which is long, and furnished with muscles of
amazing strength; but in these the greatest force
lies in the claws, which are extended with great
ease, and their gripe is so tenacious that nothing

can open it. The hinder parts in all these animals are much weaker than those before; and they seem less made for strength than agility. Nor are they endowed with the swiftness of most other animals; but generally owe their subsistence rather to catching their prey by surprise than by hunting it fairly down. They all seize it with a bound, at the same time expressing their fierce pleasure with a roar; and their first grasp generally disables the captive from all further resistance. With all these qualifications for slaughter, they nevertheless seem timid and cowardly, and seldom make an attack, like those of the dog kind, at a disadvantage: on the contrary, they fly when the force against them is superior, or even equal to their own; and the lion himself will not venture to make a second attempt, where he has been once repulsed with success. For this reason, in countries that are tolerably inhabited, the lion is so cowardly, that he is often scared away by the cries of women and children.

The cat, which is the smallest animal of this kind, is the only one that has been taken under human protection, and may be considered as a faithless friend, brought to oppose a still more insidious enemy.* It is, in fact, the only animal of this kind whose services can more than recompense the trouble of their education, and whose strength is not sufficient to make its anger formidable. The lion or the tiger may easily be tamed, and rendered subservient to human command; but even

---

* This description is nearly translated from M. Buffon: what is added by me, is marked with inverted commas.

in their humblest, and most familiar moments, they are still dangerous; since their strength is such, that the smallest fit of anger or caprice may have dreadful consequences. But the cat, though easily offended, and often capricious in her resentments, is not endowed with powers sufficient to do any great mischief. Of all animals, when young, there is none more prettily playful than the kitten; but it seems to lose this disposition as it grows old, and the innate treachery of its kind is then seen to prevail. From being naturally ravenous, education teaches it to disguise its appetites, and to watch the favourable moment of plunder; supple, insinuating, and artful, it has learnt the arts of concealing its intentions till it can put them into execution; when the opportunity offers, it at once seizes upon whatever it finds, flies off with it, and continues at a distance till it supposes its offence forgotten. The cat has only the appearance of attachment; and it may easily be perceived, by its timid approaches, and side-long looks, that it either dreads its master, or distrusts his kindness: different from the dog, whose caresses are sincere, the cat is assiduous rather for its own pleasure, than to please; and often gains confidence, only to abuse it. The form of its body, and its temperament, correspond with its disposition; active, cleanly, delicate, and voluptuous, it loves its ease, and seeks the softest cushions to lie on. " Many of its habits, however, are rather the consequences of its formation, than the result of any perverseness in its disposition; it is timid and mistrustful, because its body is weak, and its skin tender; a blow hurts it infinitely more than it does a dog, whose hide is thick, and body

muscular : the long far in which the cat is clothed,
entirely disguises its shape, which, if seen naked,
is long, feeble, and slender ; it is not to be wondered, therefore, that it appears much more fearful
of chastisement than the dog, and often flies, even
when no correction is intended. Being also the
native of the warmer climates, as will be shown
hereafter, it chooses the softest bed to lie on, which
is always the warmest."

The cat goes with young fifty-six days, and seldom brings forth above five or six at a time. The
female usually hides the place of her retreat from
the male, who is often found to devour her kittens.
She feeds them for some weeks with her milk, and
whatever small animals she can take by surprise,
accustoming them betimes to rapine. Before
they are a year old, they are fit to engender; the
female seeks the male with cries ; nor is their copulation performed without great pain, from the
narrowness of the passage in the female. They
live to about the age of ten years ; and, during
that period, they are extremely vivacious, suffering
to be worried a long time before they die.

The young kittens are very playful and amusing ;
but their sport soon turns into malice, and they,
from the beginning, show a disposition to cruelty ;
they often look wistfully towards the cage, sit
centinels at the mouth of a mouse-hole, and, in a
short time, become more expert hunters, than if
they had received the instructions of art. Indeed,
their disposition is so incapable of constraint, that
all instruction would be but thrown away. It is
true, that we are told of the Greek monks of the
isle of Cyprus teaching cats to hunt the serpents

with which the island is infested ; but this may be natural to the animal itself, and they might have fallen upon such a pursuit without any instruction. Whatever animal is much weaker than themselves, is to them an indiscriminate object of destruction. Birds, young rabbits, hares, rats and mice, bats, moles, toads, and frogs, are all equally pursued; though not, perhaps, equally acceptable. The mouse seems to be their favourite game ; and although the cat has the sense of smelling in but a mean degree, it, nevertheless, knows those holes in which its prey resides. I have seen one of them patiently watch a whole day until the mouse appeared, and continue quite motionless until it came within reach, and then seized it with a jump. Of all the marks by which the cat discovers its natural malignity, that of playing and sporting with its little captive, before killing it outright, is the most flagrant.

. The fixed inclination which they discover for this peculiar manner of pursuit, arises from the conformation of their eyes. The pupil in man, and in most other animals, is capable but of a small degree of contraction and dilatation; it enlarges a little in the dark, and contracts when the light pours in upon it in too great quantities. In the eyes of cats, however, this contraction and dilatation of the pupil, is so considerable, that the pupil, which by day-light appears narrow and small, like the black of one's nail, by night expands over the whole surface of the eye-ball, and, as every one must have seen, their eyes seem on fire. By this peculiar conformation, their eyes see better in darkness than light; and the animal is thus better adapted for spying out and surprising its prey.

Although the cat is an inhabitant of our houses, yet it cannot properly be called a dependant; although perfectly tame, yet it acknowledges no obedience; on the contrary, it does only just what it thinks fit, and no art can control any of its inclinations. In general, it is but half tamed; and has its attachments rather to the place in which it resides, than to the inhabitant. If the inhabitant quits the house, the cat still remains: and if carried elsewhere, seems for a while bewildered with its new situation. It must take time to become acquainted with the holes and retreats in which its prey resides, with all the little labyrinths through which they often make good an escape.

The cat is particularly fearful of water, of cold, and of ill smells. It loves to keep in the sun, to get near the fire, and to rub itself against those who carry perfumes. It is excessively fond of some plants, such as valerian, marum, and cat-mint; against these it rubs, smells them at a distance, and, at last, if they be planted in a garden, wears them out.

This animal eats slowly, and with difficulty, as its teeth are rather made for tearing, than chewing its aliments. For this reason, it loves the most tender food, particularly fish, which it eats as well boiled as raw. Its sleeping is very light; and it often seems to sleep, the better to deceive its prey. When the cat walks, it treads very softly, and without the least noise; and as to the necessities of nature, it is cleanly to the last degree. Its fur also is

usually sleek and glossy; and, for this reason, the
hair is easily electrified, sending forth shining
sparks, if rubbed in the dark.

"The wild cat breeds with the tame;* and,
therefore, the latter may be considered only as a
variety of the former: however, they differ in
some particulars; the cat, in its savage state, is
somewhat larger than the house-cat; and its fur
being longer, gives it a greater appearance than it
really has: its head is bigger, and face flatter: the
teeth and claws much more formidable; its muscles
very strong, as being formed for rapine; the tail
is of a moderate length, but very thick and flat,
marked with alternate bars of black and white, the
end always black; the hips, and hind part of the
lower joints of the leg, are always black; the fur
is very soft and fine: the general colour of these
animals, in England, is a yellowish white, mixed
with a deep grey. These colours, though they
appear at first sight confusedly blended together,
yet, on a close inspection, will be found to be
disposed like the streaks on the skin of the tiger,
pointing from the back downwards, rising from a
black list, that runs from the head, along the
middle of the back, to the tail. This animal is
found in our larger woods; and is the most destructive of the carnivorous kinds in this kingdom.
It inhabits the most mountainous and woody parts
of these islands, living mostly in trees, and feeding
only by night. It often happens, that the females
of the tame kind go into the woods to seek mates
among the wild ones. It should seem that these,

* British Zoology.

however, are not original inhabitants of this kingdom, but were introduced first in a domestic state,
and afterwards became wild in the woods, by ill
usage or neglect. Certain it is, the cat was an
animal much higher in esteem among our ancestors than it is at present. By the laws of Howel,
the price of a kitten, before it could see, was to
be a penny; till it caught a mouse, two-pence;
and, when it commenced mouser, four-pence. It
was required, besides, that it should be perfect in
its senses of hearing and seeing, be a good mouser,
have the claws whole, and be a good nurse. If
it failed in any of these qualities, the seller was to
forfeit to the buyer the third part of its value.
If any one stole or killed the cat that guarded the
prince's granary, he was to forfeit a milch ewe,
its fleece and lamb, or as much wheat as, when
poured on the cat, suspended by the tail (the head
touching the floor) would form a heap high enough
to cover the tip of the former. From hence we
discover, besides a picture of the simplicity of the
times, a strong argument that cats were not naturally bred in our forests. An animal that could
be so easily taken, could never have been rated so
highly; and the precautions laid down to improve
the breed, would have been superfluous, in a creature that multiplies to such an amazing degree.

" In our climate, we know but of one variety
of the wild cat; and, from the accounts of travellers, we learn that there are but very few differences in this quadruped in all parts of the world.
The greatest difference, indeed, between the wild
and the tame cat, is rather to be found internally
than in their outward form. Of all other quadru-

peds, the wild cat is, perhaps, that whose intestines are proportionably the smallest and the shortest. The intestines of the sheep, for instance, unravelled out, and measured according to their length, will be found to be above thirty times the length of its body; whereas, the wild cat's intestines, being measured out, will not be found above three times the length of its body. This is a surprising dif-ference: but we may account for it, from the nature of the food in the two animals; the one living upon vegetables, which requires a longer, and a more tedious preparation, before they can become a part of its body: the other living upon flesh, which requires very little alteration, in order to be assimilated into the substance of the creature that feeds upon it. The one, therefore, wanted a long canal for properly digesting and straining its food; the other but a short one, as the food is already prepared to pass the usual secretions: however, a difficulty still remains behind; the intestines of the wild cat are, by one third, shorter than those of the tame. How can we account for this? If we say that the domestic cat, living upon more nourishing and more plentiful provision, has its intestines enlarged to the quantity with which it is supplied, we shall find this observation contradicted in the wild boar and the wolf, whose intestines are as long as those of the hog or the dog, though they lead a savage life, and, like the wild cat, are fed by precarious subsistence. The shortness, therefore, of the wild cat's intestines, is still unaccounted for: and most naturalists consider the difficulty as inextricable. We must leave it, therefore, as one of those difficulties which future observation or accident are most likely to discover.

This animal is one of those few which are common to the new continent as well as the old. When Christopher Columbus first discovered that country, a hunter brought him one which he had discovered in the woods: it was of the ordinary size, the tail very long and thick. They were common also in Peru, although they were not rendered domestic. They are well known also in several parts of Africa, and many parts of Asia. In some of these countries they are of a peculiar colour, and inclining to blue. In Persia, Pietro della Valle informs us, that there is a kind of cat, particularly in the province of Chorazan, of the figure and form of the ordinary one, but infinitely more beautiful in the lustre and colour of its skin. It is of a grey blue, without mixture, and as soft and shining as silk. The tail is very long, and covered with hair six inches long, which the animal throws upon its back, like the squirrel. These cats are well known in France; and have been brought over into England, under the name of the *blue cat,* which, however, is not their colour.

Another variety of this animal is called by us the *lion cat,* or, as others more properly term it, the Cat of Angora. These are larger than the common cat, and even than the wild one. Their hair is much longer, and hangs about their head and neck, giving this creature the appearance of a lion. Some of these are white, and others of a dun colour. These come from Syria and Persia, two countries which are noted for giving a long soft hair to the animals which are bred in them. The sheep, the goats, the dogs, and the rabbits of Syria, are all remarkable for the fine glossy length and softness of their hair; but particularly the cat, whose nature seems to be so inflexible, conforms to the nature of the climate and soil, loses its savage colour, which it preserves almost in every other part of the world, and assumes the most beautiful appearance. There are some other varieties in this animal, but rather in colour than in form; and, in general, it may be remarked, that the cat, when carried into other countries, alters but very little, still preserving its natural manners, habits, and conformation.*

[* In addition to what is here said it may be observed, that cats in their wild state breed in hollow trees, and bring forth about four kittens at a time, which are blind for the first nine days. They have a singular facility at climbing, in consequence of their being furnished with a perfect collar-bone. In a domestic state, they have been known to acquire a considerable degree of sagacity, so as to learn to open doors, by pressing down the latch; and instances of their great attachment to man are by no means rare: but Mr. White, in his Natural History of Selborne, gives an instance of one which afforded maternal tenderness even to a leveret. " My friend had a little helpless leveret brought to him, which the servants fed with milk from a spoon; and about the same time his cat kittened, and the young were dispatched and buried. The hare was soon lost, and was supposed to have been killed by some dog or cat. However, in about a fortnight, as the master was sitting in the garden, in the dusk of the evening, he observed his cat, with tail erect, trotting towards him, and calling, with little short inward notes of complacency, such as these animals use towards their kittens, and something gamboling after her, which proved to be the leveret that the cat had nourished with her milk, and continued to support with great affection. Thus was a graminivorous animal nurtured by a carnivorous and predacious one! This strange affection was proba-

The Lion.

The influence of climate upon mankind is very small;* he is found to subsist in all parts of the earth, as well under the frozen poles, as beneath the torrid zone: but in animals, the climate may be considered as congenial, and a kind of second nature. They almost all have their particular latitudes, beyond which they are unable to subsist; either perishing with a moderate cold, or dying for want of a frozen air, even in a temperate climate. The rein-deer is never seen to depart from the icy fields of the north; and, on the contrary, the lion degenerates, when taken from beneath the line. The whole earth is the native country of man; but all inferior animals have each their own peculiar districts.

Most terrestrial animals are found larger, fiercer, and stronger, in the warmer than in the cold or temperate climates. They are also more courageous and enterprizing; all their dispositions seeming to partake of the ardour of their native soil.

bly occasioned by those tender maternal feelings which the loss of her kittens had awakened: and by the complacency and ease she derived from the procuring her teats to be drawn, which were too much distended with milk. From habit she became as much delighted with this foundling, as if it had been a real offspring."

It may likewise be mentioned that cats are not, as is commonly supposed, troubled with fleas; and that when rubbed in the dark, they emit electrical sparks.]

* This description is principally taken from M. Buffon; such parts as are added from others, I have marked with inverted commas.

16

The Lion.

The lion produced under the burning sun of Africa, is, of all others, the most terrible, the most undaunted. The wolf or the dog, instead of attempting to rival him, scarcely deserve to attend his motions, or become his providers. Such, however of these animals, as are bred in a more temperate climate, or towards the tops of cold and lofty mountains, are far more gentle, or, to speak more properly, far less dangerous than those bred in the torrid vallies beneath. The lions of Mount Atlas, the tops of which are covered in eternal snows, have neither the strength nor the ferocity of the lions of Bildulgerid or Zaara, where the plains are covered with burning sands. It is particularly in these frightful deserts, that those enormous and terrible beasts are found, that seem to be the scourge and the terror of the neighbouring kingdoms. Happily, indeed, the species is not very numerous, and it seems to be diminishing daily; for those who have travelled through these countries, assure us, that there are by no means so many there at present, as were known formerly; and Mr. Shaw observes, that the Romans carried fifty times as many lions from Lybia, in one year, to combat in their amphitheatres, as are to be found in the whole country at this time. The same remark is made with regard to Turkey, to Persia, and the Indies; where the lions are found to diminish in their numbers every day. Nor is it difficult to assign the cause of this diminution. It is obvious that it cannot be owing to the increase of the force of other quadrupeds, since they are all inferior to the lion, and, consequently, instead of lessening the number, only tend to increase

¶

the supplies on which they subsist; it must, therefore, be occasioned by the increase of mankind,
who is the only animal in nature capable of making
head against these tyrants of the forest, and preventing their increase. The arms even of a Hottentot or a Negro, make them more than a match
for this powerful creature; and they seldom make
the attack, without coming off victorious. Their
usual manner is to find out his retreat, and, with
spears headed with iron, to provoke him to the
combat; four men are considered as sufficient for
this encounter; and he against whom the lion
flies, receives him upon his spear, while the others
attack him behind. The lion, finding himself
wounded in the rear, turns that way, and thus
gives the man he first attacked an opportunity to
recover. In this manner, they attack him on all
sides; until, at last, they entirely disable, and then
dispatch him. This superiority in the numbers,
and the arts of man, that are sufficient to conquer the lion, serve also to enervate and discourage
him; for he is brave only in proportion to the
success of his former encounters. In the vast
deserts of Zaara, in the burning sands that lie between Mauritania and Negroland, in the uninha-
bited countries that lie to the north of Cafraria,
and, in general, in all the deserts of Africa, where
man has not fixed his habitation, the lions are
found in great numbers, and preserve their natural
courage and force. Accustomed to measure
their strength with every animal they meet, the
habit of conquering renders them intrepid and terrible. Having never experienced the dangerous
arts and combinations of man, they have no ap-

prehensions from his power. They boldly face him, and seem to brave the force of his arms. Wounds rather serve to provoke their rage than repress their ardour. They are not daunted even with the opposition of numbers; a single lion of the desert often attacks an entire caravan; and, after an obstinate combat, when he finds himself overpowered, instead of flying, he continues to combat, retreating, and still facing the enemy till he dies. On the contrary, the lions which inhabit the peopled countries of Morocco or India, having become acquainted with human power, and experienced man's superiority, have lost all their courage, so as to be scared away with a shout; and seldom attack any but the unresisting flocks or herds, which even women and children are sufficient to protect.

This alteration in the lion's disposition sufficiently shows that he might easily be tamed, and admit of a certain degree of education. "In fact, nothing is more common than for the keepers of wild beasts to play with this animal, to pull out his tongue, and even to chastise him without a cause. He seems to bear it all with the utmost composure; and we very rarely have instances of his revenging these unprovoked sallies of impertinent cruelty. However, when his anger is at last excited, the consequences are terrible. Labat tells us of a gentleman who kept a lion in his chamber and employed a servant to attend it; who, as is usual, mixed his blows with caresses. This ill-judged association continued for some time; till one morning the gentleman was awakened by a noise in his room, which, at first, he could not tell

the cause of; but drawing the curtains, he perceived a horrid spectacle; the lion growling over
the man's head, which he had separated from the
body, and tossing it round the floor. He immediately, therefore, flew into the next room, called
to the people without, and had the animal secured
from doing further mischief." However, this single
account is not sufficient to weigh against the many
instances we every day see of this creature's gentleness and submission. He is often bred up with
other domestic animals, and is seen to play inno-
cently and familiarly among them; and, if it
ever happens that his natural ferocity returns, it is
seldom exerted against his benefactors. As his passions are strong, and his appetites vehement, one
ought not to presume that the impressions of education will always prevail; so that it would be
dangerous in such circumstances to suffer him to
remain too long without food, or to persist in
irritating and abusing him: however, numberless
accounts assure us that his anger is noble, his
courage magnanimous, and his disposition grateful. He has been often seen to despise contemptible enemies, and pardon their insults when it was
in his power to punish them. He has been seen to
spare the lives of such as were thrown to be devoured by him, to live peaceably with them, to
afford them a part of his subsistence, and sometimes to want food himself rather than deprive
them of that life which his generosity had spared.

It may also be said that the lion is not cruel,
since he is so only from necessity, and never kills
more than he consumes. When satiated he is perfectly gentle; while the tiger, the wolf, and all the

inferior kinds, such as the fox, the pole-cat, and the ferret, kill without remorse, are fierce without cause, and, by their indiscriminate slaughter, seem rather to satisfy their malignity than their hunger.

The outward form of the lion seems to speak his internal generosity. His figure is striking, his look confident and bold, his gait proud, and his voice terrible. His stature is not overgrown, like that of the elephant, or rhinoceros; nor is his shape clumsy, like that of the hippopotamos, or the ox. It is compact, well-proportioned, and sizeable; a perfect model of strength joined with agility. It is muscular and bold, neither charged with fat or unnecessary flesh. It is sufficient but to see him in order to be assured of his superior force. His large head surrounded with a dreadful mane; all those muscles that appear under the skin swelling with the slightest exertions; and the great breadth of his paws, with the thickness of his limbs, plainly evince that no other animal in the forest is capable of opposing him. He has a very broad face, that, as some have imagined, resembles the human. It is surrounded with very long hair, which gives it a very majestic air. The top of the head, the temples, the cheeks, the under jaw, the neck, the breast, the shoulder, the hinder part of the legs, and the belly, are furnished with it, while all the rest of the body is covered with very short hair, of a tawny colour. " The length of the hair in many parts, and the shortness of it in others, serves a good deal to disguise this animal's real figure. The breast, for instance, appears very broad, but in

reality it is as narrow and contracted in proportion
as that of the generality of dogs and horses. For
the same reason, the tail seems to be of an equal
thickness from one end to the other, on account of
the inequality of the hair with which it is encom-
passed; it being shorter near the insertion, where
the flesh and bones are large, and growing longer in
proportion as its real thickness lessens towards the
point, where it ends in a tuft. The hair about the
neck and breast is not different from that on the
rest of the body, except in the length of it; nor is
each hair pointed as in most other animals, but of
an equal thickness from one end to the other. The
neck is very strong, but not composed of one solid
bone, as Aristotle has imagined; on the contrary,
though very short and muscular, it has as many
bones as the camel or the horse; for it is universal
to all quadrupeds to have seven joints in the neck;
and not one of them have either more or less.
However, the muscles in the neck of the lion, that
tie the bones together, are extremely strong, and
have somewhat the appearance of bones; so
that ancient authors, who have treated of this
animal, have mistaken the whole for a single bone.
The tongue is rough, and beset with prickles as
hard as a cat's claws; these have the grain turned
backwards; so that it is probable a lion, if it should
attempt to lick a man's hand, as we are told it
sometimes does, would tear off the skin. The
eyes are always bright and fiery; nor even in death
does this terrible look forsake them. In short, the
structure of the paws, teeth, eyes, and tongue,
are the same as in a cat; and also in the inward

parts these two animals so nearly resemble each
other, that the anatomist's chief distinction arises
merely from the size."

The lion has, as was observed before, a large
mane, which grows every year longer as the animal
grows older : the lioness is without this ornament
at every age. This mane is not coarse or rough as
in a horse, but composed of the same hair with
the rest of the body, lengthened and shining. The
mane, as well as the rest of the body, is of a yellow
colour ; nor is there ever any difference to be
found in the colour of one lion from that of another. What the ancients might have said concerning black lions, or white, or streaked like the
tiger, is not confirmed by modern experience; so
that these varieties have never been seen, or exist
no longer.

It is usually supposed that the lion is not possessed of the sense of smelling in such perfection as
most other animals. It is also observed, that too
strong a light greatly incommodes him. This is
more than probable from the formation of his eyes,
which, like those of the cat, seem fitted for seeing
best in the dark. For this reason, he seldom
appears in open day, but ravages chiefly by night;
and not only the lion, but all other animals of the
cat kind, are kept off by the fires which the inhabitants light to preserve their herds and flocks; the
brightness of the flame dazzles their eyes, which are
only fitted for seeing in the dark; and they are
afraid to venture blindly into those places which
they know to be filled with their enemies. " It is
equally true of all this kind, that they hunt rather
by the sight than the smell; and it sometimes hap-

pens that the lion pursues either the jackall or
the wild dog, while they are hunting upon the
scent; and when they have run the beast down,
he comes in, and monopolizes the spoil. From
hence, probably, may have arisen the story of the
lion's provider: these little industrious animals
may often, it is true, provide a feast for the lion;
but they have hunted merely for themselves, and
he is an unwelcome intruder upon the fruits of
their toil."

The lion, when hungry, boldly attacks all animals that come in his way; but as he is very formidable, and as they all seek to avoid him, he is often
obliged to hide, in order to take them by surprise.
For this purpose he crouches on his belly, in some
thicket, or among the long grass, which is found
in many parts of the forest; in this retreat he
continues, with patient expectation, until his prey
comes within a proper distance, and he then
springs after it, fifteen or twenty feet from him,
and often seizes it at the first bound. If he misses
the effort, and in two or three reiterated springs
cannot seize his prey, he continues motionless for
a time, seems to be very sensible of his disappoint-
ment, and waits for a more successful opportunity.
In the deserts and forests, his most usual prey are
the gazelles and the monkeys, with which the
torrid regions abound. The latter he takes when
they happen to be on the ground, for he cannot
climb trees like the cat or tiger. He devours a
great deal at a time, and generally fills himself for
two or three days to come. His teeth are so
strong that he very easily breaks the bones, and
swallows them with the rest of the body. It is

reported that he sustains hunger a very long time, but thirst he cannot support in an equal degree, his temperament being extremely hot; some have even asserted that he is in a continual fever. He drinks as often as he meets with water, lapping it like a cat; which, as we know, drinks but slowly. He generally requires about fifteen pounds of raw flesh in a day; he prefers that of live animals, and particularly those which he has just killed. He seldom devours the bodies of animals when they begin to putrefy; and he chooses rather to hunt for a fresh spoil, than to return to that which he had half devoured before. However, though he usually feeds upon fresh provision, his breath is very offensive, and his urine insupportable.

The roaring of the lion is so loud, that when it is heard in the night, and re-echoed by the mountains, it resembles distant thunder. This roar is his natural note; for when enraged he has a different growl, which is short, broken, and reiterated. The roar is a deep hollow growl, which he sends forth five or six times a day, particularly before rains. The cry of anger is much louder, and more formidable. This is always excited by opposition; and upon those occasions, when the lion summons up all his terrors for the combat, nothing can be more terrible. He then lashes his sides with his long tail, which alone is strong enough to lay a man level. He moves his mane in every direction; it seems to rise and stand like bristles round his head; the skin and muscles of his face are all in agitation; his huge eye-brows half cover his glaring eye-balls; he discovers his teeth, which are formed rather for destruction

than chewing his food; he shows his tongue.
covered with points, and extends his claws, which
appear almost as long as a man's fingers. Prepared
in this manner for war, there are few animals that
will venture to engage him; and even the boldest
of the human kind are daunted at his approach.
The elephant, the rhinoceros, the tiger, and the
hippopotamos, are the only animals that are not
afraid singly to make opposition.

" Nevertheless, neither the leopard nor the wild
boar, if provoked, will shun the combat; they do
not seek the lion to attack, but will not fly at his
approach; they wait his onset, which he seldom
makes, unless compelled by hunger; they then
exert all their strength, and are sometimes successful. We are told of the combat of a lion and a wild
boar, in a meadow near Algiers, which continued for a long time with incredible obstinacy.
At last both were seen to fall by the wounds they
had given each other; and the ground all about
them was covered with their blood. These instances, however, are very rare, for the lion is in
general the undisputed master of the forest. Man
is the only creature that attacks him with almost
certain success, with the assistance of dogs and
horses, which are trained to the pursuit. These
animals that, in a state of nature, would have fled
from the presence of the lion, in an agony of consternation, when conscious of the assistance of
man, become pursuers in turn, and boldly hunt
their natural tyrant. The dogs are always of the
large breed; and the horses themselves, as Gesner
assures us, must be of that sort called Cherossi, or
lion-eyed, all others of this kind flying at the

sight of the lion, and endeavouring to throw their riders. When the lion is rouzed, he recedes with slow proud motion; he never goes off directly forward, nor measures his paces equally, but takes an oblique course, going from one side to the other; and bounding rather than running. When the hunters approach him, they either shoot or throw their javelins; and in this manner disable him before he is attacked by the dogs, many of whom he would otherwise destroy. He is very vivacious, and is never killed at once, but continues to fight desperately, even after he has received his mortal blow. He is also taken by pit-falls; the natives digging a deep hole in the ground, and covering it slightly over with sticks and earth; which, however, give way beneath his weight, and he sinks to the bottom, from whence he has no means of escape. But the most usual manner of taking this animal is while a cub, and incapable of resistance: The place near the den of the lioness is generally well known by the greatness of her depredations on that occasion; the natives, therefore, watch the time of her absence, and, aided by a swift horse, carry off her cubs; which they sell to strangers, or to the great men of their country."

The lion, while young and active, lives by hunting in the forest, at the greatest distance from any human habitation; and seldom quits this retreat while able to subsist by his natural industry; but when he becomes old, and unfit for the purposes of surprise, he boldly comes down into places more frequented, attacks the flocks and herds that take shelter near the habitation of the shepherd or the husbandman, and depends rather upon his courage than his address for support. It is remarkable,. however, that when he makes one of these desperate sallies, if he finds men and quadrupeds in the same field, he only attacks the latter, and never meddles with men, unless they provoke him to engage. It is observed that he prefers the flesh of camels to any other food; he is likewise said to be fond of that of young elephants; these he often attacks before their trunk is yet grown; and unless the old elephant comes to their assistance, he makes them an easy prey.

The lion is terrible upon all occasions, but particularly at those seasons when he is incited by desire, or when the female has brought forth. It is then that the lioness is seen followed by eight or ten males, who fight most bloody battles among each other, till one of them becomes victorious over all the rest. She is said to bring forth in spring, and to produce but once a year. "With respect to the time of gestation, naturalists have been divided, some asserting that the lioness went with young six months, and others but two. The time also of their growth and their age have hitherto been left in obscurity; some asserting that they acquired their full growth in three years, and others that they require a longer period to come to perfection; some saying (and among this number is M. Buffon) that they lived to but twenty, or twenty-two years at most; others making their lives even of shorter duration. All these doubts are now reduced to certainty; for we have had several of these animals bred in the Tower; so that the manner of their copulation, the time of their gestation, the number they bring forth, and the

17

De Séve del.   Warner sculp.

The Lionefs.

time they take to come to perfection, are all pretty
well known. Although the lion emits his urine
backwards, yet he couples in the ordinary manner;
and, as was said before, his internal structure
in almost every respect resembles that of a cat.
The lioness, however, is upon these occasions
particularly fierce, and often wounds the lion
in a terrible manner. She goes with young, as
I am assured by her keeper, no more than five
months; the young ones, which are never more
than two in number, when brought forth are
about the size of a large pug dog, harmless, pretty,
and playful; they continue the teat for twelve
months, and the animal is more than five years in
coming to perfection. As to its age, from its imprisoned state, we can have no certainty; since
it is very probable that, being deprived of its
natural climate, food, and exercise, its life must be
very much abridged. However, naturalists have
hitherto been greatly mistaken as to the length of
its existence. The great he-lion, called Pompey,
which died in the year 1760, was known to have
been in the Tower for above seventy years; and
one lately died there, which was brought from the
river Gambia, that died above sixty-three. The
lion, therefore, is a very long-lived animal; and,
very probably, in his native forests, his age exceeds
even that of man himself."

In this animal, all the passions, even of the
most gentle kind, are in excess, but particularly
the attachment of the female to her young. The
lioness, though naturally less strong, less courageous, and less mischievous than the lion, becomes terrible when she has got young ones to

provide for. She then makes her incursions with even more intrepidity than the lion himself; she throws herself indiscriminately among men and other animals; destroys without distinction; loads herself with the spoil, and brings it home reeking to her cubs; whom she accustoms betimes to cruelty and slaughter. She usually brings forth in the most retired and inaccessible places; and when she fears to have her retreat discovered, often hides her tracks, by running back her ground, or by brushing them out with her tail. She sometimes, also, when her apprehensions are great, transports them from one place to another, and, if obstructed, defends them with determined courage, and fights to the last.

The lion is chiefly an inhabitant of the torrid zone; and, as was said, is always most formidable there; nevertheless, he can subsist in more temperate climates; and there was a time when even the southern parts of Europe were infested by him. At present, he is only found in Africa and the East Indies; in some of which countries he grows to an enormous height. The lion of Bildulgerid is said to be nearly five feet high, and between nine and ten feet from the tip of the nose to the insertion of the tail. We have in the Tower, at present, one of above four feet high, that was brought from Morocco, which is the largest that for some time past has been seen in Europe. The ordinary size is between three and four feet; the female being, in all her dimensions, about one third less than the male. There are no lions in America; the Puma, which has received the name of the American Lion, is, when com-

pared, a very contemptible animal, having neither
the shape, the size, nor the mane of the lion;
being known to be extremely cowardly, to climb
trees for its prey, to subsist rather by its cunning
than its courage, and to be inferior even to the
animal that goes by the name of the American
Tiger. We ought not, therefore, to confound
this little treacherous creature with the lion, which
all the ancients have concurred in denominating the
king of beasts, and which they have described as
brave and merciful. " Indeed, the numerous
accounts which they have given us of this animal's
generosity and tenderness, show that there must
be some foundation for the general belief of its
good qualities; for mankind seldom err when they
are all found to unite in the same story. However,
perhaps, the caution of Aristophanes, the comic
poet, is better followed in practice, who advises us
to have nothing to do with this creature, but to let
the lioness suckle her own whelps."*

[In Dr. Sparrman's Voyage to the Cape, he
relates that one of the Namaaqua Hottentots,
endeavouring to drive his master's cattle into a pool
of water, enclosed between two ridges of rock,
espied a huge lion couching in the midst of the pool.
Terrified at the unexpected sight of such a beast,
which seemed to have its eyes fixed upon him, he
instantly took to his heels. In doing this, he had
presence of mind enough to run through the herd;
concluding, that if the lion should pursue, he would
take up with the first beast that should present
itself. In this, however, he was mistaken. The

* Ου χρη λεοντος σκυμνον εν πολει τρεφειν

lion broke through the herd, making directly
after the Hottentot; who, on turning round, and
perceiving that the monster had singled him out,
breathless and half dead with fear, scrambled up
one of the tree-aloes, in the trunk of which had
luckily been cut out a few steps, the more readily
to come at some birds' nests that the branches
contained. At the same moment the lion made a
spring at him, but missing his aim fell upon the
ground. In surly silence he walked round the
tree, casting at times a dreadful look towards the
poor Hottentot, who had crept behind the nests.
I should here remark, that these nests belong to
a small bird of the genus Loxia, that lives in a
state of society with the rest of its species, con-
structing a whole republic of nests in one clump,
and under one cover. One of these clumps of
nests sometimes extends a space of ten feet in
diameter, and contains a population of several
hundred individuals. It was under the cover of one
of these structures, that the Hottentot screened
himself from the view of the lion. Having remained silent and motionless for a length of time,
he ventured to peep over the side of the nest,
hoping that the lion had departed; when, to his
great terror and astonishment, his eyes met those
of the animal, which, as the poor fellow afterwards
expressed himself, flashed fire at him. In short,
the lion laid himself down at the foot of the tree,
and did not move from the place for four-and-
twenty hours. At the end of this time, becoming
parched with thirst, the beast went to a spring at
some distance, in order to drink. The Hottentot,
with trepidation, ventured to descend, and ran

18

The Tiger.

off to his home, which was not more than a mile distant, as fast as his feet could carry him, where he arrived in safety. The perseverance of the lion was such, that it appeared afterwards he returned to the tree, and finding the man had descended, hunted him, by the scent, to within three hundred paces of the house.

Lions have been occasionally made a part of the establishment of royal pomp in the East. The monarch of Persia, we are informed by Mr. Bell in his Travels, had, on his days of audience, two large lions chained on each side the passages of the hall of state; being led there by proper officers, in chains of gold.]

The Tiger.

" The ancients had a saying, *That as the peacock is the most beautiful among birds, so is the tiger among quadrupeds.** In fact, no quadruped can be more beautiful than this animal; the glossy smoothness of his hair, which lies much smoother, and shines with greater brightness than even that of the leopard; the extreme blackness of the streaks with which he is marked, and the bright yellow colour of the ground which they diversify, at once strike the beholder. To this beauty of colouring is added an extremely elegant form, much larger indeed than that of the leopard, but more slender, more delicate, and be-

* Tantum autem præstat pulchritudine tygris inter alias feras, quantum inter volucres pavo.

†

speaking the most extreme swiftness and agility. Unhappily, however, this animal's disposition is as mischievous as its form is admirable, as if Providence was willing to show the small value of beauty, by bestowing it on the most noxious of quadrupeds. We have, at present, one of these animals in the Tower, which to the view appears the most good-natured and harmless creature in the world: its physiognomy is far from fierce or angry; it has not the commanding stern countenance of the lion, but a gentle placid air; yet for all this it is fierce and savage beyond measure; neither correction can terrify it, nor indulgence can tame."

The chief and most observable distinction in the tiger, and in which it differs from all others of the mottled kind, is in the shape of its colours, which run in streaks or bands in the same direction as his ribs, from the back down to the belly. The leopard, the panther, and the ounce, are all partly covered like this animal, but with this difference, that their colours are broken in spots all over the body; whereas in the tiger they stretch lengthwise, and there is scarcely a round spot to be found on his skin. Besides this, there are other observable distinctions: the tiger is much larger, and often found bigger even than the lion himself: it is much slenderer also in proportion to its size; its legs shorter, and its neck and body longer. In short, of all other animals, it most resembles the cat in shape; and if we conceive the latter magnified to a very great degree, we shall have a tolerable idea of the former.

In classing carnivorous animals, we may place

the lion foremost.;* and immediately after him follows the tiger, which seems to partake of all the noxious qualities of the lion, without sharing any of his good ones. To pride, courage, and strength, the lion joins greatness, clemency, and generosity; but the tiger is fierce without provocation, and cruel without necessity. The lion seldom ravages except when excited by hunger; the tiger, on the contrary, though glutted with slaughter, is not satisfied, still continues the carnage, and seems to have its courage only inflamed by not finding resistance. In falling in among a flock or a herd, it gives no quarter, but levels all with indiscriminate cruelty, and scarcely finds time to appease its appetite, while intent upon satisfying the malignity of its nature. It thus becomes the scourge of the country where it is found; it fears neither the threats nor the opposition of mankind; the beasts both wild and tame fall equally a sacrifice to its insatiable fury; the young elephant and the rhinoceros become equally its prey, and it not unfrequently ventures to attack the lion himself.

Happily for the rest of nature, that this animal is not common, and that the species is chiefly confined to the warmest provinces of the East. The tiger is found in Malabar, in Siam, in Bengal, and in all the countries which are inhabited by the elephant or the rhinoceros. Some even pretend that it has a friendship for, and often accompanies the latter, in order to devour its excrements, which serve it as a purge. Be this as it will, there

* The remainder of this description is taken from M. Buffon, except where marked with inverted commas.

is no doubt but that they are often seen together at
the sides of lakes and rivers; where they are probably both compelled to go by the thirst which in that
torrid climate they must very often endure. It
is likely enough, also, that they seldom make war
upon each other, the rhinoceros being a peaceable
animal, and the tiger knowing its strength too well
to venture the engagement. It is still more likely
that the tiger finds this a very convenient situation,
since it can there surprise a greater number of animals, which are compelled thither from the same
motives. In fact, it is generally known to lurk
near such places where it has an opportunity of
choosing its prey, or rather of multiplying its mas-
sacres. When it has killed one, it often goes to
destroy others, swallowing their blood at large
draughts, and seeming rather glutted than satiated
with its abundance.

However, when it has killed a large animal,
such as a horse or a buffalo, it immediately begins
to devour it on the spot, fearing to be disturbed.
In order to feast at its ease, it carries off its prey
to the forest, dragging it along with such ease,
that the swiftness of its motion seems scarcely re-
tarded by the enormous load it sustains. From
this alone we may judge of its strength; but, to
have a more just idea of this particular, let us stop
a moment to consider the dimensions of this most
formidable creature. Some travellers have compared it for size to a horse, and others to a buffalo,
while others have contented themselves with saying that it was much larger than a lion. We have
recent accounts of this animal's magnitude that deserve the utmost confidence. M. Buffon has been

assured by one of his friends that he saw a tiger, in the East Indies, of fifteen feet long. "Supposing that he means including the tail, this animal, allowing four feet for that, must have been eleven feet from the tip of the nose to the insertion of the tail. Indeed, that which is now in the Tower is not so large, being, as well as I could measure, six feet from the tip to the insertion, and the tail was three feet more. Like all the rest of its kind, its motions are irregular and desultory; it bounds rather than runs; and like them rather chooses to take its prey by surprise than to be at the troub'e of hunting it down." How large a leap it can take at once we may easily judge, by comparing what it might do to what we see so small an animal as the cat actually perform. The cat can leap several feet at a bound; and the tiger, who is ten times as long, can no doubt spring proportionably.

"The tiger is the only animal whose spirit seems untameable. Neither force nor constraint, neither violence nor flattery, can prevail in the least on its stubborn nature. The caresses of the keeper have no influence on their heart of iron; and time, instead of mollifying its disposition, only serves to increase its fiercenes and malignity. The tiger snaps at the hand that feeds it as well as that by which it is chastised; every object seems considered only as its proper prey, which it devours with a look: and, although confined by bars and chains, still makes fruitless efforts, as if to show its malignity when incapable of exerting its force."*

[* In the beginning of the present century, says Mr. Pennant,

To give a still more complete idea of the strength of this terrible creature, we shall quote a passage from Father Tachard, who was an eye-witness of a combat between a tiger and two elephants at Siam. For this purpose, the king ordered a lofty palisade to be built of bambou cane, about a hundred feet

a company seated under the shade of some trees, near the banks of a river in Bengal, were alarmed with the unexpected sight of a tiger, preparing for its fatal spring ; when a lady, with almost unexampled presence of mind, unfurled a large umbrella in the animal's face : which, being confounded by so extraordinary and sudden an appearance, instantly retired, and thus gave them an opportunity of escaping from its terrible attack.

But the fatal accident which a few years ago occurred in the East Indies to Mr. Monro, son of sir Hector Monro, must be still fresh in the memory of all who have read the dreadful description given by an eye-witness of the scene. " We went," says the relator, " on shore on Sangar island to shoot deer, of which we saw innumerable tracks, as well as of tigers : we continued our diversion till near three o'clock, when, sitting down by the side of a jungle to refresh ourselves, a roar like thunder was heard, and an immense tiger seized our unfortunate friend, and rushed again into the jungle, dragging him through the thickest bushes and trees, every thing giving way to its monstrous strength : a tigress accompanied his progress. The united agonies of horror, regret, and fear, rushed at once upon us. I fired on the tiger ; he seemed agitated. My companion fired also ; and in a few moments after this, our unfortunate friend came up to us, bathed in blood. Every medical assistance was vain ; and he expired in the space of twenty-four hours ; having received such deep wounds from the teeth and claws of the animal, as rendered his recovery hopeless. A large fire, consisting of ten or twelve whole trees, was blazing near us at the time this accident took place, and ten or more of the natives were with us. The human mind can scarcely form any idea of this scene of horror. We had but just pushed our boat from this accursed shore, when the tigress made her appearance, almost raging mad, and remained on the sand all the while we continued in sight."]

square; and in the midst of this were three elephants appointed for combating the tiger. Their heads and a part of their trunks were covered with a kind of armour, like a mask, which defended that part from the assaults of the fierce animal with which they were to engage. As soon, says this author, as we were arrived at the place, a tiger was brought forth from its den, of a size much larger than we had ever seen before. It was not at first let loose, but held with cords, so that one of the elephants approaching, gave it three or four terrible blows with its trunk, on the back, with such force, that the tiger was for some time stunned, and lay without motion as if it had been dead. However, as soon as it was let loose, and at full liberty, although the first blows had greatly abated its fury, it made at the elephant with a loud shriek, and aimed at seizing his trunk. But the elephant, wrinkling it up with great dexterity, received the tiger on his great teeth, and tossed it up into the air. This so discouraged the furious animal, that it no more ventured to approach the elephant, but made several circuits round the palisade, often attempting to fly at the spectators. Shortly after, three elephants were sent against it, and they continued to strike it so terribly with their trunks, that it once more lay for dead; and they would certainly have killed it, had there not been a stop put to the combat.

From this account we may readily judge of the strength of this animal, which, though reduced to captivity, and held by cords, though first disabled, and set alone against three, yet ventured to

continue the engagement, and even that against
animals covered and protected from its fury.

" Captain Hamilton informs us, that in the Sun-
dah Rajah's dominions there are three sorts of tigers
in the woods, and that the smallest are the fiercest.
This is not above two feet high, appears to be
extremely cunning, and delights in human flesh.
The second kind is about three feet high, and
hunts deer and wild hogs, besides the little animal
which has been already described, under the name
of the Chevrotain, or Guinea deer. The tiger of
the largest sort is above three feet and a half high ;
but, although endowed with greater powers, is by
no means so rapacious as either of the former.
This formidable animal, which is called the Royal
Tiger (one of which we have at present in the
Tower) does not seem so ravenous nor so dangerous, and is even more cowardly. A peasant in that
country, as this traveller informs us, had a buffalo
fallen into a quagmire, and while he went for assistance, there came a large tiger, that, with its single
strength drew forth the animal, which the united
force of many men could not effect. When the
people returned to the place, the first object they
beheld was the tiger, who had thrown the buffalo
over its shoulder, as a fox does a goose, and was
carrying it away, with the feet upward, towards
its den ; however, as soon as it saw the men, it
let fall its prey, and instantly fled to the woods :
but it had previously killed the buffalo, and sucked
its blood ; and, no doubt, the people were very
well satisfied with its retreat. It may be observed,
that some East-Indian buffaloes weigh above a

thousand pounds, which is twice as heavy as the ordinary run of our black cattle; so that from hence we may form a conception of the enormous strength of this rapacious animal, that could thus run off with a weight at least twice as great as that of itself.

" Were this animal as common as the panther, or even as the lion himself, thus furnished as it is with the power to destroy, and the appetite for slaughter, the country would be uninhabitable where it resides. But luckily the species is extremely scarce ; and has been so since the earliest accounts we have had of the tiger. About the times of Augustus, we are assured by Pliny,* that when panthers were brought to Rome by hundreds, a single tiger was considered as an extraordinary sight ; and he tells us, that the emperor Claudius was able to procure four only; which shows how difficultly they were procured. The incredible fierceness of this animal may be, in some measure, the cause of the scarcity which was then at Rome, since it was the opinion of Varro, that the tiger was never taken alive :† but its being a native only of the East Indies, and that particularly of the warm regions, it is not to be wondered that the species should be so few."

We may therefore consider the species of the true streaked tiger as one of the scarcest of animals, and much less diffused than that of the lion. As to the number of its young, we have no cer-

* Plin. Hist. Nat. lib. viii. c. 17.

† Tigris vivus capi adhuc non potuit. Var. de Ling. Lat.

tain accounts; however, it is said, that it brings
forth four or five at a time. Although furious at
all times, the female, upon this occasion, exceeds
her usual rapacity; and, if her young are taken
from her, she pursues the spoiler with incredible
rage; he, to save a part, is contented to lose a part,
and drops one of her cubs, with which she immediately returns to her den, and again pursues him;
he then drops another, and by the time she has
returned with that, he generally escapes with
the remainder. If she loses her young entirely,
she then becomes desperate, boldly approaches
even the towns themselves, and commits incredible
slaughter. The tiger expresses its resentment in
the same manner with the lion; it moves the muscles and skin of its face, shows its teeth, and
shrieks in the most frightful manner. Its note is
very different from that of the lion; being rather
a scream than a roar: and the ancients expressed
it very well when they said, that, *tigrides inda-
gine raucant rugiuntque leones.*

  The skin of these animals is much esteemed all
over the East, particularly in China; the Manda-
rins cover their seats of justice in the public places
with it, and convert it into coverings for cushions
in winter. In Europe, these skins, though but
seldom to be met with, are of no great value, those
of the panther and the leopard being held in much
greater estimation. This is all the little benefit
we derive from this dreadful animal, of which so
many falsehoods have been reported; as, that its
sweat was poisonous, and the hair of its whiskers
more dangerous than an envenomed arrow. But
the real mischiefs which the tiger occasions while

19

The Cougar.

living are sufficient, without giving imaginary
ones to the parts of its body when dead. In fact,
the Indians sometimes eat its flesh, and find it neither disagreeable nor unwholesome.

There is an animal of America, which is usually
called the Red Tiger, but M. Buffon calls it the
Cougar, which, no doubt, is very different from
the tiger of the East. Some, however, have
thought proper to rank both together; and I will
take leave to follow their example, merely because
the cougar is more like a tiger in every thing, except the colour, than any other animal I know,
having the head, the body, and the neck shaped
very much in the same manner. Of these slight
differences, words would give but a very faint idea;
it will be, therefore, sufficient to observe, that
they are both equally slender, and are smaller where
the neck joins the head, than others of the panther
kind. There is one at present in the Tower; and
it seemed to me, as well as I could see it through
the bars, that were it properly streaked and
coloured, it would in all things resemble a small
tiger. It is, however, of a very different colour,
being of a deep brown, and the tail very long and
pointed. It is rather darker on the back; under
the chin it is a little whitish, as also on the lower
part of the belly.

Of all the American animals, this is the most
formidable and mischievous; even their pretended
lion not excepted. It is said, there are several
sorts of them; and, as well as I can remember, I
have seen one or two here in England, both differing from the present, in size and conformation.
It is, indeed, a vain endeavour to attempt to de-

scribe all the less obvious varieties in the cat kind. If we examine them minutely, we shall find the differences multiply upon us so much, that, instead of a history, we shall only be paid with a catalogue of distinctions. From such of them as I have seen within these last six years, I think I could add two animals of this species, that have not been hitherto described, and with the names of which he that showed them was utterly unacquainted. But it is a poor ambition, that of being eager to find out new distinctions, or adding one noxious animal more, to a list that is already sufficiently numerous. Were the knowing a new variety to open an unknown history, or in the least to extend our knowledge, the inquiry would be then worth pursuing; but what signifies mentioning some trifling difference, and from thence becoming authors of a new name, when the difference might have originally proceeded either from climate, soil, or indiscriminate copulation?

The cougars are extremely common in South America, and, where the towns border upon the forest, these make frequent incursions by night into the midst of the streets, carrying off fowls, dogs, and other domestic creatures. They are, however, but weak and contemptible, compared to the great tiger, being found unable to cope with a single man. The Negroes and Indians are very dextrous in encountering them; and some, even for the sake of their skins, seek them in their retreats. The arms in this combat, seemingly so dangerous, are only a lance of two or three yards long, made of heavy wood, with the point hardened in the fire; and a kind of scimitar of about three

quarters of a yard in length. Thus armed, they
wait till the tiger makes an assault against the left
hand, which holds the lance, and is wrapped up in a
short cloak of baize. Sometimes the animal, aware
of the danger, seems to decline the combat; but
then its antagonist provokes it with a slight touch
of the lance, in order, while he is defending himself, to strike a sure blow. As soon, therefore, as
the creature feels the lance, it grasps it with one
of its paws, and with the other strikes at the arm
which holds it. Then it is that the person nimbly
aims a blow with his scimitar, which he kept concealed, with the other hand, and hamstrings the
creature, which immediately draws back enraged,
but instantly returns to the charge. But then,
receiving another stroke, it is totally deprived of
the power of motion : and the combatant, killing
it at his leisure, strips the skin, cuts off the head,
and returns to his companions, displaying these as
the trophies of his victory.

This animal, as we are assured, is often more
successful against the crocodile ; and it is the only
quadruped in that part of the world that is not
afraid of the engagement. It must be no un-
pleasant sight to observe, from a place of safety,
this extraordinary combat, between animals so
terrible and obnoxious to man. Such as have seen
it, describe it in the following manner. When
the tiger, impelled by thirst, that seems continually to consume it, comes down to the river side to
drink, the crocodile, which makes no distinction
in its prey, lifts its head above water to seize it;
the tiger not less rapacious than the other, and
unacquainted with the force of the enemy, boldly

ventures to seize it, and plunges its claws into the
eyes of the crocodile, which is the only vulner-
able part of its body : upon this the crocodile
instantly dives under water, and the tiger goes
down with him, for it will sooner die than let go
its hold. In this manner the combat continues
for some time, until the tiger is drowned, or
escapes, as is sometimes the case, from its disabled
enemy.

These animals are common in Guiana.* They
were formerly seen swimming over, in great numbers, into the island of Cayenne, to attack and
ravage the flocks and herds of the inhabitants. In
the beginning, they were a terrible scourge to the
infant colony : but, by degrees, they were repulsed
and destroyed, and are now seen no longer at that
place. They are found in Brazil, in Paraguay, in
the country of the Amazons, and in several other
parts of South America. They often climb trees
in quest of prey, or to avoid their pursuers. They
are deterred by fire, like all other animals of the
cat kind ; or more properly speaking, they seldom
venture near those places where they see it kindled,
as they are always sure of their enemies being near,
and their nocturnal eyes are dazzled by the brightness of the blaze. From the description of this
animal, one would be hardly led to suppose, that
its flesh was good for food ; and yet we have
several accounts which allege the fact, some asserting it to be superior even to mutton; however,
what Monsieur Des Marchais observes, is most
likely to be true; namely, that the most valuable

* Buffon, vol. xix, p.

20

The Male Panther.

part of this animal is its skin, and that its flesh is
but indifferent eating, being generally lean, and
usually having a strong fume.*

The Panther, and the Leopard.

We have hitherto found no great difficulty in
distinguishing one animal from another, each carrying its own peculiar marks, which, in some measure, serve to separate it from all the rest. But it
is otherwise, when we come to these of the cat
kind, that fill up the chasm between the tiger and
the cat. The spots with which their skins are
diversified are so various, and their size so equivocal,
that it is no easy matter to distinguish the species,
particularly as we have little else but the spots and
the size to guide us in making the distinction. If we
regard the figure and diversity of the spots, we shall
find many varieties not taken notice of by any naturalist; if we are led by the size, we shall find an
imperceptible gradation from the cat to the tiger.
It would be in vain, therefore, to make as many
varieties in these animals as we see differences in
spots or stature; it will be sufficient to seize the
most general distinctions, and leave the rest to such
as are fond of more minute disquisitions.

Of all this tribe, whose skins are so beautifully
spotted, and whose natures are so mischievous, the
Panther may be considered as the foremost. This
animal has been by many naturalists mistaken for

[* This animal is said sometimes to climb trees, like a cat,
and watch the opportunity of springing on its prey, as it passes
underneath.]

the tiger; and, in fact, it approaches next to it in size, fierceness, and beauty. It is distinguished, however, by one obvious and leading character; that of being spotted, not streaked; for, in this particular, the tiger differs from the panther, the leopard, and almost all the inferior ranks of this mischievous family.

This animal, which M. Buffon calls simply the Panther, Linnæus the Pard, Gesner the Pardalis, and the modern Latins the Leopardus; this animal, I say, which goes by too many names; and which the English have indiscriminately called by the name of the Panther or the Leopard, may be considered as the largest of the kind, and is spotted in a manner somewhat different from those that are smaller. As those spots, however, make the principal difference between it and the lesser animals, which it otherwise resembles in shape, size, disposition, and beauty, I will first show these slight distinctions; and mention the names each animal has received in consequence thereof; and then proceed to give their history together, still marking any peculiarity observable in one of the species, which is not found in the rest.

Next to the great panther, already mentioned, is the animal which M. Buffon calls the Leopard, a name which he acknowledges to be given arbitrarily, for the sake of distinction. Other naturalists have not much attended to the slight differences between this and the great panther, nor have they considered its discriminations as sufficient to entitle it to another name. It has hitherto, therefore, gone under the name of the Leopard, or Panther of Senegal, where it is chiefly found. The

differences between this animal and the former are
these: the large panther is often found to be six
feet long, from the tip of the nose to the insertion
of the tail; the panther of Senegal is not above
four. The large panther is marked with spots in
the manner of a rose, that is, five or six make a
kind of circle, and there is generally a large one in
the middle. The leopard of Senegal has a much
more beautiful coat, the yellow is more brilliant,
and the spots are smaller, and not disposed in rings
but in clusters. As to the rest, they are both
whitish under the belly; the tail in both is pretty
long, but rather longer in proportion in the latter
than the former. To these two animals, whose
differences seem to be so very minute, we may add
a third; namely, the Jaguar or Panther of America. This, in every respect, resembles the two
former, except in the disposition of its spots, and
that its neck and head are rather streaked than
spotted. The jaguar is also said to be lower upon
its legs, and less than the leopard of Senegal.
These three quadrupeds, as we see, have but very
slight differences, and the principal distinction
used by M. Buffon is taken from the size; the
first, as he says, is usually six feet long; the second
four feet; and the last, about three: however, it
appears from the particular subjects of his description, that the panther in his possession was not
above three feet seven inches long; that the leopard's skin which he describes was about four;
and that the jaguar, at two years old, was between
two and three feet long, which, when come to its
full growth, would, no doubt, be four feet long, as
well as the two former. From hence, therefore,

we may conclude, that the size in these animals is
not sufficient to make a distinction among them;
and that those who called them all three by the
indiscriminate names of the leopard and the panther, if not right, were at least excusable. Of
those which are now to be seen in the Tower, the
jaguar, or the American panther, is rather the largest
of the three; and is by no means the contemptible
animal which M. Buffon describes it to be: the
leopard is the least of them, and has, by some
travellers, been supposed to be an animal produced
between the panther and the ounce, an animal
which resembles, but is less than any of the former. These three animals we may, therefore,
rank together, as they agree pretty nearly in their
robe, their size, their dispositions, and their ferocity.*

[* The Panther is distinguished by its superior size, measuring
about six feet and a half from the nose to the tail; by its brighter
tawny yellow colour; and by the spots on the upper parts of
the body being disposed into circles, each consisting of four
or five separate spots, in the centre of which circle there is commonly a distinct spot; while the spots on the lower parts of the
body are lengthened out into lines. The leopard is smaller in
size, and has the spots smaller, and placed closer together,
without the central one, and they are not disposed in continuous
lines on the lower parts. The jaguar is about the size of a wolf,
marked on the upper parts with streaks of open oblong black
spots or patches; the top of the back with long interrupted
stripes, and the sides with rows of regular open marks; the
thighs and legs variegated with black spots without central
spaces: the tail is not so long as the body.

Mr. Pennant describes a leopard, which he calls the Hunting
Leopard. It is a native of India, is about the size of a greyhound, and of a more slender make than the leopard. On its
neck it is said to have a slight mane. It is tamed, and used in

21

Do Savo del.   Hussar fe.

The Lynx.

We come next to an animal confessedly different from any of the former, being much smaller, and its colour more inclining to white. Its name, however, in our language, has caused no small confusion. It has been generally called by foreigners, the Onza, or the Ounce, and this name some of our own writers have thought proper to give it; but others of them, and these the most celebrated, such as Willughby, have given this name to a different animal with a short tail, and known to the ancients and moderns by the name of the Lynx. I confess myself at a loss, in this case, whom to follow; the alteration of names should be always made with great caution, and never but in cases of necessity. If we follow Willughby, there will be an animal of the panther kind, very distinguishable from all the rest, left without a name; and if we recede from him, it will serve to produce some confusion among all the numerous class of readers and writers who have taken him for their guide: however, as he seems himself to have been an innovator, the name of the lynx having been long adopted into our language before, it was unnecessary to give the animal that bore it another name, and to call that creature an ounce, which our old writers had been accustomed to know by the Latin appellation; for this reason, therefore, we may safely venture to take a name that has been long misapplied from the lynx, and restore it to the animal in question. We will, therefore, call that animal of the panther

the chase of antelopes and other animals; being carried into the field chained and hooded, and afterwards let loose upon its prey.]

kind, which is less than the panther, and with a longer tail, the Ounce; and the lynx may remain in possession of that name by which it was known among all our old English writers, as well as by all antiquity.

The Ounce, or the Onca of Linnæus, is much less than the panther, being not, at most, above three feet and a half long: however, its hair is much longer than that of the panther, and its tail still more so. The panther of four or five feet long, has a tail but of two feet, or two feet and a half. The ounce, which is but about three feet, has a tail often longer than the rest of its body. The colour of the ounce is also apparently different, being rather more inclining to a cream colour, which is deeper on the back, and whiter towards the belly. The hair on the back is an inch and a half long; that on the belly, two inches and a half; which is much longer than that of the panther. Its spots are disposed pretty much in the same manner as the large panther, except that on the haunches it is rather marked with stripes than with spots.

Descending to animals of this kind that are still smaller, we find the Catamountain, which is the Ocelot of M. Buffon, or the Tiger Cat of most of those who exhibit it as a show. It is less than the ounce, but its robe more beautifully variegated. It is an American animal, and is about two feet and a half in length, from the nose to the insertion of the tail. It is extremely like a cat, except that it is larger and slenderer, that its colours are more beautiful, and its tail rather shorter. The fur is of a reddish colour, the whole beautified with black spots and streaks of different figures. They are

long on the back, and round on the belly and
paws. On the ears are black stripes, which run
across; but, in other respects, they entirely resemble those of a cat. These colours, however, which
naturalists have taken great pains minutely to
describe, are by no means permanent, being differently disposed in different animals of the same
species. I remember to have seen an animal of
this size, but whether of this species I will not
pretend to say, some years ago, that was entirely
brown, and was said also to have come from
America.

-. From this tribe of the cat kind, with spotted
skins and a long tail, we come to another with
skins diversified in like manner, but with a shorter
tail. The principal of these is the Lynx, the name
by which the animal was known to Ælian, among
the ancients; and to all our old English writers
among those of a more modern date. This name
has been corrupted by the Portuguese into the
word Ouze; and this corruption has been adopted
by Ray, who has improperly called this animal
the Ounce, after some of the foreign travellers.
The first striking distinction between the lynx and
all those of the panther kind, is in its tail, which
is at least half as short in proportion, and black at
the extremity. Its fur is much longer, the spots
on the skin less vivid, and but confusedly mingled
with the rest. Its ears are much longer, and
tipped at the points with a black tuft of hair. The
colour round the eyes is white, and the physiognomy more placid and gentle. Each hair of this
animal is of three different colours: the root is of
a greyish brown; the middle red, or of an ash

colour; and the ends white. This whiteness of the ends takes up so small a part of the particular hair, that it does not prevent us from seeing the principal colour, which is that of the middle part; so that it only makes the surface of the body appear as if it was silvered over: however, the hair of which the spots consist has no white at the ends, and at the roots it is not quite so black as the other part. This animal is not above the size of the ounce, but is rather stronger built; and it has but twenty-eight teeth; whereas all the rest of the cat kind already mentioned have thirty.

Another animal of this kind is called the Syagush, or, as M. Buffon names it, the Carecal. It is a native of the East Indies, and resembles the lynx in size, in form, and even in the singularity of being tufted at the tips of the ears. However, the syagush differs in not being mottled as the lynx is; its fur, or rather hair, is rougher and shorter; its tail is rather longer, its muzzle more lengthened, its physiognomy more fierce; and its nature more savage.

The third and last animal that need be mentioned of this kind, is that which M. Buffon calls the Serval, and which he has first described. It is a native of Malabar, resembling the panther in its spots, but the lynx in the shortness of its tail, in its size, and in its strong-built form.

These seem to be all the principal distinctions among animals of the panther kind, from the largest of this tribe down to the domestic cat, which is the smallest of all these fierce and mischievous varieties. In all, their nature seems pretty much the same; being equally fierce, subtle, cruel, and

22

De Sere del.   Werner sc.

The Syagush.

cowardly. The panther, including the leopard and the jaguar, or American panther, as they are the largest, so also are they the most dangerous of this kind; for the whole race of cats are noxious in proportion to their power to do mischief. They inhabit the most torrid latitudes of India, Africa, and America, and have never been able to multiply beyond the torrid zone. They are generally found in the thickest and the most entangled forests, and often near remote habitations, where they watch to surprise all kinds of domestic animals. They very seldom attack man, even though provoked by him; they seem rather desirous of finding safety by flight, or by climbing trees, at which they are very expert. In this manner also they often pursue their prey; and, being expert at seizing it, as well above as below, they cause a vast destruction. Of all other animals, these are the most sullen, and, even to a proverb, untameable. They still preserve their fierce and treacherous spirit; and at those places where they are exposed to be seen among others, we often observe, that while their keeper is familiar with the lion or the bear, yet he is apprehensive of the large panther, and keeps it bound with the shortest chain.

As the ounce differs from these in figure and size, so also it seems to differ in disposition, being more mild, tractable, and tame. These we frequently see as harmless and innocent as cats; and there is one at present in the Tower, with which the keeper plays without the smallest apprehension. I own I was not a little uneasy, at first, for the man, when he put his hand through the bars, and called the animal by its name; but was a good deal surprised to see the creature, which one might suppose irritated by long confinement, come gently up to him, stroke his hand with his face, in the manner of a cat, and testify the utmost gentleness of disposition. The ounce, therefore, is remarkable for being easily tamed; and, in fact, it is employed all over the East for the purposes of hunting. Not, indeed, but that panthers themselves are sometimes used for this purpose; but they are never thoroughly subdued like the former; being usually brought to the field in a carriage, and kept chained and caged until they are shown the gazelle or the leveret, which is their prey. This they pursue rather by three or four great springs, than by running. If they seize it by this sudden effort, it finds no mercy; but if it escapes from their first effort, they never attempt to pursue, and appear quite disappointed and confounded at their mischance. It sometimes happens that they are so much enraged at it, that they attack even their employer, and his only resource to avoid their fury, is to throw them some small pieces of meat, which he has brought with him for that purpose.

The ounce, however, is not so dangerous; and is treated with more confidence and familiarity. It is usually brought to the field hoodwinked behind one of the horsemen. When the game appears, the ounce is instantly uncovered, and shown where it lies; upon which the fierce creature darts like an arrrow to the place, and seizes it at once; or, missing it, remains motionless in the place. It would be vain to attempt retrieving its disgrace by continuing the pursuit; for although it bounds

with greater agility than most other animals, yet
it is slow and awkward in running, and has no
means of finding the animal it pursues by the smell,
as is common among those of the dog kind. From
hence, therefore, it appears how much superior
the European method of hunting is to that of the
Asiatic; since whatever amusement this exercise
affords must arise from the continuance of the
chase, and from the fluctuation of doubt and expectation, which raise and depress the pursuers by
turns. All this an Asiatic hunter is deprived of;
and his greatest pleasure can scarcely be more
than what among us is called coursing, in which
the dog pursues the animal, and keeps it constantly
in view.

But it must not be supposed that it is from
choice the Asiatics use this method of chase; for,
no doubt, were dogs serviceable among them, as
they are in Europe, they would be employed for
the same purposes. But the fact is, that the extreme heat of the tropical climates, produces such
universal putrefaction, and sends up such various
and powerful scents, that dogs are at first bewildered in the chase, and at last come to lose the
delicacy of their scent entirely. They are, therefore, but little used in those warm countries; and
what could they avail in places where almost every
other animal of the forest is stronger and more
rapacious? The lion, the tiger, the panther, and
the ounce, are all natural enemies to the dog, and
attack him wherever he appears, with ungovernable fury. The breed, therefore, in those places,
would quickly be destroyed; so that they are
obliged to have recourse to those animals which

are more fitted to serve them; and thus convert
the ounce to those purposes for which dogs are employed in Europe.

The Catamountain, or Ocelot, is one of the
fiercest, and, for its size, one of the most destructive animals in the world. It is, as was before
observed, a native of South America, and by no
means capable of the same education as the ounce,
which it more approaches in size than in disposition. Two of these, from whom Mr. Buffon has
taken his description, were brought over from
Carthagena, and having been taken from the dam
when very young, were afterwards suckled by a
bitch. But, before they were three months old,
they had strength and ingratitude sufficient to kill
and devour their nurse. Their succeeding fierceness and malignity seemed to correspond with their
first efforts; for no arts could tame or soften their
natures; and while they continued in their cages,
they still testified an unceasing disposition for
slaughter. When their food was given them, the
male always served himself before the female ventured to touch a bit; and it was not till he was
satisfied that the other began. In their savage
state, these animals are still more destructive;
having great strength and agility, they very easily
find and overtake their prey, which they pursue
among the tops of the trees, as well as on the
ground; but what renders them still more mischievous, is their increasing appetite rather for the
blood than the flesh of their prey. They suck this
with the greatest avidity, but frequently leave the
carcass otherwise untouched, in order to pursue
other animals for the blood in like manner. They

represent what they wish than what they know;
and exalt human strength, to fill up the whole
sphere of their limited conceptions. Great strength
is an accidental thing; two or three in a country
may possess it; and these may have a claim to
heroism. But what may lead us to doubt of the
veracity of these accounts is, that the heroes of antiquity are represented as the sons of heroes; their
amazing strength is delivered down from father to
son; and this we know to be contrary to the
course of nature. Strength is not hereditary, although titles are: and I am very much induced to
believe, that this great tribe of heroes, who are all
represented as the descendants of heroes, are more
obliged to their titles than to their strength, for
their characters. With regard to the shining characters in Homer, they are all represented as
princes, and as the sons of princes; while we are
told of scarcely any share of prowess in the meaner
men of the army; who are only brought into the
field for these to protect or to slaughter. But nothing can be more unlikely than that those men,
who were bred in the luxury of courts, should be
strong; while the whole body of the people, who
received a plainer and simpler education, should be
comparatively weak. Nothing can be more contrary to the general laws of nature, than that all the
sons of heroes should thus inherit not only the
kingdoms, but the strength of their forefathers;
and we may conclude, that they owe the greatest
share of their imputed strength rather to the dignity of their stations than the force of their arms;
and, like all fortunate princes, their flatterers happened to be believed. In later ages, indeed, we

have some accounts of amazing strength, which we
can have no reason to doubt of. But in these, nature is found to pursue her ordinary course; and
we find their strength accidental. We find these
strong men among the lowest of the people, and
gradually rising into notice, as this superiority had
more opportunity of being seen. Of this number
was the Roman tribune, who went by the name of
the second Achilles; who, with his own hand, is
said to have killed, at different times, three hundred of the enemy; and when treacherously set
upon, by twenty-five of his own countrymen, although then past his sixtieth year, killed fourteen
of them before he was slain. Of this number was
Milo, who, when he stood upright, could not be
forced out of his place. Pliny, also, tells us of one
Athanatus, who walked across the stage at Rome,
loaded with a breast-plate weighing five hundred
pounds, and buskins of the same weight. But of
all the prodigies of strength, of whom we have
any accounts in Roman history, Maximin, the
emperor, is to be reckoned the foremost. Whatever
we are told relative to him is well attested; his
character was too exalted not to be thoroughly
known; and that very strength, for which he was
celebrated, at last procured him no less a reward
than the empire of the world. Maximin was above
nine feet in height, and the best proportioned man
in the whole empire. He was by birth a Thracian;
and, from being a simple herdsman, rose through
the gradations of office, until he came to be Emperor of Rome. The first opportunity he had of
exerting his strength, was in the presence of all the
citizens in the theatre, where he overthrew twelve

of the strongest men in wrestling, and outstript two of the fleetest horses in running, all in one day. He could draw a chariot loaden that two strong horses could not move; he could break a horse's jaw with a blow of his fist; and its thigh with a kick. In war he was always foremost and invincible; happy had it been for him and his subjects, if, from being formidable to his enemies, he had not become still more so to his subjects; he reigned, for some time, with all the world his enemy; all mankind wishing him dead; yet none daring to strike the blow. As if fortune had resolved that through life he should continue unconquerable, he was killed at last by his own soldiers, while he was sleeping. We have many other instances, in later ages, of very great strength, and not fewer of amazing swiftness; but these, merely corporeal perfections, are now considered as of small advantage, either in war or in peace. The invention of gunpowder has, in some measure, levelled all force to one standard; and has wrought a total change in martial education through all parts of the world. In peace, also, the invention of new machines every day, and the application of the strength of the lower animals to the purposes of life, have rendered human strength less valuable. The boast of corporeal force is, therefore, consigned to savage nations, where those arts not being introduced, it may still be needful; but, in more polite countries, few will be proud of that strength which other animals can be taught to exert to as useful purposes as they.

" If we compare the largeness and thickness of our muscles with those of any other animal, we

shall find that, in this respect, we have the advantage; and if strength or swiftness depended upon
the quantity of the muscular flesh alone, I believe
that, in this respect, we should be more active and
powerful than any other. But this is not the
case; a great deal more than the size of the muscles goes to constitute activity or force; and it is
not he who has the thickest legs that can make the
best use of them. Those, therefore, who have
written elaborate treatises on muscular force, and
have estimated the strength of animals by the
thickness of their muscles, have been employed to
very little purpose. It is, in general, observed that
thin and raw-boned men are always stronger and
more powerful than such as are seemingly more
muscular; as, in the former, all the parts have
better room for their exertions."

Women want much of the strength of men;
and, in some countries, the stronger sex have
availed themselves of this superiority, in cruelly
and tyrannically enslaving those who were made
with equal pretensions to a share in all the advantages life can bestow. Savage nations oblige their
women to a life of continual labour; upon them
rest all the drudgeries of domestic duty; while the
husband, indolently reclined in his hammock, is
first served from the fruits of her industry. From
this negligent situation he is seldom roused, except
by the calls of appetite, when it is necessary,
either by fishing or hunting, to make a variety
in his entertainments. A savage has no idea of
taking pleasure in exercise; he is surprised to see
an European walk forward for his amusement, and
then return back again. As for his part, he could

their ground against him ; and which may be said to keep some kingdoms of the earth in their own possession. How many extensive countries are there in Africa, where, the wild beasts are so numerous, that man is deterred from living amongst them ; reluctantly giving up to the lion and the leopard, extensive tracts, that seem formed only for his delight and convenience !

END OF THE SECOND VOLUME.

Printed by T. C. Hansard, Peterborough-court, Fleet-street, London.

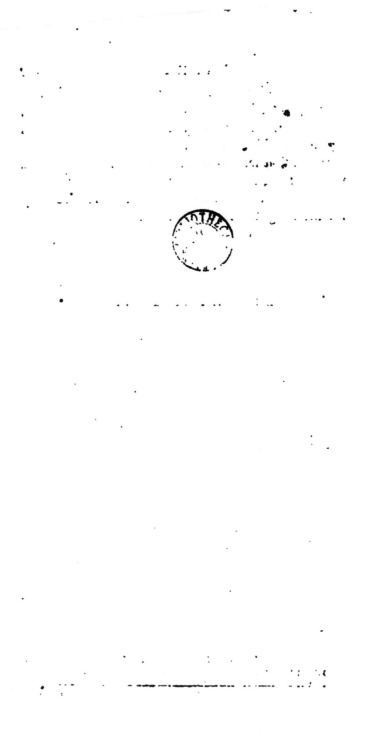